THE STATE *of* FAMILIES

LYNN A. CURTIS

Family, Employment and Reconstruction

Policy Based on What Works

Families International, Inc.
Publishing in association with
Family Service America, Inc.
Milwaukee, Wisconsin

Copyright 1995
Families International, Inc.
11700 West Lake Park Drive
Milwaukee, Wisconsin 53224

ISBN 0–87304–270–0

All rights reserved. No part of this book may be reproduced, stored in a retrieval system, or transmitted in any form or by any means (electronic, mechanical, photo-copying, recording, or otherwise) without permission in writing from the publisher.

Library of Congress Cataloging-in-Publication Data
(Revised for volume 4)

The State of families.

    Vols. 4–   published by Familes International, Inc.
    Includes bibliographical references.
    Contents: — v. 2. Work and family — v. 3. Losing direction / Ray Marshall — 4. Family, employment, and reconstruction / by Lynn A. Curtis.
    1. Work and family—United States. 2. United States—Social conditions—1980– . 3. Unemployment—Canada. I. Marshall, Ray, 1928– . II. Family Service America.
HD4904.25.S83   1987   306.85'0973   87–24374
ISBN 0–87304–226–3 (pbk. : v. 2)
ISBN 0–87304–249–2 (v. 3)

Contents

Acknowledgments		5
Foreword		7
Executive Summary		9
1	Acknowledging Trends over Time	17
2	Reducing Child Poverty	33
3	Nurturing Children and Their Schools	45
4	Creating Opportunities for Youth and Young Adults	61
5	Generating Jobs for Inner-City Families Through Economic Development	89
6	Increasing Public Safety to Secure Economic Development and Jobs for Families	107
7	Investing in Inner-City Families to Scale: Finding the Money	119
8	Mobilizing Citizens and Families to Reform Congress and the Media	131
Sources		141
Tables & Figures		145
Bibliography		147

Acknowledgments

Publication of *The State of Families*, 4 is made possible by grants from the Helen Bader Foundation, Inc., and The William and Flora Hewlett Foundation.

The author wishes to acknowledge the guiding role in this report of Yvonne Scruggs, Director of the Urban Policy Institute of the Joint Center for Political and Economic Studies and Vice Chair of the Milton S. Eisenhower Foundation. Ms. Scruggs reviewed the entire manuscript and provided valuable feedback with her customary eloquence. The first part of chapter 1 is based on Ms. Scruggs' chapter, "The Cities," in *Eyes on the President*, Leo E. Heagerty, editor.

The Author

Lynn A. Curtis is President of the Milton S. Eisenhower Foundation in Washington, D.C. The Foundation is the private-sector continuation of President Lyndon B. Johnson's National Advisory Commission on Civil Disorders (the 1967 Kerner Riot Commission) and National Commission on the Causes and Prevention of Violence (the 1968 National Violence Commission). Other recent Foundation reports include *Youth Investment and Community Reconstruction* (1990), a twenty-five year update of the Kerner Riot Commission (1993), and *Youth Development and Community Policing* (1995). Stories on the reports have appeared in the *New York Times*, *Washington Post*, *Los Angeles Times*, *Boston Globe*, *Christian Science Monitor*, and USA *Today* and on CBS, ABC CNN, and CSPAN. The Foundation replicates and evaluates successful programs, provides management and leadership training, and communicates what works to citizens and policymakers.

Foreword

For years we have talked about the plight of America's cities—how they have deteriorated; how they have become centers of crime with poor housing, poor schools, and poor economic infrastructure; and how we need to fix them. A generation ago, following the burning of a number of our cities in the riots of the late 1960s, the Kerner Commission issued a report detailing the degradation of life in the inner cities and provided numerous recommendations on how conditions could be improved. In 1993, the Milton S. Eisenhower Foundation issued a follow-up report showing that little, if anything, had been accomplished since 1969 and that conditions were worse than ever.

Today, as middle-class Americans of all races continue to flee to the suburbs and exurbs and many lower-skilled manufacturing jobs are being moved overseas, we are faced with the enormous job of not only physically rebuilding our cities, but of rebuilding their economic structures and living environments as well. Another generation has been left behind with few resources and with eroded public and private policies that offer little hope for improvement.

In the face of these disheartening conditions, we are pleased to offer this document, both as a chronicle of the policies of the past 20 years and as a testament to the commitment and good work of many organizations and people who have found ways to bring hope and promise to so many—especially youth—who might otherwise have found less desirable ways to survive their condition. I thank Dr. Lynn Curtis, president of the Eisenhower Foundation, for his work and commitment in writing this book. It is historically instructive about the failed policies of the past and hopeful in its descriptions of programs that work.

Necessarily, not all the good, helpful programs are included here. Those described in this book are distinctive for their scope and success, as documented by their scientific evaluations. Many other programs and services touch and help people in need on a daily basis. That is the business of family service agencies everywhere, whether acting singly or in partnership with other community resources. I am proud to honor them along with the many fine programs mentioned in this book for the essential work they are doing.

But as Dr. Curtis indicates, more must be done. I trust this book will be received as a thoughtful contribution to the discourse on how to restore our cities to being models of livability and productivity so necessary for our civilization. The alternative simply is not acceptable.

Peter B. Goldberg
President and Chief Executive Officer
Family Service America

Executive Summary

After the Los Angeles riots in 1992, a *New York Times*/CBS News poll asked a national sample of citizens whether they were prepared to have more tax dollars spent on effective programs that reduce child poverty and related American dilemmas. A majority said they were willing to pay more for effective programs that work. The poll then asked what was the greatest obstacle to achieving effective programs. Fifty-one percent of the respondents said that the greatest obstacle was "lack of knowledge."

The message of *Family, Employment, and Reconstruction* is that we *do* have the knowledge. But presently America lacks the political will.

No one should overstate. Yet, to a considerable extent, we already know a great deal about what works for children, youth, families, and the inner city. And we know a great deal about what doesn't work.

In many ways, then, our national policy ought to be as American as apple pie. We need to stop doing what doesn't work and use the money saved to replicate what does work—but funded at a scale that is equal to the dimensions of the problem.

Scale is important. Solutions are at hand. But we are told by politicians that there is not enough money to expand them nationally to all children, youth, and families who qualify for them. That is not so. This report lays out how much money we need to expand success to all who qualify. And it specifies where the money ought to come from.

What Doesn't Work?

In the 1980s, trickle-down, supply-side economics reduced taxes on the rich so they would, we were told, invest more. This, the country was assured, would reduce the debt and help the middle class and the poor. Benefits would trickle down to them.

Instead, in the words of conservative analyst Kevin Phillips, "The rich got richer and the poor got poorer." From 1977 to 1988, the income of the richest 1% of the United States increased by 122%. The income of the poorest fifth declined by 10%. Child poverty increased significantly.

Over the same period, the real incomes (adjusted for inflation) of the working class and the middle class also declined. The national debt that the children of these families would have to pay back rose from $800 billion in 1981 to $3 *trillion* in 1991.

There appeared to be many other costs associated with trickle-down, supply-side economics. The defaults that resulted from congressional deregulation of the savings and loan industry cost the taxpaying voter over $500 billion—more than enough to finance the policy of comprehensive interdependence over a decade proposed in these pages. Along similar lines, as a result of the supply-side scandal over the 1980s, which cost taxpayers over $5 billion, an independent prosecutor convicted the federal housing commissioner and several other top officials at the U.S. Department of Housing and Urban Development of awarding money to "benefit their friends, their families, and themselves without regard to the actual housing needs of this nation or its low-income families." And a scientific evaluation commissioned by the Reagan administration of the nation's primary job-training program for the poor, the Job Training Partnership Act, which was based on supply-side economics, found that young people in the program did *worse* than a comparison group of youth who did not participate at all.

Did trickle-down economics bring the nation closer to class war? Some thought so. The rich were pleased that, in the 1980s, their tax rate was reduced well below their counterparts in Germany and Japan. According to some, the middle class became the "anxious class"—worried that the new, high-tech global economy was benefiting only the fortunate few at the top—who could, for example, disinvest from American workers and get workers in China to do their jobs for much less. The anxiety might have been alleviated if middle-class workers had the opportunity to upgrade their skills through new technologies, so they could work in sectors where Americans had a comparative advantage. But no such plan was legislated to invest in the human capital of the middle class. This was even more true for the poor, who expressed their views, for example, in the 1992 Los Angeles riot and in a dramatic rise in violent crime among youth in the 1980s.

Woven into the increased class tension of the 1980s was increased racial tension. The prophecy of the 1968 Kerner Riot Commission—of "two societies, Black and White, increasingly separate and less equal"—came to pass. The English spoken by African Americans became more and more different from the English spoken by white Americans. "Hypersegregation" became a term to describe housing patterns in cities like Newark and Milwaukee. Prison building became part of American civil-rights policy. Even though there was no proof that more and more prisons resulted in less and less crime, the number of prison cells tripled from 1981 to 1991. The cost was up to $100,000 per cell built and up to $30,000 to keep someone in that cell for a year. *One of four young African American males in America was in prison, on probation, or on parole by the late 1980s.* That, we believe, is an astounding proportion. The proportion was one in three in California, which usually leads the rest of the nation (for better or worse), and almost one in two in some major cities, like Washington, D.C. The new prisons tended to be in rural areas. Some saw parallels to the rural "homelands" policy of South Africa during apartheid. The new rural prisons disproportionately incarcerated minorities, but heavily employed whites as prison personnel. Small rural cities began lobbying for prisons, as an economic stimulus package to employ family breadwinners. The prison-building surge coincided with a decrease by 80% in federal appropriations for housing the poor. So in some ways, prison building became America's national low-income housing policy, already decimated by the supply-side scandal at the U.S. Department of Housing and Urban Development.

In spite of the destructiveness of trickle-down, supply-side economics and prison building in the 1980s, the house majority leader concluded, in 1995, "I think

Reaganomics was an incredible success. We ought to stand up and be proud of the '80s." It was *déjà vu* all over again.

What Works?

Based on existing scientific evaluation (with comparison or control groups) over the past quarter century, the principles that appear to underlie what works, especially at the grass-roots level, include safe haven sanctuaries off the street after school where kids get mentoring, social support, and discipline from big brothers and big sisters; educational innovations (like computer-based remedial education) that motivate youth to obtain a high school degree; job training (which continues social support and discipline) carefully linked to job creation; feasible options for continuing on to college; employment linked to economic development (like housing rehabilitation); and problem-oriented, community-based policing, which helps secure a neighborhood for the economic development that creates the jobs.

Not all successful ventures illustrate all of these principles, but multiple solutions usually are evident in the most enduring models. And to be able to identify the underlying principles means we can begin to replicate them, with variations based on local needs.

Similarly, the successes tend to have multiple good outcomes. Not uncommonly, in programs evaluated as successful, these outcomes include some combination of less crime, less gang-related behavior, less drug abuse, less welfare dependency, fewer adolescent pregnancies, fewer school dropouts, more school grades completed, more successful school-to-work transitions, more employability, better parenting among targeted high-risk youth, and more stable families. The communities where young people live can experience less fear, fewer drug dealers, and more business, job, and economic development. Not all model programs achieve all of these good outcomes. But the point is that multiple outcomes are the rule, not the exception.

"Enough is known about the lives of disadvantaged high-risk youth to mount an intensive campaign to alter the trajectories of these children," says Joy Dryfoos in *Adolescents at Risk*. "Enough has been documented about the inability of fragmented programs to produce the necessary changes to proceed toward more comprehensive and holistic approaches."

"We know how to intervene to reduce the rotten outcomes of adolescence and to help break the cycle that reaches into succeeding generations," says Lisbeth Schorr in *Within Our Reach*. "Unshackled from the myth that nothing works, we can assure that the children without hope today will have a real chance to become the contributing citizens of tomorrow."

What Should We Do?

With a knowledge of what works, we propose a plan for truly disadvantaged urban families—which constitute about 10% of all families in the United States. The policy centers on educational opportunity, job opportunity, and job creation.

Chapter 3 recommends expansion of Head Start to all poor children who are eligible. Such preschool improves educational achievement and employability. Many middle-class and upper-class kids already have this advantage, through private preschool arranged by their parents. Chapter 3 has proven initiatives—like the James Comer Yale University School Development Plan, Project Prepare in Chicago, and boys and girls club-type safe havens after school across the nation. These cutting-edge, scientifically evaluated successes increase the likelihood that children and youth will stay in school and so qualify later for legal labor-market employment.

Chapter 4 sets forth a job training and placement system to replace the failed Job Training Partnership Act for high-risk youth. The alternative is based on job ventures that *have* succeeded at the grass-roots community level—like YouthBuild USA and the Argus Community Learning for Living Center.

Chapter 5 calls for placement of poor people so trained—in jobs that rebuild inner-city housing and inner-city infrastructure. The jobs created also would be for associated essential inner-city services—like teaching, child care, and policing. Based on the past experiences, chapter 5 concludes that reconstruction should be carried out, in particular, by local private-sector, nonprofit community-development corporations—which receive grants and loans via private national nonprofit institutions like the Ford Foundation's Local Initiatives Support Corporation (LISC) and developer James Rouse's Enterprise Foundation. LISC and the Enterprise Foundation already rehabilitate and build more housing for the poor than the U.S. Department of Housing and Urban Development. Chapter 5 shows how the development ought to be financed through expansion of community-development banking, based on the successful model of the South Shore Bank in Chicago, and secured through community-based problem-oriented policing, based on models scientifically evaluated as successful by the Police Foundation, the Police Executive Research Forum, and the Eisenhower Foundation.

With an eye to estimates made by the 1968 Kerner Riot Commission, this plan to reduce child poverty (i.e., to reform welfare), and to achieve many other goals to restore human capital and revive inner cities, will cost roughly $30 billion per year in new investments in children, youth, workers, families, housing, and urban infrastructure. We believe that the plan ought to be sustained for at least 10 years, or better, for a full generation of inner-city children who, over that time, transition into good workers—taxpaying voters who take responsibility for instilling the solid values in their children. *Employment* is the best way to create such family values.

We assert in chapter 7 that, notwithstanding rhetoric in Washington, D.C., there really are no technical, financial obstacles against generating the resources needed. Financing is a matter of political will and leadership. Among other sources, the financing ought to come from reducing corporate welfare (which costs taxpaying voters at least $40 billion per year and probably more), reducing military spending (based on the recommendations of former Joint Chiefs of Staff and of former Reagan Assistant Defense Secretary Lawrence Korb, now at the Brookings Institution), and increasing taxes significantly on the richest 1% of Americans. (Taxes on the poor, the working class, and the middle class ought to be reduced.)

Our plan assumes health-care reform that allows adults to function as good parents and workers. Because there presently is so much political discord over health-care reform, the costs of such reform are not included in our $30 billion per year education investment, job investment, and housing/infrastructure reconstruction budget.

Chapter 8 concludes that our plan can be attained if American citizens realize that the problem is not so much the Boyz N the Hood as the boys on the Hill. It calls for a citizen revolt to reverse what some view as the betrayal by Congress of American democracy. In the words of William Greider in *Who Will Tell the People*, "Rehabilitating democracy will require citizens to devote themselves first to challenging the status quo, disrupting the contours of power and opening the way to renewal." Common people must "engage their surrounding realities" and "question the conflict between what they are told and what they see and experience."

Reversing the betrayal must begin with campaign finance reform and control of special-interest lobbyists, based on the plan set forth by Common Cause. Then we will have the money to implement what works for inner-city families and children on a scale equal to the dimensions of the problem. The new citizen movement that is needed should be financed by American foundations.

Our plan is for the federal government to raise money, create guidelines based on what works, and enforce standards. At the same time, to a considerable extent, we favor decentralized day-to-day implementation of the investments in children, youth, families, and inner cities that form our plan to reduce child poverty. If something federal works—like Head Start—don't fix it. But localities, and especially private-sector, nonprofit community-based organizations, are closest to the people and have had the most success. Decentralization and "devolution," to use the ungainly word now fashionable inside the Washington, D.C., beltway, are to *this*, community and neighborhood, level in our plan. As Walt Whitman wrote in *Leaves of Grass*, "The genius of the United States is not best or most in its executives or legislatures, nor in its ambassadors or authors or colleges or churches . . . nor even in its newspapers or inventors . . . but always most in the common people."

Where Are the Jobs?

There are few words less popular with the common people than "welfare." Next to "build prisons," the two most salable words for politicians today are "cut welfare." Yet "welfare" is a program that tries to remove poor children from poverty. The main federal welfare program is, of course, Aid to Families with Dependent Children (AFDC). Children make up two-thirds of its 14 million recipients. Nearly one child in four lives in poverty in America. That leaves many citizens ashamed. "Poor children" have always been a subject of bipartisan concern.

Public opinion is full of contradictions. A December 1994 *New York Times*/CBS *News* poll asked a national sample of citizens about government spending on welfare. Forty-eight percent of those polled said it should be cut. Only 13% advocated increases. Yet, when asked about "spending on programs for poor children," 47% of all respondents nationally called for increases, while only 9% wanted cuts.

Regardless of the words used, none of the current welfare reform plans finances the changes in the Job Training Partnership Act and the job creation that is central to our plan.

One reason job training and creation are not being linked to child poverty and welfare reform in other plans has to do with the nature of capitalism. In 1995, most politicians were calling for the welfare poor to work. At the same time, many were agreeing with Wall Street that the economy, having reduced overall unemployment to 5% (and about twice that for African Americans), had overheated. Interest rates had to go up. The Federal Reserve increased interest rates in a series of increments. That began to increase the unemployment rate above 5%. Yet how could we employ more AFDC mothers and increase unemployment at the same time?

When they have to trade off, the power brokers of our system prefer more unemployment and less inflation. Those who get most unemployed are the poor at the bottom—with inadequate representation in a political system in which influence is based on how much money one has to buy lobbyists. Inflation is worse for the power brokers because it affects not just the poor, but the rich as well.

Alternatively, the plan set forth in this report recognizes that conventional, incremental monetary and fiscal policy *always* will fail the poor—because, among other reasons, even in the best of times some unemployment is needed by the system to avoid overheating. Our plan sees the need for a national industrial policy that deals with the *structurally* unemployed—those low-income, often AFDC poor persons and families stuck in the mud, who don't benefit from a conventional monetary and fiscal policy that pretends to promise a rising tide that lifts all boats. Our plan is to employ those people at the bottom, even at the expense, if necessary, of a bit more inflation than thought appropriate by those who *say* they simultaneously want AFDC mothers to work and Wall Street markets to be secured against overheating.

Why Not Devolve beyond State Bureaucracy?

Notwithstanding their failure to create jobs, most present plans for child poverty and welfare reform decentralize control from the federal government to the states—through block grants. In our view, this does not devolve far enough. Based on what works, we propose a Walt Whitman-type policy based more on Jeffersonian democracy.

Discretionary block-grant funding means that AFDC and related benefits lose their entitlement status. The poor would lose their safety net. We believe Americans have a right to an entitlement safety net. That was the thinking of President Roosevelt when he instituted Social Security and other reforms and when he told the nation, "People who are hungry and out of a job are the stuff of which dictatorships are made." It is hypocritical for Congress to reverse President Roosevelt, unless members of Congress are prepared also to remove their many safety nets, like stellar medical insurance and retirement plans. Abolishing entitlements also would drop America even further behind many Western European countries, which incorporate safety nets because they are viewed as human rights. Governors need to remember, as well, that entitlements have the virtue of adjusting to economic conditions—if a state has more poor people, federal benefits go up. But Congress can cut a discretionary block-grant program at will.

Executive Summary

Plans to eliminate entitlements and create state block grants also are carefully crafted to decrease the overall level of benefits. Some applaud further tightening the belts of the poor, because, they say, it will lead to more "self-sufficiency." Yet there is little evidence that cutting benefits or increasing taxes on the poor makes them more self-sufficient and better off. Over the past 20 years, welfare benefits have in fact been falling in real spending power—with little positive effect on the poor and considerable negative effect.

Some states have been "creative laboratories for change," to use currently fashionable language. An illustration is the success of southern states in reducing infant mortality. Yet there is great variability among states. There are innovative states—like New York and California. There also are states which are much less innovative—like Texas and Ohio. Some states, like Vermont, have true participatory democracy, while other states, like Louisiana, are entrenched with cronyism. Nor is there any proof that states attract more qualified people than the federal government—or than the successful, private-sector, community-based nonprofit organization.

Experience has shown that, when the federal government makes state block grants that affect high-risk children and youth, governors do not always distribute block grants proportionately to the populations in need. There have been recent years, for example, when the State of California did not grant Los Angeles nearly its proportionate share of drug block-grant money. The same held for Wisconsin and its distribution to Milwaukee. In these and other states, existing misallocations could be magnified if the low-income population increases at a high rate. In such instances, block-grant funds may not cover rising administrative costs in AFDC, food stamps, and Medicaid. Federal block-grant funding to states also tends to erode over time.

Nor have states established a good record in the kind of education, employment training, and job creation that we believe is the first priority in reducing child poverty. For example, a report by the United States General Accounting Office released in December 1994 found that only about 11% of the 4 million parents receiving AFDC were participating in the state-level education and training program known as JOBS (Job Opportunities and Basic Skills). This study was undertaken from 1991 through 1993. The study observed that state education and training programs for AFDC mothers were failing to reach many women at highest risk of long-term dependency, particularly teenagers and drug abusers. The state-run programs were simply not establishing strong links to local employers who could help AFDC recipients find jobs, the GAO concluded. This raises additional doubts about two-years-and-out welfare reform plans by states, like Wisconsin, if they are unaccompanied by comprehensive, or even minimal, job training and placement.

The arguments by some governors today that they are closer to the people when it comes to child poverty and minorities harken back to the arguments of governors George Wallace, Ross Barnett, and Orval Faubus not so long ago that their states could handle racial problems better than the federal government because they were closer to their black citizens. It is hard to believe, but many Americans, including many new members of Congress, seem to have forgotten that "states rights" was a slogan that encouraged people like Bull Conner, facilitated the Ku

Klux Klan, and justified a system of apartheid that denied basic rights to African Americans. The federal government had to overturn their injustice and inaction. This is particularly relevant for child poverty and welfare reform today because the governors are white. Yet there are large numbers of nonwhite leaders at the levels of local government and private nonprofit community organizations, where many more examples of success can be found than at the state level.

For all the talk about devolution to the state level, the contemporary political dialogue suggests that people on both the left and the right do not necessarily, or wholly, trust states. This mistrust exists because most block-grant proposals give each state a fixed pool of money and leave the states with great autonomy to decide who gets support and when. Some conservatives are worried about giving all the responsibility to the states. They are afraid that some states won't undertake what they consider reform—a reform *without* job-training reform or job creation. Progressives are worried that some states will reform the system out of existence and replace it with an alternative that is expensive and ineffective, like orphanages and prison building. It also is possible that a state legislature could cut services and taxes as a lure to business. This could force other states into doing the same, to compete. A downward spiral would be created. As Russell Baker has noted, state legislators "are for sale cheap, at least compared with the prices for Members of the U.S. House and Senate. . . . Consider for example, the splendid character of your own state legislator. You do know who he is, don't you? Ah . . . I see."

Decentralization, say some politicians, is justified by the Tenth Amendment, which concludes that "the powers not delegated to the states by the Constitution, nor prohibited to the states, are reserved to the states respectively, or to the people." Yet those last words—"or to the people"—open the door to power at a more grass-roots level—the level of the private nonprofit community organizations that have had more success with the poor than the states. The Tenth Amendment rationale also overlooks the dictum by Alexander Hamilton that Congress should provide for the "general welfare."

This means that, in our view:

■ No serious child poverty and welfare reform is possible in America without a new employment-training system and a job-creation plan for poor mothers and fathers who qualify. To be able to work, poor parents need adequate health and day care. Greater job opportunity for fathers should be linked to increased financial responsibility by them.

■ Under such reform, a two-years-and-you're-out policy is feasible, as long as the poor have at least as much entitlement safety net status as members of Congress and the poor in many Western European countries.

■ To avoid presenting the taxpaying, voting citizen with another double standard, child-poverty welfare reform should be accompanied by corporate welfare reform, to help finance the new employment-training and job-creation system that is needed.

■ The federal government should finance, oversee, and enforce child-poverty reform, but day-to-day program operations should be devolved in large part to the most creative proven laboratories for change—private-sector nonprofit community organizations. Conservatives ought to approve the *private* nature of these ventures, while progressives always have been attracted to their grass-roots democracy.

Chapter 1

Acknowledging Trends over Time

Only a few years ago the National Commission on Children concluded its deliberations and issued an optimistic view that prospects for improved family life indeed existed. Yet, during those four years, turbulence within the family as well as in communities has increased dramatically, as the impact of the rich getting richer and the poor getting poorer has been felt.

For many families and their children, unprecedented levels of violence regularly disrupt family and community life. Violence has been more evident and frequent in inner-city, low-income black and Latino neighborhoods. But no communities have been spared, regardless of their economic and racial composition or geographic location. Those children and families least equipped to overcome adversity and the uncertainty of environmental instability are increasingly becoming "ghettoized" as a result of economic adversity and disinvestment, the physical and social deterioration of their environments, and instability of their educational and parenting systems.

> [In the 1980s as a result of Reaganomics] the rich got richer and the poor got poorer.
> Kevin Phillips
> *The Politics of the Rich and Poor*

> "I think Reaganomics was an incredible success," representative Dick Armey, the Texas Republican who is now the House majority leader, told reporters. "We ought to stand up and be proud of the 80's."
> David E. Sanger
> *The New York Times*
> January 15, 1995

This report looks at the experiences of such children and families. They represent approximately 10% of all families in the United States. We propose a comprehensive policy. Our concern is primarily with urban populations composed of long-term disadvantaged persons. But rural families living under comparable conditions will benefit equally from a comprehensive policy.

That the majority of those whom this report addresses are families and children of color reflects the disproportionate concentration of poverty in low-income non-white communities. These conditions include high juvenile-arrest and long-term incarceration rates, high rates of school dropouts, high levels of underemployment and unemployment, the increasing number of single-parent households, teen pregnancies, and drug-related dependencies and crimes of violence.

The report looks at federal policy because the potential exists only at the federal level for generating sufficient resources at a scale equal to the dimensions of the

Chapter 1

problem—even though we believe that actual implementation of programs should be at the local (not federal or state) level, especially in the private (but nonprofit) sector.

This report also is about our national will and the resolve of our institutions to make a difference in families. Organizations and agencies throughout the United States traditionally have been at the cutting edge of social change. The War on Poverty and other components of the Great Society's programs were pioneered and piloted in local communities, under the auspices of nonprofit agencies funded by foundations and other nonprofit organizations. Similarly, many of the remedies to family and youth problems are being piloted on a small scale in local communities. But such efforts do not yet have a national political constituency. We lack a guiding national policy to replicate successful programs. And we lack a national policy to facilitate dialogue about what works and how it works.

Thirty Years of Inner-City Family Policy

The 1960s was a watershed decade for family and youth policies. Various statutory tools and policy efforts focused on debilitating conditions that affect selected racial and economic groups. Conditions of deprivation inspired the Civil Rights Act, the Voting Rights Act, and the Economic Opportunity Act, to name a few. Presidential commissions were put together to explore the problems of inner-city youth who acted out their frustration with deplorable conditions of poverty and racism.

How have conditions changed in the past 30 years and how have these changes affected urban family life? The inner core of urban areas and large cities have become balkanized, neglected outposts of deterioration, joblessness, and self-destruction for children and their families. Families earn less than they did 30 years ago (see Table 1). Fifty percent of African American children and 40% of Hispanic children younger than six years of age live in poverty.

> **The inner core of urban areas and large cities have become balkanized, neglected outposts of deterioration, joblessness, and self-destruction for children and their families.**

Some of these communities could benefit as much from an arms-control agreement as could international communities in the news today. More violent, gun-related deaths have occurred in American inner cities than occurred during the entire Vietnam War. Even infants younger than one year old face brutal lives and the possibility of early death. The life expectancy of African American males between 15 and 34 years of age is 10 times shorter than it is for white males: The death rate from homicide is nearly 110/100,000 population for African American males and approximately 12/100,000 for white males (see Table 2).

Household Income Less Than $15,000	Then (1970)	Now (1990)
White	22.5%	22.0%
African American	41.5%	42.4%
Hispanic	26.2% (1972)	34.0%

Table 1. Household income less than $15,000, 1970–1990.

The Joint Center for Political and Economic Studies reports that urban areas are home to 75% of African Americans, 60% of American Indians, and 95% of immigrants of color. Between 1980 and 1990, roughly 40% of population growth in the United States resulted from immigration. Seventy-five percent of those immigrants were either Latino or Asian, and 95% of these immigrants have settled in and around the 10 largest American cities—where African Americans and American Indians already live.

Racism has adverse effects on communities where people of color are concentrated. So the continuing economic and physical decline of cities comes as no sur-

Acknowledging Trends over Time

Age	African American Males	African American Females	White Males	White Females
Less than 1 year	19.3	23.5	5.6	6.0
1 - 4 years	7.5	6.3	2.2	1.6
5 - 14 years	4.2	3.1	1.0	0.8
15 - 24 years	101.8	17.4	11.5	3.9
25 - 34 years	108.8	25.5	13.2	4.4
35 - 44 years	79.2	14.6	10.4	3.2
45 - 54 years	45.2	7.7	7.6	2.5
55 - 64 years	29.1	6.8	6.0	2.0
65 - 74 years	26.2	9.0	4.1	2.3
75 - 84 years	30.5	9.9	4.3	3.0
85 years plus	31.4	12.7	5.1	2.9

Table 2. Death rates due to homicide, per 100,000 population among African Americans and whites.

prise. The 1992 riots in Los Angeles resulting from the Rodney King trial as well as the potential for civil unrest in inner-city communities throughout the country attest to the instability of urban environments for primarily nonwhite families that live there.

The current unemployment rate for African Americans and other people of color is approximately 14%, well above the national average of approximately 7%. It is estimated that urban African American, Latino, and American Indian unemployment exceeds 60% in many inner-city communities, on reservations, and in poor rural areas (see Table 3). The poverty status for whites and African Americans has improved slightly in the past 30 years. But it has worsened for Latinos and is higher for Asians than for whites (see Table 4).

A disproportionate number of Americans of color are involved with the criminal-justice system at both the state and federal levels. For example, although African

Unemployment Rates	Then (1963)	Now (1992)
White	5.0%	6.5%
African American/Other	10.8%	14.1%

Table 3. Unemployment rates among whites, African Americans, and others, 1963–1992.
Note: Estimates for unemployed urban African Americans and Hispanics exceed 50% in some localities.

Chapter 1

Poverty Status	1966	1991
White	12.2%	10.7%
African American	41.8%	32.7%
Hispanic Origin (1973)	21.9%	28.7%
Asian American (1980)	-------	12.1%*

Table 4. Poverty status among whites, African Americans, Hispanics, and Asian Americans, 1966–1991.
*Note: Includes Laotian, 65.9%, and Cambodian, 48.7%.

Americans make up only 12% of the population, they constitute nearly 50% of inmates (see Tables 5–8). Juveniles are increasingly being charged with violent crimes of murder, rape, robbery, and assault.

The Joint Center for Political and Economic Studies has found that

> arrests of black males on violent crime charges did increase in the latter part of the 1980s, but arrests of white males for violent crime offenses showed exactly the same pattern of growth. The black share or proportion of violent crime arrests has not increased over the decade. The increase in youthful violence should be cause of grave concern to our society. [But] the search for effective ways to reduce this violence must begin with the recognition that violence among young people is not a problem exclusive to young black males.

City and Family Policies of the 1980s and Early 1990s

Large cities are burdened with especially difficult challenges. They have the oldest housing stock and the highest rates of unemployment. In some cities, unemployment is higher than it was at the peak of the Great Depression. In these cities fewer students complete high school than did 20 years ago.

More babies are born to single mothers in cities than occurs elsewhere, thus stacking the odds against economic survival for these urban children. Industry has abandoned cities for nonurban locations. Drug abuse and increasing incidents of violent crime against person and property characterize many of these communities. Economic and social problems in the nation's cities are compounded by the fact that cities are the main locations for newly arrived immigrants, most of whom are Asians and nonwhite Latinos.

Metropolitan cities are the primary residence for 75% of African Americans, for whom cities remain their best chance to rise out of poverty into the American main-

Prison Status	1964	1986
TOTAL	81,099	183,769
White	65%	55%
African American	33%	44%
Hispanic	2%	1%

Table 5. Admissions to state and federal prisons, 1964–1986.

Prison Status	1964	1986
TOTAL	67,879	167,474
White	63%	53%
African American	35%	46%
Hispanic	2%	1%

Table 6. Admissions to state prisons, 1964–1986.

TOTAL	White	Black	African American	Native American	Asian
2,588	1,316	1,008	185	47	19
100%	51%	39%	7%	2%	.7%

Table 7. Prisoners under sentence of death–1992.

stream. As a result of unyielding attitudes toward diversity, which isolate whites from nonwhites and well-to-do from poor, cities remain the only real alternative for persons who are neither white nor well-to-do.

■ Blocking Decentralization

The Reagan and Bush administrations blocked decentralization of decision making at the level closest to the people—the city and community level. Federal assistance and economic aid programs to cities and their residents were dismantled. Between 1978, the high point of federal aid to cities, and 1988, when President Bush began his term of office, direct aid to cities decreased by nearly one-third—from 28% of the total federal aid distributed in 1978 to 17% of the total distribution in 1988.

At the same time, aid from the federal government to states and noncity localities (counties, suburbs, and rural districts) increased nearly 100% during that same period—from $69 billion to more than $114 billion. Yet, state decision making was further from the people than city decision making.

One explanation was that the Reagan and Bush administrations owed substantial political debts to their supporters, who were primarily suburban and rural conservatives and self-made "New Federalists."

At the beginning of the Bush presidency, 600 local officials who were surveyed gave the Reagan/Bush administration "a lousy report card" on Washington's han-

TOTAL	White	African American	Native American	Asian/Pacific
774,375	369,485	367,122	6,251	2,806
100%	48%	47%	.8%	.4%

Table 8. Prisoners under jurisdiction of state and federal authorities–1992.

> Between 1978, the high point of federal aid to cities, and 1988, when President Bush began his term of office, direct aid to cities decreased by nearly one-third.

Chapter 1

dling of city-related issues such as drugs, housing, disposal of hazardous materials, unemployment, poverty, and the federal deficit.

■ The Bush Policy on Cities

A bipartisan panel of mayors from cities such as Newark, Indianapolis, Dallas, Hartford, and New York called for a new urban agenda for the 1990s, stating that "education, housing, drugs, AIDS, transportation, and the elderly are problems that the federal government cannot continue to distance itself from." They challenged President Bush to create a national council of urban advisers to handle urban issues. He did.

President Bush's 1988 campaign promised "a kinder, gentler nation." But the Interagency Task Force that he appointed to study problems of poverty did not propose new strategies to assist cities, but instead stated that President Bush should do as President Reagan had advised—just make things work better. One task force member stated that "it was fun to think about" things that might "do something about poverty," but that there was no money. No new initiatives were recommended.

The Bush administration was not completely silent on the subject of cities. In the first year of the Bush presidency, Secretary of Housing and Urban Development (HUD) Jack Kemp advanced his perennial (since 1980) solution to urban decline: enterprise zones. In a 1989 HUD report, Secretary Kemp proposed enterprise zones as an alternative to direct budgeting of federal dollars for urban economic development. Nevertheless, enterprise zones failed (see page 12).

The urban explosion in south central Los Angeles following the trial verdict exonerating four L.A. police officers who beat Rodney King highlighted the frustration and hopelessness of inner-city residents. Cutbacks in urban dollars had inhibited the development of new urban and poverty strategies. Urban advocates described the grim conditions of south central Los Angeles as the plight of major urban centers throughout the country.

The president's traditional supporters also were outraged, although for different reasons, over the events in Los Angeles. A Republican representative from California stated, "There's resentment from the rural areas . . . that the administration was about to send the wrong message that urban terrorism brings federal largess." Vice President Dan Quayle charged the Democrats with promoting mayhem and inertia through welfare-state, tax-and-spend urban solutions.

Under attack from both progressives and conservatives, President Bush came late and ill prepared to the same dilemma that has confronted every president since Franklin Roosevelt: How do we help cities and their residents create and sustain a decent quality of life? For the first time since Bush took office, the White House issued a formal statement on urban policy—a news release captioned "President Bush's Initiatives for Strengthening Urban Areas." These initiatives suggested the following actions:

■ *Weed and seed*: $500 million to "weed out" the criminals and drug dealers from the streets and to "seed" social programs and assistance, thus reducing crime and drug use.

■ *Home ownership for people everywhere* (H.O.P.E.): $1 billion to help 100,000 families living in public housing and other government-owned properties to purchase their housing units.

Education, housing, drugs, AIDS, transportation, and the elderly are problems that the federal government cannot continue to distance itself from.

Under attack from both liberals and conservatives, Bush came late and ill prepared to the same dilemma that has confronted every president since Franklin Roosevelt: How do we help cities and their residents create and sustain a decent quality of life?

■ *Enterprise zones*: Initiate HUD's urban economic-development program as described earlier.

■ *America 2000*: Primarily noncash incentives for educational reform resulting from summit conference recommendations (including the controversial proposal for parental choice of private, religious, or public schools).

■ *Welfare reform*: Flexibility in welfare administration and relaxation of welfare restrictions at both state and federal levels.

■ *Youth jobs*: Congressional passage of a jobs and training program, long supported by urban and poverty activists.

Commenting on the overall effect of this agenda on urban communities and their residents, Eddie N. Williams, president of the Joint Center for Political and Economic Studies, stated:

> Today, after the L.A. riot, President Bush and Congress are contemplating Band-Aids to deal with a problem which requires a tourniquet. Our cities are literally bleeding to death. It is now an ethical, moral and survival requirement that a serious approach to urban policy be advanced, implemented and sustained. The problems of our cities, and of blacks and other minorities who live there, can no longer be swept under the rug.

■ Trickle-Down Economics

The trickle-down supply-side economics of the 1980s had a devastating effect on inner-city families. Tax rates for the poor increased and tax rates for the wealthy decreased (Figure 1). By 1992, the lowest income tax rate was 15% and the highest rate was 31%, a spread of just 16 points. By comparison, in 1968 the bottom rate was 14% and the top rate was 75%, a spread of 61 points. Thus, income tax in the United States regressed. By comparison, tax rates in France, Germany, Italy, and Japan are more progressive (Figure 2).

African Americans especially felt that the Bush administration's position on civil rights and urban relief were ambivalent and insubstantial at best, mean spirited at worst.

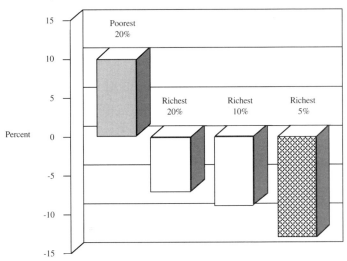

Fig. 1. *Changes in tax rates between 1980–1990 in the United States.*

Chapter 1

Sources of Revenue

Various taxes as a percentage of total revenue. The largest component of each country's tax system is shown in boldface.

	Britain	Canada	France	Germany	Italy	Japan	United States
Personal income	26.6%	**38.4%**	11.8%	**29.5%**	26.7%	**24.7%**	**35.7%**
Corporate	12.3	8.5	5.5	5.5	10.1	24.4	8.5
Social Security employee	7.5	4.4	13.0	15.6	6.4	10.1	11.5
Social Security employer	9.5	8.4	27.2	18.5	23.8	14.5	16.5
Goods and services	**30.9**	29.5	**28.7**	25.6	**26.9**	12.6	16.2
Other	13.2	10.8	13.7	5.3	6.1	13.7	11.5

Total

All taxes, as a percentage of the gross domestic product.

	36.5	35.3	43.8	38.1	37.8	30.6	30.1

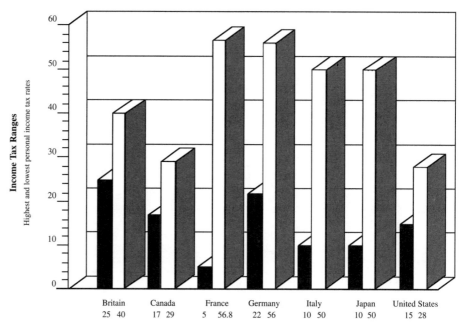

Fig. 2. Taxation by nation–1989.

■ Military Investment and Human Disinvestment

While trickle-down, supply-side economic policy, which included disinvestment in programs for the poor, was implemented throughout the 1980s and early 1990s, the federal government invested heavily in the military. Between 1979 and 1992, appropriations for job training and employment fell from nearly $12 billion per year to less than $5 billion per year. During that same period, federal appropriations on Star Wars research climbed from $0 to almost $4 billion per year. Over several years in the 1980s, funding for Star Wars research actually exceeded funding for job training (Figure 3). From 1980 to 1990 community-development block grants to the cities were cut from more than $6 billion to less than $3 billion. During approximately the same period, overall federal outlays for defense skyrocketed

> Over several years in the 1980s, funding for Star Wars research actually exceeded funding for job training.

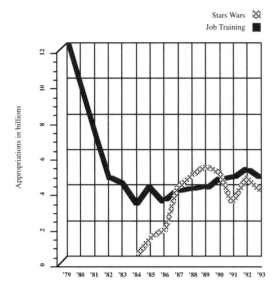

Fig. 3. Federal Appropriations for Star Wars and Job Training, 1979–1993.

from approximately $200 billion per year to nearly $300 billion per year, while overall federal outlays for education, job training, employment, and social services declined from approximately $50 billion per year to less than $40 billion per year—a decrease of more than 20% (Figure 4.)

The huge increases in military expenditures were financed only minimally through cuts in domestic spending. Most of it was paid for by running up the national debt. From 1980 to 1993, the deficit climbed from $74 billion to $331 billion (Figure 5). As the nation entered the 1990s, annual federal spending to cover the interest on the debt was approximately the same as annual spending by government at all levels on public education for grades K through 12. Thirty percent of a typical family's total tax dollars was used to pay interest on the debt (Figure 6).

■ Prison Building and the War on Drugs

Prison building constituted one exception to the federal government's domestic disinvestment policies. Throughout the 1980s, the United States moved past South Africa and the former Soviet Union to achieve the highest rate of incarceration among industrialized nations in the world (Figure 7). Federal and state prison building cost $37 billion over the decade. A new prison cell in New York State cost between $75,000 and $100,000, and the cost of maintaining a prisoner skyrocketed to $30,000 a year. It now costs more to go to jail than to Yale.

Prison building became part of the nation's education policy as well. More that 70% of the prison space available today was built in the mid-1980s and early 1990s, whereas only approximately 10% of the schools open today have been built or repaired since the mid-1980s. Has funding for prison building diminished funding for school building?

The prison population tripled while funding for housing for the poor was cut by more than 80% from 1978 to 1991. The cost of a new prison cell in New York State

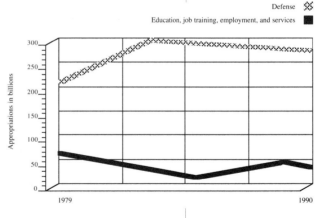

Fig. 4. Federal outlays for defense, job training, employment, and social services in the United States, 1979–1990.

Chapter 1

> The cost of a new prison cell in New York State equals the average cost of a new home in the United States.

equals the average cost of a new home in the United States. So prison building might also be viewed as the nation's low-income-housing policy of the 1980s.

Expenditures for the War on Drugs increased from less than $2 billion per year in 1980 to approximately $11 billion per year in 1991 (Figure 8). Throughout this period, however, the proportion of monies spent on supply-side law enforcement and interdiction policies re-mained at approximately 70%, whereas the proportion spent on demand-side prevention and treatment remained at approximately 30%. There exists no scientific evidence to justify these policies. By way of comparison, France, for example, spends 30% of budgeted monies on law en-forcement and interdiction and 70% on prevention and treatment.

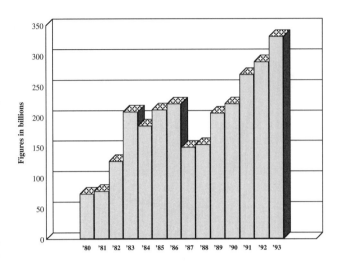

Fig. 5. The federal deficit in the United States, 1980–1993.

■ Oversimplification and Neglect

From 1981 to 1992, there was little talk about possible connections among inner-city family policy, tax policy, inner-city disinvestment, drug problems, prison building, school building, and low-income housing construction. Nor was there much enthusiasm for civil-rights enforcement or for reform of child poverty programs (the main such program being Aid to Families with Dependent Children) through job training. In the absence of inner-city funding, however, the government advocated volunteerism, self-sufficiency, self-help, and empowerment. "Family values" became a catch phrase admonishing citizens to become more self-disciplined.

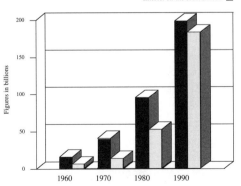

Fig. 6. Spending on debt interest and public education in the United States, 1960–1990.

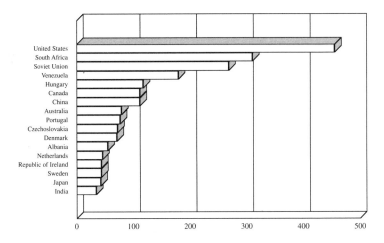

Fig. 7. Prison incarceration rate per 1,000,000 by nation in 1990 or 1991 (1989 in the Soviet Union).

Failure

By most objective measures, these federal domestic policies from 1981 to 1992 were a stunning failure.

■ Trickle-Down Economics

As a result of supply-side tax policy, the income of the poor declined 10% between 1977 and 1988. By contrast, the income of the middle class changed little and the income of the wealthiest 1% increased by more that 120% (Figure 9). As conservative analyst Kevin Phillips concluded in The Politics of the Rich and Poor, the rich got richer and the poor got poorer. The rich who got richer tended to be white, and the poor who got poorer tended to be minority. Racial divisions as well as class divisions widened.

In his The Economy of Nations, Secretary of Labor Robert Reich views the upper-income group—the "fortunate fifth"—as, in effect, seceding from the rest of American society. For example, 85% of the richest families in the greater Philadelphia area live outside the city limits, whereas 80% of Philadelphia poor live in the inner city. This city–suburb split had a tremendous impact on the tax base of Philadelphia. Such differences are common across the nation. In Texas, for example, the richest school district in the state spends more

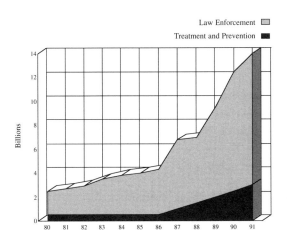

Fig. 8. Federal spending in the "war on drugs" in the United States from 1980–1991.

> Acknowledging Trends over Time

> "Family values" became a catch phrase admonishing citizens to become more self-disciplined.

Chapter 1

than $19,000/year/pupil; the poorest district spends approximately $2,000/year/pupil. Increasingly, according to Secretary of Labor Robert Reich, the fortunate fifth is linked by jet aircraft, fax machines, telephones, satellites, and fiber optic cable to their commercial and political counterparts throughout the nation and the world, while becoming less connected or concerned with the bottom four-fifths of America in their own hometowns.

> According to Secretary of Labor Robert Reich, the fortunate fifth is linked to their commercial and political counterparts throughout the nation and the world, while becoming less connected or concerned with the bottom four-fifths of America in their own hometowns.

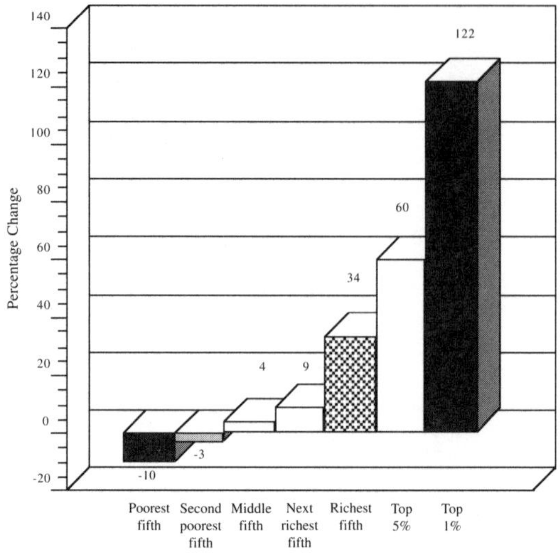

Fig. 9. Average after-tax income gains and losses by various household income groups in the United States, 1977–1988.

■ Enterprise Zones

In 1992, the Urban Institute reported that

> extensive evaluations of state enterprise zone programs have found no evidence that incentives have contributed to employment or investment growth in designated areas.... Most proposed enterprise zone incentives are poorly targeted on the poor. Few of the tax benefits in the leading proposals accrue directly to the disadvantaged residents of enterprise zones. Instead much of it goes to reward businesses for behavior that will not necessarily benefit the poor.

The Urban Institute examined proposals for 50 enterprise zones submitted each year by the Bush administration. The study estimated that, even if the proposals met the administration's standards—an outcome considered quite unlikely by the Urban Institute—the program would have affected at most 1.5% of the poor in the United States. The administration's own budget indicated that the enterprise zone program would lose $1.8 billion in revenues over five years.

The Urban Institute study concluded that federal resources used to provide generous tax subsidies in the 50 enterprise zones could be better utilized by developing effective programs for low-income children. Similarly, a U.S. General Accounting Office evaluation concluded that the Maryland enterprise zone program "did not stimulate economic growth as measured by employment or strongly influence most employers' decisions about business location." According to *Business Week*, one study found that infrastructure, low crime rates, and access to labor markets were more important factors in business-site selection than were tax rates. And according to the *Economist*, a conservative publication, "There is evidence that [enterprise zones] are often wasteful and tend to displace rather than create business activity."

■ Federal Disinvestment from Education and Job Training

Combined with the increased disparity between rich and poor, federal disinvestment from education and job training has yielded undesirable outcomes. For example,

- During the 1980s, college enrollment among African American males declined.
- In 1960 the ratio of African American to white unemployed young adults 20–24 years of age was 1:6; in 1989, the ratio was 2:3.
- For all African American households, the median family income was 59% that of whites in 1966 compared with 56% in 1989.
- By the end of the 1980s, the poverty rate was 33% for African Americans, 29% for Hispanic Americans, 14% for Asian Americans, and 11% for whites. The poor were increasingly concentrated in the nation's cities.
- Nationwide, the number of children living in poverty increased by 22% throughout the 1980s. Most of these children lived in the inner city. According to the Children's Defense Fund, one of five American children now lives in poverty. In Canada, Germany, and the United Kingdom, the child poverty rate is approximately half that of the United States.
- Among industrialized countries, the United States has the highest incidence of poverty among the nonelderly and the widest distribution of poverty across all age and family groups. Compared with industrialized countries, the poor in the United States experience the longest spells of poverty.
- Poverty in the United States is generally more severe than is poverty in continental Europe. In the United States, most poor families fall far below half the poverty line. In contrast, among European countries a large percentage of poor households remain close to the poverty line.

Civil Rights and Racial Tension

Politicians tell us that the African American middle class has grown throughout the past two decades while a growing hard-core disadvantaged class has been left behind. But even the African American middle class experiences inequalities in the private sector. For example, African Americans make up 10% of the nation's work force but only 4% of doctors and 3% of lawyers. African American male lawyers 35 to 45 years of age earn on average $790 for every $1,000 of their white counterparts. (African American female lawyers in the same age group do better, earning $930 for every $1,000 of their white female counterparts.)

Within metropolitan areas, whites, African Americans, Hispanic Americans, and other minorities have become increasingly isolated from one another. In the 1980s, sociologists coined the term "hypersegregation" to describe this pattern. One indicator, based on the research of sociolinguist William Labov, is that the English spoken by inner-city African Americans has become more and more different from the English spoken by whites. A more stark indicator was the 1992 riot in Los Angeles.

In his recent book *Two Nations, Black and White, Separate, Hostile and Unequal*, Andrew Hacker paints a grim picture of racial interaction. A sense of white superiority still haunts America. Hacker concludes that the condition is chronic and cancer-like.

> There remains an unarticulated suspicion might there be something about the Black race that suited them for slavery? This is not to say anyone argues that human bondage was justified. Still, the facts that slavery existed for so long and was so taken for granted cannot be erased from American minds.

Chapter 1

Senator Bill Bradley of New Jersey, one of the few white members of Congress who has talked honestly and openly about race relations, adds:

> I don't think politics has dealt honestly with race in 25 years. . . . Republicans have used race in a divisive way to get votes, speaking in code words to targeted audiences. Democrats have essentially ignored self-destructive behavior of parts of the minority population and covered self-destructive behavior in a cloak of silence and self-denial.

Tension exists not only between African Americans and whites. Hispanics are the fastest growing ethnic group, generally, and in some cities, especially on the West Coast, the Asian population also is growing rapidly. In a few central cities, Los Angeles among them, the African American proportion of the population declined between 1980 and 1990. According to the Urban Institute, these changes have contributed to new social tension "in which different minority groups collide with one another in economic and political competition."

Overall, despite gains incurred since the 1960s, the atmosphere of greed and disinvestment in the 1980s has sustained the 1968 Kerner Riot Commission's conclusion that in the United States there exist "two societies, one Black, one White—separate and unequal." In fact, the commission's conclusion may be even more relevant today than it was in 1968 with the emergence of multiracial disparities and growing segregation.

■ Prison Building

Despite unprecedented increases in prison building, violent crime reported to police increased by more than 40% between 1981 and 1991 (Figure 10). Reports of homicide increased, and homicide is more accurately reported to police than is any other crime. (Crime rates based on interviewing victims remained about the same throughout the decade, although such surveys encounter some reporting problems in the inner city.) Partly as a result of drugs and gangs, the homicide rate among young men exploded in the 1980s. For example, between 1984 and 1991, homicide arrest rates for males 14 to 17 years of age increased more than 60%, and arrest rates for males 18 to 24 years old increased by approximately 150% (Figure 11). The young persons arrested were disproportionately from minority groups.

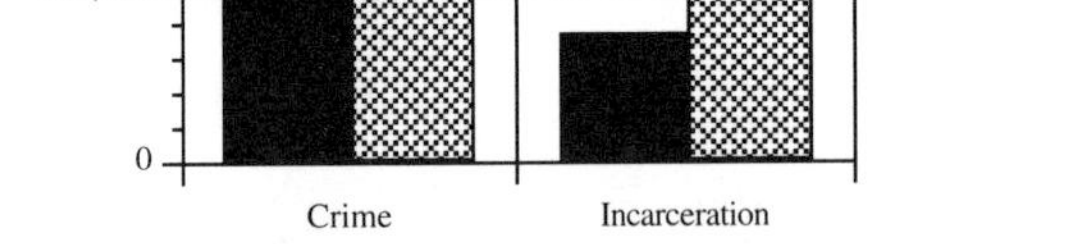

To justify prison building to citizens, whose taxes finance new prisons, politicians might try to show that countries with higher rates of im-

> Despite gains incurred since the 1960s, the atmosphere of greed and disinvestment in the 1980s has sustained the 1968 Kerner Riot Commission's conclusion that in the United States there exist "two societies, one Black, one White—separate and unequal."

Fig. 10. Trends in violent crime (murder, aggravated assault, forcible rape, robbery) and incarceration in the United States, 1981–1991.

prisonment have lower rates of crime. The opposite is true. The United States has the highest rates of violent crime in the industrialized world (Figure 12) as well as the highest rate of incarceration (Figure 7, page 27).

So it is difficult to justify to American taxpayers that prison building is an effective or cost-effective way to stop crime.

Prison building may protect inner-city residents from the small number of violent, repeat offenders who commit a large proportion of serious crime. Prison building also may make family building and cohesion more difficult. The reason is that offenders who commit less serious crimes are imprisoned without receiving remedial education and job training. So they leave prison more hardened against society as well as less able to find work to support their families.

Studies conducted by the U.S. General Accounting Office and the National Center for Institutions and Alternatives have not shown that military-style boot-camp imprisonment is effective. Such studies do document, however, that brutality and racism often occur in boot-camp-style prisons.

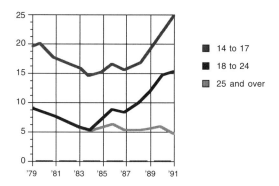

Fig. 11. Homicide arrests per 100,000 people, by age of suspect in the United States, 1979–1991.

■ "Empowerment" and "Family Values"

Throughout the 1980s, the word *empowerment* became particularly fashionable among politicians. For example, in public housing communities, empowerment was used to describe programs for tenant management and tenant ownership. With few resources available, however, such programs were limited to a few demonstra-

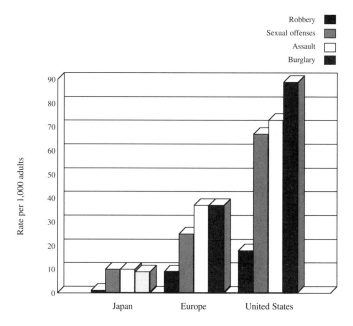

Fig. 12. Rates of violent crime victimization by nation, 1988.

The United States has the highest rates of violent crime in the industrialized world as well as the highest rate of incarceration.

Chapter 1

tions. For example, one demonstration in Washington, D.C., was used as a showcase for visiting dignitaries. Even the Queen of England visited it. But without sufficient resources to train all or most tenants in all or most public housing, such empowerment did not have any national impact. Similarly, to provide the training and resources necessary for tenants throughout all public housing to own their own housing, should they wish, little national impact could be expected.

Care also was taken throughout the 1980s *not* to use the word empowerment in many areas where it *did* make sense. For example, the word was not used to describe innovative ways to invest in remedial education linked to job training and placement, which might provide a way out of poverty for high-risk teen fathers. There was no used of the word empowerment to describe tax changes that would encourage more nonprofit organizations to create safe havens—places to go after school, where youth could work with big brothers and big sisters in an extended family setting. And there was no use of the word empowerment to describe increased access by poor families to the legal system.

One consequence is that some American psychologists invented a new term—*post-empowerment syndrome*. This term refers, for example, to programs run by an inner-city nonprofit organization that is funded for, say, two years and then encouraged to become "self-sufficient" through "volunteerism," "partnerships" with other nonprofits and for-profit businesses in areas with little commercial infrastructure, like south central Los Angeles. When such initiatives fail, as is usually the case, and when participants realize that they are not truly empowered, they become even more frustrated and angry. As a result, they may be less likely to accept subsequent strategies, however well-intentioned and well-designed.

As part of the same kind of rhetoric as "empowerment" and "self-sufficiency," the emphasis on "family values" without educational and employment opportunities in the 1980s did not have an impact. For example, in 1960, 20% of all African American children were living in fatherless families. *Today, the figure is an astounding 60%.* Fatherless families have increased among minorities and whites, the poor, and the middle class. But the increase is the greatest for the minority poor.

Reversing Trends and Doing What Works

But if things got worse in the last quarter century, we also learned about programs that worked. This report identifies those programs and proposes that they be replicated to a scale equal to the dimensions of the problem. By so doing, we will create a comprehensive and interdependent policy for poor families, employment, and urban reconstruction.

Chapter 2

Reducing Child Poverty

Back in the early part of this century, when the Supreme Court had taken back the three great post-Civil War amendments, when blacks were at the mercy of lawless courts, lawless police forces and lawless gangs, three black children were born in St. Louis, Missouri. When the youngest was born their mother died. They were poor people. They were very poor. Their grandparents had been slaves.

The oldest was six, he was a little boy. There was a little girl who was four, and then there was a baby. These are what you would call children at-risk. Their father was not the kind of guy who was going to be able to take care of them.

Fortunately, their uncle by marriage, who had a job, took them in. It was a working-class job. It was a good job by black standards in those days. He was a railroad waiter. Their lives were organized around that man's job. Money came in. They had a sense of being connected to the economy. The man had authority in the family because he brought the money in. Their aunt who took care of them gave them daily lessons in values and studying hard and working hard. They went to public schools, they went to the public university.

The girl became a terrific and very popular student, before she died while she was a junior. The baby became a journalist of a segregated newspaper. He interviewed President Roosevelt and Governor Landon and wrote a series of brilliant analyses of the campaign in 1936 before he died at an early age. The oldest of the three went on to become a public service executive. These people were my Uncle Roy Wilkins, my Aunt Armeta, and my father. They were saved from being children at-risk. They were given values. They were given a future by one thing—my Great-Uncle Sam's job.

Roger W. Wilkins
Remarks made at the
Presidential Commission Anniversary Dinner
Milton S. Eisenhower Foundation
Washington, D.C.
January 27, 1994

Chapter 2

In America today policy on poor American families usually is taken to be policy on welfare reform.

There are few words less popular in America than "welfare." Next to "build prisons," the two most salable words for a politician today are "cut welfare." Yet "welfare" is a program that tries to remove poor children from poverty. The main federal welfare program is, of course, called Aid to Families with Dependent Children (AFDC). Children make up two-thirds of its 14 million recipients. Nearly one child in four lives in poverty in America. That leaves many citizens ashamed. "Poor children" have always been a subject of bipartisan concern.

Public opinion is full of contradictions. A December 1994 New York Times/CBS News poll asked a national sample of citizens about "government spending on welfare." Forty-eight percent of those polled said it should be cut; only 13% advocated increases. Yet, when asked about "spending on programs for poor children," 47% of all respondents nationally called for increases, while only 9% wanted cuts.

Our Plan

Accordingly, this chapter is about how to reduce child poverty. We agree with Roger Wilkins, in the quote above, that the best way is through jobs. Most of this report is centered on programs that already have proven to work and that, in one way or another, are about educational opportunity, job opportunity, and job creation. Chapter 3 recommends expansion of Head Start to all poor children who are eligible. Such preschool improves educational achievement and employability. Many middle-class and upper-class kids already have this advantage, through private preschool arranged by their parents. Chapter 3 has proven initiatives like the James Comer Yale University School Development Plan, Project Prepare, and boys and girls club-type safe havens after school. These cutting-edge successes increase the likelihood that children and youth will stay in school and so qualify later for legal labor-market employment. Chapter 4 notes that America's major job-training program for high-risk youth, the Job Training Partnership Act (JTPA), begun in the early 1980s, has failed—based on scientific evaluations commissioned by the Reagan administration. Chapter 4 recommends an alternative job training and placement system based on programs that *have* succeeded at the grass-roots community level—like YouthBuild USA, the Argus Community Learning for Living Center, and Job Corps. Chapter 5 calls for placement of poor people so trained—in jobs that rebuild inner-city housing and inner-city infrastructure. The jobs created also would be for associated essential inner-city services—like teaching, child care, and policing. Based on the past experiences, chapter 5 concludes that reconstruction should be carried out, in particular, by local private-sector, nonprofit community-development corporations—which receive grants and loans via private national nonprofit institutions like the Ford Foundation's Local Initiatives Support Corporation (LISC) and developer James Rouse's Enterprise Foundation. LISC and the Enterprise Foundation already rehabilitate and build more housing for the poor than the U.S. Department of Housing and Urban Development (HUD). Chapter 5 shows how the development ought to be financed through expansion of communi-

Nearly one child in four lives in poverty in America.

ty-development banking, based on the successful model of the South Shore Bank in Chicago and secured through community-based problem-oriented policing, based on models scientifically evaluated as successful by the Police Foundation, the Police Executive Research Forum, and the Eisenhower Foundation.

With an eye to estimates made by the 1968 Kerner Riot Commission, this plan to reduce child poverty (i.e., to reform welfare), and to achieve many other goals to restore human capital and revive inner cities, will cost roughly $30 billion per year in new investments in children, youth, workers, and infrastructure. Our best estimate is that the plan ought to be sustained for at least 10 years, and better, a full generation of inner-city children who, over that time, transition into good workers—taxpaying citizens who take responsibility for instilling the same values in their children as Roger Wilkins's Great-Uncle Sam instituted in the children he and his wife raised. We assert in chapter 6 that, notwithstanding rhetoric in Washington, D.C., there really are no technical, financial obstacles to generating those resources. It just takes political will. The financing ought to come from reducing corporate welfare (which is at least $40 billion per year and may be considerably higher), reducing military spending (based on the recommendations of former Joint Chiefs of Staff and of former Reagan Assistant Defense Secretary Lawrence Korb, now at the Brookings Institution), and increasing taxes significantly on the richest 1% of Americans, who saw their incomes go up by 122% from 1977 to 1988 as a result of trickle-down, supply-side economics. (The real incomes of the poor, the working class, and the middle class declined over these same years, and so we believe they now should receive tax cuts.)

Our plan assumes health-care reform, as outlined in chapter 4, that allows adults to function as good parents and workers. (Because the issues are so complex and there presently is so much political discord over health-care reform, the costs of such reform are not included in our $30 billion per year education investment, job investment, and housing/infrastructure reconstruction budget.)

Chapter 8 concludes that our plan can be attained if American citizens realize that the problem is not so much the Boyz N the Hood as the boys on the Hill. It calls for a citizen revolt to reverse what some view as the betrayal of American democracy. For example, among other citizen-instigated actions, we need to put tight controls on the lobbyists with those thousand dollar suits and alligator shoes, and we need to reform campaign financing. Then we will have the money to implement what works for our children on a scale equal to the dimension of the problem.

Our plan is for the federal government to raise money, create guidelines based on what works, and enforce standards. At the same time, to a considerable extent, we favor decentralized day-to-day implementation of the investments in children, youth, families, and inner cities that form our plan to reduce child poverty. If something federal works—like Head Start—don't fix it. But localities, and especially private-sector, nonprofit community-based organizations, are closest to the people and have had the most success. Decentralization and "devolution," to use the ungainly word now in fashion inside the beltway in Washington, D.C., are to *this*, community and neighborhood, level in our plan. As Walt Whitman wrote in *Leaves of Grass*, "The genius of the United States is not best or most in its executives or leg-

> **Notwithstanding rhetoric in Washington, D.C., there really are no technical, financial obstacles to generating the resources recommended here. It just takes political will.**

Chapter 2

islatures, nor in its ambassadors or authors or colleges or churches . . . nor even in its newspapers or inventors . . . but always most in the common people."

Examples of Community Solutions

Our report is filled with more details of our kind of decentralization, to private-sector, community-based nonprofit organizations, run by Whitman's common people, in inner cities. Here, we give just two illustrations—one for young AFDC mothers and one for the absent fathers—to try to provide the reader with a sense of the promise they hold for reducing child poverty, *if* they are replicated on a sufficient scale as part of a coordinated, comprehensive plan financed at the federal level and implemented day-to-day at the private, grass-roots neighborhood level.

■ Project Redirection

The Ford Foundation's Project Redirection was for teen mothers 17 years of age or younger who lacked a high school diploma or an equivalency degree. Most were eligible for AFDC. Implemented by private, nonprofit community-based organizations in 11 locations during the 1980s, this comprehensive program sought to enhance teens' educational, job-related, parenting, conflict-resolution, and life-management skills while encouraging them to delay further childbearing until they were more financially independent.

Project Redirection linked participants with existing opportunities in the community and supported these "brokered" services by organizing workshops, peer-group sessions, and individual counseling. Teens were paired with female adult mentors in the community who volunteered to provide ongoing support and friendship to convey values both within and outside the normal program structure. Five years after entering the program (and four years, on average, after leaving it), Project Redirection participants, although still disadvantaged, showed more favorable outcomes than did a comparison group of young mothers in terms of employment, earnings, welfare dependency, and parenting skills. Their children were more advanced developmentally *vis-à-vis* the comparison group.

Project Redirection provides a good illustration of private, nonprofit community-based "extended family" initiatives. Underlying this example is the conclusion by Professor Lisbeth Shorr at the Harvard School of Public Health that we *do* know much about what works for AFDC populations, and that the answer lies in programs that are comprehensive and interdependent—multiple solutions to multiple problems:

> Knowing now that effective social interventions can reduce the number of children hurt by cruel beginnings and simultaneously promote the national welfare, we must be certain that these newly available tools are put to work. We have the knowledge we need. We know how to organize health programs, family supports, child care, and early education to strengthen families and to prevent casualties in the transition from childhood to adulthood. We know how to intervene to reduce the rotten outcomes of adolescence and to help break the cycle that reaches into succeeding generations. Unshackled from the myth that nothing works, we can assure that children without hope today will have a real chance to become the contributing citizens of tomorrow.

The Ford Foundation's Project Redirection sought to enhance teens' educational, job-related, parenting, conflict-resolution, and life-management skills while encouraging them to delay further childbearing until they were more financially independent.

■ Responsive Fathers

Project Redirection helps to disprove uninformed, media-generating, political rhetoric in Washington, D.C., that nothing works for AFDC mothers. But we need to initiate more effective programs to bring absent fathers back into the family picture. This, we admit, is more difficult. Although later chapters show plenty of good programs that improve education, lead to jobs, and reduce crime, such breakthroughs are not yet adequately linked to increased responsibility by young fathers. But at least these are some promising beginnings.

Disproportionately, young fathers absent from AFDC households live in the inner city and have poor educational backgrounds, spotty work experience, and few job prospects. For young mothers to become economically independent within two years, as we discuss below, fathers must meet their child-support obligations.

Street-savvy observers often say that many of these young men want to be good parents, especially in the critical period immediately after the child is born—a time when they often feel the most pride. But young, unmarried, inner-city fathers face daunting obstacles. If a young man acknowledges paternity or is named the father by the child's mother, he is expected to start child payments immediately. In our view he must be made to take responsibility. Because these young men typically lack the education and skills to command more than the minimum wage and sporadic employment, some young fathers take dead-end jobs to keep up with payments. But many others do not take responsibility and attempt to avoid the system.

To address these realities and change stultifying regulations, Public/Private Ventures (P/PV), the research and evaluation organization in Philadelphia, currently is evaluating a Responsive Fathers program that has been initiated in various locations throughout the United States. Some aspects of the program appear to be promising, consistent with many of the strategies that worked in Project Redirection. Changes in local child-support bureaucracies and policies are being instituted to allow a father to take financial responsibility and also to obtain remedial education, intensive job training and job placement.

Tough talk from older male mentors is important. Before they can become good fathers, these young men—most of whom have had little or no fathering themselves—need guidance from role models who can help them deal with feelings of anger, confusion, and poor self-esteem. One mentor observed, "Our biggest challenge is to make them aware of their responsibilities, to show them how to negotiate the system and not quit when they feel frustrated."

Our priority in child-poverty welfare reform is training and jobs. For any new system to work, both mothers and fathers must equally qualify for jobs that have the potential for upward mobility. The Clinton administration and Congress, in our view, must carefully review the results of the P/PV Responsive Fathers program and incorporate its lessons into child-poverty reform. The key is linking quality job opportunity to increased paternal responsibility.

Bringing absent fathers back into the family picture may help at least some of the fathers and mothers to function more like a family, which in turn might improve their economic and social stability. The Project Redirection mentoring initiative suggested that a coordinated training and job-placement program for single teen fathers would help stabilize the couples. Importantly, recent research at the

University of Chicago indicates that single, teen, high-risk parents are more likely to marry if the father is employed and the mother has completed high school. Marriage encourages stable two-parent family life and reduces the risk of their children's involvement in crime and other negative behavior. However, in our experience, AFDC reform should not create a system in which single mothers *must* depend on the fathers. The mothers need options.

Comparisons with Other Plans for Reducing Child Poverty and Reforming Welfare

How do other plans to reduce child poverty—that is, in particular, reform AFDC—measure up to our plan?

AFDC is an entitlement program. Anyone who meets the eligibility criteria set by federal and state laws is entitled to monthly cash payments, regardless of the number of people who apply or the total cost. In hard times, when more people are unemployed, the amount of federal aid automatically increases. The average AFDC family receives a monthly payment of about $380, as well as food stamps and Medicaid. Fewer than 15 % of those on welfare receive AFDC continuously for five years, according to the American Public Welfare Association. Much more typical is a family that cycles on and off. Half of single parents who apply for AFDC leave the program within a year, but nearly half of those return to the program within a year of departing.

■ The Clinton Administration Plan

The core of the Clinton administration's reform plan is that no one be allowed to collect AFDC benefits for longer than two years. This represents the biggest change in AFDC since the program was established. A two-year limit would cut the number of recipients by approximately 70%. The proposal includes education and job-training initiatives, and its goal is to help single AFDC mothers become economically independent.

We do not object to two-years-and-you're-out—as long as reform includes a quality job training and placement program for all mothers and fathers who are eligible. However, no such comprehensive program has yet been set forth by the Clinton administration. In part recognizing only limited resources, at present, to upgrade job training and placement opportunities, the Clinton administration would let AFDC mothers continue to receive some aid as long as they worked.

■ More Punitive Plans

The point of departure for more punitive proposals is to end the entitlement status of AFDC and associated programs, including food stamps, child nutrition, Medicaid, foster care, child-support enforcement, and Supplemental Security Income. Instead, there would be block grants to the states. The level of block-grant funding could be changed by Congress. The states would have wide discretion. States could end all benefits to a family in as little as two years, even if the mother were willing to join a work program. Some proposals want to end AFDC payments for unwed mothers younger than 18 and their children. These plans also give states the option of denying aid to unwed mothers younger than 21. States then could use the money to establish orphanages for children whose mothers could not care for them. Such plans would require teenage mothers on AFDC to live with their custodial parent rather than establish their own homes. They would deny additional payments to AFDC mothers who have children while they are in the program. Benefits would also be denied to children for whom paternity had not been established.

■ Public Opinion

Public opinion is against these more punitive proposals. In a *New York Times*/CBS poll in December 1994, 71% of the respondents agreed with the Clinton plan—to continue benefits as long as the poor worked.

A recent analysis of the kind of more punitive plans, by the Center on Budget and Policy Priorities, concluded that they would push 2.5 million families and more than 5 million children currently receiving AFDC out of the program. About half of the current case load would lose eligibility. The Center concluded that the negative consequences of such legislation would be extreme. "Poverty would deepen, homelessness and hunger would rise. Temporary and permanent out-of-home placements and institutionalization of children could increase." *Importantly, the report found that the real need was to provide better jobs, child care, and health insurance.*

■ Orphanages

As for orphanages, they are cost-ineffective, just as prisons are cost-ineffective. For example, the Child Welfare League of America estimates that the price of maintaining a child in an orphanage, with support services, is $36,000 a year. By contrast, the average cost for foster care is $4,800 per year, and a child's share of AFDC and food stamps is $2,644 per year. Some politicians talk about the private sector providing the resources for orphanages, but even the head of Boy's Town in Nebraska doubts the money will be available. The result, we believe, is that the burden of supporting orphanages would be left to the states.

To point out the ineffectiveness and cost-ineffectiveness of orphanages is not to say that children in trouble should always stay with their parents. Experience suggests a range of alternatives, tailored to individual needs, work best—counseling for troubled parents, family reunification programs, foster parents and transitional facilities, like those offered by Project Prepare and other private-sector, non-profit community-based extended families that are discussed in chapters 3 and 4 of this report.

Where Is JTPA Reform and Job Creation?

In comparison with our plan, the more punitive proposals, in particular, fail to create jobs. The rhetoric is that we should put welfare chiselers to work—or the chiseler must face the consequence. The reality is that no financed plan is set forth for *what* work, employed by *whom*, and *where*.

> Orphanages are cost-ineffective, just as prisons are cost-ineffective.

Chapter 2

By contrast, as Katherine McFate has written:

> Policies for lone-parent families in France and Sweden are more effective than American policies in reducing *dependency* as well as poverty because the former countries invest public funds in universal programs that subsidize the costs of child rearing (through free medical care, child allowances, advanced child support maintenance) *and* they simultaneously invest in programs to promote work among mothers (subsidized child care, paid parental leave, greater wage equality, employment in the public sector) [Emphasis in the original].

One reason American politicians won't fix the JTPA that has failed to train high-risk youth and won't create jobs at a scale equal to the dimension of the problem for those trained is, they say, that it costs too much money. Our plan costs about $30 billion per year for at least 10 years—and we estimated it provides adequate training and creates many of the jobs needed. We don't think that costs too much. For example, Congress unwisely deregulated the savings and loan industry in the 1980s, as part of trickle-down, supply-side economics. The result was a bailout by Congress that has cost the voting taxpayer over $500 billion—and Congress does not seem to think *that* was too much.

A more troubling reason job creation is not being linked to child poverty and welfare reform has to do with the nature of capitalism. In 1995, most politicians were calling for the welfare poor to work. At the same time, many were agreeing with Wall Street that the economy, having reduced unemployment to 5%, had overheated. Interest rates had to go up. The Federal Reserve increased interest rates in a series of increments. That began to increase the unemployment rate above the unacceptably low rate of 5%. How could we employ more AFDC mothers and increase unemployment at the same time?

When they have to trade off, the power brokers of our system prefer more unemployment and less inflation. Those who get most unemployed are the poor at the bottom—with inadequate representation in a political system in which influence is based on how much money one has to buy lobbyists. Inflation is worse for the power brokers because it affects not just the poor, but them as well.

Alternatively, the plan set forth in this report recognizes that conventional, incremental monetary and fiscal policy *always* will fail the poor—because, even in the best of times, some unemployment is needed by the system to avoid overheating. Our plan sees the need for a national industrial policy that deals with the structurally unemployed—those low-income, often welfare poor persons and families stuck in the mud, who don't benefit from a conventional monetary and fiscal policy that pretends to promise a rising tide that lifts all boats. Our plan is to employ those people at the bottom, even at the expense, if necessary, of a bit more inflation than thought appropriate by those who say they simultaneously want the poor to work and Wall Street markets to be secured against overheating.

As Roger Wilkins made clear in the reflections opening this chapter, job security for parents helps stabilize homes, which can lead to education and jobs for the children as they grow up. The education and employment teach more solid values and more responsibility—about when to have children and how to financially provide for them. Such lessons are more motivating than any of the punitive plans that seek to impose moral standards without providing educational and employment opportunity.

If poor fathers and mothers are to work, they need to be healthy and their children need to be cared for when the adults are away. Neither the Clinton plan nor the more punitive plans create such comprehensive interdependence—of child poverty, health, and child-care reform. The linkage appears all the more necessary in light of a multiyear study of hundreds of child-care centers released in 1995 by a team headed by the University of Colorado. The study concluded that the vast majority of the 5 million American children who spend their days in child-care centers are receiving "poor to mediocre" care. One in eight are in poor-quality settings where health and safety are threatened. The study concluded that, for child care to improve, we need:

- Higher staff–to–child ratios
- Higher levels of staff education
- More experienced administrators
- Higher teacher wages
- Lower teacher turnover

The Old, New Federation

Notwithstanding their failure to create jobs, the more punitive plans for child poverty and welfare reform decentralize control from the federal government to the states—through block grants. This is unwise in our view. The poor have the same right to entitlement safety nets as do members of Congress, with their many perks. Government benefits will decline, in state block grants plans, in spite of any proof that this will lead to "self-sufficiency" by the poor. Innovativeness varies greatly by state. States do not always distribute block grants proportionately to populations in need. States have poor records in employment training and placement. Americans easily forget that "states rights" was the slogan for apartheid in the South. There is ample evidence that both conservatives and progressives do not wholly trust states. Decentralization is far more effective at the level of private-sector nonprofit community-based organizations run by Walt Whitman's "common people."

Consider each of these points. First and foremost, discretionary block-grant funding means that AFDC and related benefits lose their entitlement status. The poor would lose their safety net. In the process, the more punitive proposals lower overall spending. We believe Americans have a right to an entitlement safety net. That was the thinking of President Roosevelt when he instituted Social Security and other reforms, and when he told the nation, "People who are hungry and out of a job are the stuff of which dictatorships are made." It is hypocritical for Congress to reverse President Roosevelt, unless members of Congress are prepared also to remove their many safety nets, like stellar medical insurance and retirement plans. Abolishing entitlements also would drop America even farther behind many Western European countries, which incorporate safety nets as human rights. Governors need to remember, as well, that entitlements have the virtue of adjust-

If poor fathers and mothers are to work, they need to be healthy and their children need to be cared for when the adults are away.

Chapter 2

ing to economic conditions—if a state has more poor people, federal benefits go up. But Congress can cut a discretionary block-grant program at will.

Plans to eliminate entitlements and create state block grants also are carefully crafted to decrease the overall level of benefits. Some applaud further tightening the belts of the poor, because, they say, it will lead to more "self-sufficiency." Yet there is little evidence that cutting benefits or increasing taxes on the poor makes them more self-sufficient and better off. Over the past 20 years, welfare benefits have in fact been falling in real spending power—with little positive effect on the poor and considerable negative effect. For example, there was a significant rise in child poverty in the 1980s. This was made worse by trickle-down, supply-side economics, which reduced the income of the poorest fifth of the population by 10% from 1977 to 1988 (chapter 1).

Some states have been "creative laboratories for change," to use currently fashionable language. An illustration is the success of southern states in reducing infant mortality. Yet there is great variability among states. There are innovative states—like New York, and California. There also are states which are much less innovative—like Texas and Ohio. Some states, like Vermont, have true participatory democracy, while other states, like Louisiana, are entrenched with cronyism. Nor is there any proof that states attract more qualified people than the federal government—or than the successful, private-sector, community-based nonprofit organization which we discuss in chapters 3, 4, and 5 as key implementors in true decentralization based on already demonstrated success.

Experience has shown that, when the federal government makes state block grants that affect high-risk children and youth, governors do not always distribute block grants proportionately to the populations in need. There have been recent years, for example, when the State of California did not grant Los Angeles nearly its proportionate share of drug block-grant money. The same held for Wisconsin and its distribution to Milwaukee. In these and other states, existing misallocations could be magnified if the low-income population increases at a high rate. In such instances, block-grant funds may not cover rising administrative costs in AFDC, food stamps, and Medicaid. Federal block-grant funding to states also tends to erode over time.

Nor have states established a good record in the kind of education, employment training, and job creation that we believe is the first priority in reducing child poverty. For example, a report by the United States General Accounting Office (GAO) released in December 1994 found that only about 11% of the 4 million parents receiving AFDC were participating in the state-level education and training program known as JOBS (Job Opportunities and Basic Skills). This study was undertaken from 1991 through 1993. The study observed that state education and training programs for AFDC mothers were failing to reach many women at highest risk of long-term dependency, particularly teenagers and drug abusers. The state-run programs were simply not establishing strong links to local employers who could help AFDC recipients find jobs, the GAO concluded. This raises additional doubts about two-years-and-out welfare-reform plans by states like Wisconsin, which are unaccompanied by comprehensive, or even minimal, job training and placement.

> **Plans to eliminate entitlements and create state block grants are carefully crafted to decrease the overall level of benefits. Yet there is little evidence that cutting benefits or increasing taxes on the poor makes them more self-sufficient and better off.**

> **Experience has shown that, when the federal government makes state block grants that affect high-risk children and youth, governors do not always distribute block grants proportionately to the populations in need.**

In a similar way, states have a spotty track record in running orphanages, prisons, mental hospitals, and nursing homes in a cost-effective way.

The arguments by some governors today that they are closer to the people when it comes to child poverty and minorities harken back to the arguments of governors George Wallace, Ross Barnett, and Orval Faubus not so long ago that their states could handle racial problems better than the federal government because they were closer to their black citizens. It is hard to believe, but many Americans, including many new members of Congress, seem to have forgotten that "states rights" was a slogan that encouraged people like Bull Conner, facilitated the Ku Klux Klan and justified a system of apartheid that denied basic rights to African Americans. The federal government had to overturn their injustice and inaction. This is particularly relevant for child poverty and welfare reform today because the governors are white. Yet there are large numbers of nonwhite leaders at the levels of local government and private nonprofit community organizations, where many more examples of past success can be found than at the state level.

For all the talk about "devolution" to the state level, the contemporary political dialogue suggests that people on both the left and the right do not necessarily, or wholly, trust states. This mistrust exists because most block-grant proposals give each state a fixed pool of money and leave the states with great autonomy to decide who gets support and when. Some conservatives are worried about giving all the responsibility to the states. They are afraid that some states won't undertake what they consider reform—a reform *without* JTPA reform or job creation. Progressives are worried that some states will reform the system out of existence and replace it with an alternative that is expensive and ineffective, like orphanages and prison building. It also is possible that a state legislature could cut services and taxes as a lure to business. This could force other states into doing the same, to complete. A downward spiral would be created. As Russell Baker has noted, state legislators "are for sale cheap, at least compared with the prices for Members of the U.S. House and Senate. . . . Consider for example, the splendid character of your own state legislator. You do know who he is, don't you? Ah . . . I see."

The argument for the states presumes that a state is a kind of community with shared interests and values. In the early days of the nation, this made some geographic sense. For example, Virginia was in fact different from Pennsylvania, and Pennsylvania was different from Rhode Island. However, today, the New York Borough of Brooklyn and rural western New York State have little in common except language (and that just barely). The suburbs of Atlanta and Washington, D.C., are more similar than the suburbs of Atlanta and downtown Atlanta.

Decentralization, say some politicians, is justified by the Tenth Amendment, which concludes that "the powers not delegated to the states by the Constitution, nor prohibited to the states, are reserved to the states respectively, or to the people." Yet those last words—"or to the people"—open the door to power at a more grass-roots level—the level of the private nonprofit community organizations that have had more success with the poor than the states. The Tenth Amendment rationale also overlooks the dictum by Alexander Hamilton that Congress should provide for the "general welfare."

> **For all the talk about "devolution" to the state level, the contemporary political dialogue suggests that people on both the left and the right do not necessarily, or wholly, trust states.**

Chapter 2

There are, then, a host of arguments for avoiding state bureaucracy and state red tape. The chapters of this report suggest, alternatively, an array of funding mechanisms, including federal grants and loans to private nonprofit intermediaries that grant and loan monies to decentralized private, nonprofit neighborhood organizations; federal grants and loans to city governments with the stipulation that substantial monies be made available to private neighborhood nonprofit organizations; and federal grants and loans made directly to private nonprofit organizations.

Conclusions

In sum:

■ No serious child poverty and welfare reform is possible in America without a new employment-training system and a job-creation plan for poor mothers and fathers who qualify. To be able to work, poor parents need adequate health and day care. Greater job opportunity for fathers should be linked to increased financial responsibility by them.

■ Under such reform, a two-years-and-you're-out policy is feasible, as long as the poor have at least as much entitlement safety net status as members of Congress and the poor in many European countries, like France and Sweden.

■ To avoid presenting the taxpaying, voting citizen with another double standard, child-poverty welfare reform should be accompanied by corporate welfare reform, to help finance the new employment-training and job-creation system that is needed.

■ The federal government should finance, oversee, and enforce child-poverty reform, but day-to-day program operations should be devolved in large part to the most creative proven laboratories for change—private-sector nonprofit community organizations.

Chapter 3

Nurturing Children And Their Schools

Decades of experience and research have taught us that at-risk inner-city children's chances of becoming well-functioning family members, responsible taxpaying citizens, and nurturing parents increase substantially if they are nurtured by warm and responsive adults who guide them through the critical early stages of their lives. This chapter provides examples of preschool, elementary, middle school, and high school initiatives that help high-risk children make the transition to responsible adulthood. These initiatives need to be expanded on a scale equal to the dimensions of the problem.

A wide-ranging, three-year study of young American children (*Starting Points: Meeting the Needs of Our Youngest Children*, by the Carnegie Corporation of New York) confirms some of society's worst fears: millions of infants and toddlers are so deprived of medical care, loving supervision and intellectual stimulation that their growth into healthy and responsible adults is threatened.
Susan Chira
Washington Post
April 4, 1994

Preschool Programs

The Head Start program is administered by the Department of Health and Human Services (HHS). It provides multiple solutions to the multiple problems of disadvantaged preschoolers and their low-income families. Head Start enables children to deal more effectively with both their present environment and later responsibilities in the school and community. Solutions embrace education; social services; medical, dental, nutrition, and mental health services; and parent involvement with the goal of enabling children to develop to their highest potential. Head Start is implemented through a nationwide network of 1,321 grantees serving approximately 2,050 communities. The program employs approximately 97,000 persons and enlists the aid of approximately 800,000 volunteers in these communities. Head Start grants are awarded by HHS regional offices and HHS Indian and Migrant Program branches to local public agencies, private nonprofit organizations, and school systems.

Head Start has been evaluated as perhaps the most cost effective inner-city prevention strategy ever developed. In 1985, the Committee for Economic Development, which is composed of conservative corporate executives, concluded,

> It would be hard to imagine that society could find a higher yield for a dollar of investment than that found in preschool programs for its at-risk children. Every $1.00 spent on early prevention and intervention can save $4.75 in the costs of remedial education, welfare, and crime further down the road.

Chapter 3

Head Start has been evaluated as perhaps the most cost effective inner-city prevention strategy ever developed.

Over the years, scientific evaluations have illustrated the cost–benefit ratio of Head Start. Figure 13 compares disadvantaged kids in the Perry Preschool program in Michigan to similar children who do not attend preschool. The preschoolers had significantly fewer arrests, school dropouts, cases of mental retardation, and experience with welfare system as well as significantly higher literacy, employment, and attendance rates in vocational school or college by age 19. All of those welcome outcomes appeared to be interrelated with one another.

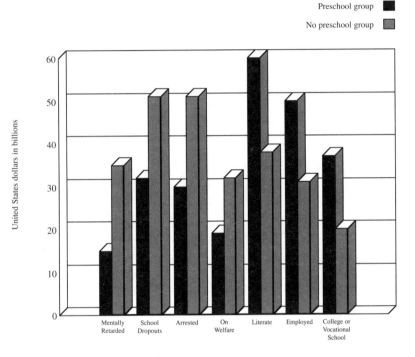

Fig. 13. Comparison between preschool and nonpreschool at age 19. Perry Preschool Program in Ypsilanti, Michigan

The Family Development Research Program operated between 1969 and 1975 in Syracuse, New York. Its major program goal was "the support of child and familial behaviors that sustain growth and development after intervention ceases." By age five, children in the experimental program showed statistically meaningful gains in their cognitive functioning compared with control children. Based on a longitudinal study undertaken when the Syracuse children were 15 years old, it was apparent that peer pressure from their classmates, particularly for the program boys, had militated against their continuing to do well in cognitive performance. The program girls retained their superior records, but the boys did not. However, the principal measurable difference for the program boys was their functioning in society. For the 60 experimental program children who could be found years later, only 6% had been placed under supervision of the probation department, contrasted with 22% of the 54 children in the control group who could be located. This translated into an estimated cost to society for court processing, probation services, supervision, and detention of $186 per child in the program group compared with an estimated $1,985 per child in the control group—more than ten times as much.

As a final example, the Yale Child Welfare Research Program assessed coordinated pediatric child care, social work, and psychological services provided to low-income mothers and their first child during the 30 months following birth. Ten years after the services were terminated, the boys in the program were statistically less likely to be involved in predelinquent behavior (e.g., truancy) than were comparison group boys.

■ Full Funding

Yet only less than 40% of all eligible lower-income children aged three to five presently are served by Head Start, whereas the percentage is considerably more than double for middle-income-family ($35,000 and more) children of the same ages whose parents pay for private preschool and related child care. (The enrollment rate of three-year-olds eligible for Head Start is especially low.)

The Congressional Budget Office estimates that the present level of Head Start funding, $2.2 billion per year, will need to be increased by $6 billion to $7 billion per year to provide eligibility for all who qualify, with the exact amount depending on how quickly the additional funding is phased in.

We recommend full funding of Head Start for all eligible three- to five-year-olds as well as funding for at least some two-year-olds (based, for example, on the experience of Project Beethoven, which is described later). At the same time, the quality of Head Start staff and programming should be improved. Upgrading quality includes better training, pay, and benefits. In the late 1980s, half of all Head Start workers earned less than $10,000 a year:

> As it stands, the low pay leads to rapid and disruptive staff turnover, which diminishes the quality of care; and not enough staff have sufficient training to cope with the increasingly complex problems (including parental drug abuse) children are bringing with them to the program.

We concur with the recommendations of a Ford Foundation panel that at least one-half of all new slots be full-day programs for children with working parents. And we endorse the conclusion of the Children's Defense Fund that state and local governments and private employers should increase their investments in child care and early childhood development.

■ Child and Family Support in France

France has the most comprehensive system of child and family support and care in the world. For example, in France preschool is available for all eligible children. In addition, $123 per month of child benefits is provided for families with two children, compared with zero dollars per month in the United States.

The French, as well as most other Europeans, were amused throughout the 1994 American election debates on "family values," which they viewed as empty talk. The French are willing to back rhetoric on family values with programs and funding. They view their children as conservators of family traditions and culture:

We recommend full funding of Head Start for all eligible three- to five-year-olds as well as funding for at least some two-year-olds.

Chapter 3

All the continental European systems have one common feature: they provide income security to families with children. All offer universal access to health care. If women are expected to work, high-quality public day care is provided. Parental leave policies that allow mothers to easily move back into the labor force after child-bearing (or in the case of Sweden, while child rearing) are also common. Perhaps the most important lesson we can learn from the Europeans is the concept of "social solidarity," the belief that children and young people belong to the entire community, not just to their individual families.

Table 9 compares "family values" among European nations and the United States as defined by terms of maternity leave allowed, child benefits, and percent of taxes paid for child benefits. The United States is consistently last in all categories.

What Every Citizen Gets	Maternity Leave Number of weeks	Child Benefits Per month, for two children	Taxes Percent for family benefits, including Social Security
Belgium	14	$230	34%
France	16	$123	44%
Germany	14	$120	36%
Italy	20	$48	33%
U.S.	0	$0	29%

Table 9. Measures of family values, by nation in recent years.

The Sobering Experience of Project Beethoven

Preschool and coordinated services are not easy to initiate and operate in deteriorated American inner-city areas. Project Beethoven, which was created by Chicago businessman and philanthropist Irving B. Harris in the notorious Robert Taylor Homes Housing Project, provides a good example of an ambitious project designed to serve inner-city families.

When Project Beethoven began in 1986, Mr. Harris's dream was that the family of every baby born in six buildings of Robert Taylor Homes might be enriched by an assortment of services, including home visits, medical care, advice on child development and nutrition, and a supportive, safe environment. The project's goal was to deliver to the local Beethoven Elementary School after five years a kindergarten class packed with confident and healthy children who were eager to learn and comparable to kids in the wealthy Chicago suburbs of Highland Park and Winnetka. The project was a beacon of hope in the increasingly desperate fight to save inner-city children, a concentrated effort to prevent tragedies such as suffered by a seven-year-old who was caught in cross fire between drug dealers at the housing project in 1992.

Beginning in 1986 with 100 children, Project Beethoven's goal was to prepare 90% to 95% of these children for kindergarten in Beethoven School. By the fall of 1992, however, only 20 of the 100 children reached kindergarten; only one of these children attended Beethoven School. Many families had moved out of Robert Taylor Homes; some had bettered themselves and others had not. The program lost touch with them. Of the first 100 families recruited, more than 50% moved at least once.

One reason for these outcomes was that Project Beethoven was not an easy sell to a community hardened by years of watching well-meaning programs come and go. Some families did not let representatives from the program through their front door. To counter this problem, the program hired Taylor residents to try to communicate and recruit families. As it turned out, the families that remained involved with the program did so in large part because of these home visits.

Crime was another major impediment to the program. Between 1986 and 1991, violent crime in the Robert Taylor housing project increased by 43%. Violence traumatized both parents and children, who often kept behind locked doors in their own apartments. Terror also made it difficult for Project Beethoven to hire and retain staff, who were understandably frightened. The gangs in the housing project actually forced the program to close down once a month. Presumably, these were days when gang activities increased, thus threatening injury to parents and children.

For those who have stayed with the program, success has been subtle but evident. For example, the first baby born into the program, prematurely as it turned out, started kindergarten at Beethoven School with above-average scores on a standard school-readiness test. "He has a lot of confidence and follows the classroom rules well," said his teacher. "He's one of the few children in my room who knows all his letters and all his numbers. He came in knowing more than what we teach in the first semester." The youngster's mother has been hired as an assistant teacher in one of the Head Start classes at the Beethoven Project. His father has recently married his mother and says he has given up drugs and sleeping in shelters.

■ Ongoing Concerns

Mr. Harris remains committed to Project Beethoven. But he believes that we need to know more about programs like Project Beethoven: "We are at a very, very early stage of learning, and it is misleading to overstate what we think we know." He believes, for example, that we need to learn what motivates mothers in such dire circumstances to seek prenatal care and to take precautions against bearing more children into high-risk situations. He concludes, "We have not learned how to train paraprofessionals satisfactorily to do the highly difficult work that professional social workers in child development and health providers need to perform." He is especially concerned about the dramatic increase in violence, much of it drug related, and its relation to post-traumatic stress disorders among the Robert Taylor population, especially children. Such violence has caused low attention spans, hyperactivity, additional violent behavior, and poor school behavior.

■ Guarded Optimism

These sobering observations drawn from the Project Beethoven experience must be factored into our national policy. Although Mr. Harris's commitment and insight deserve respect, available scientific evidence allows for guarded optimism on the potential success of innovative programs for low-income inner-city residents. For example, the Ford Foundation's Project Redirection (discussed in chapter 2) has been replicated in various locations. The program achieved considerable success over a five-year evaluation period that tested and compared populations of low-income mothers and their infants. Many of the outcome measures were similar to those of Project Beethoven.

Training staff *is* of crucial importance. University-trained professionals have a key role in other successful inner-city programs that deal with issues similar to Project

Chapter 3

Beethoven. But these programs, for example, the Argus Community in the South Bronx (see chapter 4), have found that training people from the community—including graduates of the program—is central, because success seems to proceed far beyond the traditional conceptions, and preconceptions, of "professionals." Success also requires crossing the boundaries of traditional disciplines to create multiple, interrelated solutions tailored to individual needs. Sometimes university-trained professionals are not sufficiently attuned to, and therefore resent, this street reality.

Security of participants and staff from violence and drug dealers is a major concern. But here, again, there are at least some model programs already in existence that have created that security. For example, in chapter 4 we discuss how, in San Juan, Puerto Rico, Centro Sister Isolina Ferre has created a residential police ministation on the grounds of a dynamic, multipurpose community program, which includes early intervention and which has reduced crime dramatically, based on police statistics. In chapter 6, we discuss how young male police officers now are living in the public housing they patrol in places like Alexandria, Virginia, and Columbia, South Carolina.

■ A Broader Vision

The experience of the Beethoven Project highlights the need to assure adequate prenatal care and proper developmental care of infants and toddlers, especially if signs of developmental disability are evident. But more is needed. We need more programs like James Comer's School Development Plan, as discussed later in this chapter. We need a reformed national job training and placement program that employs all eligible project residents and provides support and discipline to them (see chapter 4). Some residents need to be employed by nonprofit, community-based housing corporations similar to those sponsored by the Ford Foundation's Local Initiatives Support Corporation and developer James Rouse's Enterprise Founda-tion (see chapter 5). Neighborhood homes need to be rehabilitated or rebuilt. City and federal government leaders may need to follow the lead of the St. Louis Housing Authority, which demolished the Pruitt-Igo Public Housing high-rise dec-ades ago, and destroy inner-city housing projects such as Robert Taylor and Cabrini Green. High-rises should be replaced with low-rises that are integrated with commercial development as part of a new national initiative to invest in our urban communities. Residents can be employed as neighborhood police to patrol their neighborhoods. These new police can be assisted by young adult advocates who serve as mediators between police and at-risk youth as is done at the Centro Sister Isolina Ferre program in Puerto Rico (chapter 4).

Project Beethoven was initiated in a public housing environment that is a monument to government stupidity. Robert Taylor homes is block upon block of high rises, with elevators that seldom work, run by a public housing authority that, until recently, had an inexcusably poor management record to say the least. This we must change for good.

■ Expectations and Ted Williams

To date, in our view, the real issue with Project Beethoven is expectations. Ted Williams was the last baseball player ever to bat over .400. Such a feat is consid-

Nurturing Children
And Their Schools

ered virtually unobtainable by sports writers today. How, then, with much tougher pitching against it, could Project Beethoven ever expect to bat .900 or .950? In the South Bronx, at the Argus community (discussed in chapter 4), Elizabeth Sturz, the founder, concludes, "Twenty-two percent completion rates seem to be what Argus is achieving with Harbor House, our drug free therapeutic community enhanced with psychiatric services, and with several other community mental health residences for homeless substance abusers who are also seriously mentally ill." This is about what Argus expected. Beethoven has batted .200, and a reasonable improvement, in our judgment, would be to end up somewhere between Argus and Ted Williams.

One of the positions in this report, then, is that the citizens who pay the taxes and the politicians who appropriate the money should not have a double standard. They cannot canonize Ted Williams and then expect initiatives for the truly disadvantaged in places devastated by multiple problems, many caused by the politicians and the public bureaucracy, to succeed at a far higher rate.

Nothing in the experience of Project Beethoven, in our view, for example, should argue against full funding of Head Start for all eligible three- to five-year-olds (as well as younger children, as Mr. Harris advocates). At 100% funding, we should also expect a lower cost–benefit ratio than the $1.00 to $4.75 reported by the Committee for Economic Development. At the present rate of funding, which covers about 25% of those eligible, there has been considerable self-selection. That is, kids now in Head Start probably have parents who are more savvy and more adept at working the system than the kind of mothers with more problems and less going for them who are the clientele of Project Beethoven. So if there is full eligibility, including such mothers and their children, we cannot necessarily expect them to succeed as well as those more able and motivated. But, even if the cost–benefit ratio falls to $1 to $1, good progress will have been made with these troubled populations, in our view.

	U.S.	Switzerland	France	Korea
Math Scores*	55	71	64	73
Science Scores*	67	74	69	78
Graduation Rate**	74	88	85	Not Available

Inner-City School System Innovation

Table 10 shows how American 13-year-olds lag behind their counterparts in European and Asian countries. The performance gap is much greater for poor, inner-city American kids.

We believe that the United States must save its inner-city public schools, as part of a comprehensive policy, and use them as institutional vehicles for change working with nonprofit community organizations. Beyond Head Start, we believe that new national policy for the inner city should be based on reform of the Elementary and Secondary Education Act of 1965, adaptation of the National Urban Schools Program and other structural school innovations proposed by the Carnegie Foundation for the Advancement of Teaching and the Carnegie Council on Adolescent Development, replication much more widely of the James Comer School Development Plan, replication of variations on the Eugene Lang "I Have a Dream"

Table 10. School performance, by nation.

*Percent of questions answered correctly on a standardized test given to a random sample of 13-year-olds in these countries in 1991.
**Students finishing secondary school as a percent of the graduation-age population.

Chapter 3

Program and the Cities in Schools Program if evaluations prove them successful, further development of high school apprenticeships and vocational training, replication of successful desegregation plans like that of St. Louis, and experimentation with community service to repay college loans—but initially for inner-city students only.

■ Reform of the Elementary and Secondary Education Act of 1965

Funded by the Edna McConnell Clark Foundation and the John D. and Catherine T. MacArthur Foundation, an independent commission has released a new report, *Making Schools Work for Children in Poverty*, that calls for reforms in Chapter 1 of the Elementary and Secondary Education Act of 1965. Chapter 1 is the federal government's main program for helping to improve basic academic skills of poor children. Chapter 1 presently allocates more than $6 billion per year, one-fifth of the federal education budget, to about two-thirds of the nation's schools.

The report praises Chapter 1 for helping a generation of impoverished students improve in reading, writing, and math since it was created in 1965. However, the commission finds that too little money reaches the poorest of the nation's schools and that the program's key element—pulling poor children out of class for 25 minutes of tutoring each day—is not in touch with current educational thinking. Accordingly, the commission's main recommendations are that:

- States should set higher academic standards for all children.
- States must develop and enforce a system of rewards for schools that succeed and assistance for those that fail.
- Schools should spend 20% of their Chapter 1 allocations on curriculum and staff development.
- Schools should be free to spend Chapter 1 money to meet their perceived needs, unlike the more rigid present system.
- Schools should develop better ways to assess students, instead of the standardized test now used.
- Parents should receive clearer reports than at present on their children's academic progress.
- States must better co-target their health and social services with public schools that receive Chapter 1 support.

Several other reports have made similar recommendations on reform of Chapter 1. We endorse such reforms.

■ The Carnegie Proposals

Much of the Chapter 1 reform proposed by the commission in *Making Schools Work for Children in Poverty* is consistent with the report *Saving Urban Schools* by the Carnegie Foundation for the Advancement of Teaching. The Carnegie Foundation calls for strong national leadership backed by federal financing for a proposed National Urban Schools Program, modeled in spirit on the Rural Extension Act that was passed decades ago to assist American farmers. Although federal funds would seed local reform, Carnegie believes that state and local governments have the prime responsibility for the fiscal health of public education. One reasonable guideline is one new

The United States must save its inner-city public schools, as part of a comprehensive policy, and use them as institutional vehicles for change working with non-profit community organizations.

federal reform dollar for each eight state and local dollars. This is a modest increase over the 7% the federal government currently pays for public education.

Carnegie advocates a national policy of greater equity in urban school financing, which means more money for inner-city schools and a commitment to educate all children, even those from the most difficult backgrounds. Beyond early education, Carnegie calls for new local governance procedures. If, after a reasonable period, a specific urban school fails to meet objectives that have been clearly agreed upon in advance, officials from the school system have the power to intervene. The Carnegie Foundation believes that the range of such intervention should include professional consultation, new leadership in the specific school, and, in the extreme, the closing of the school.

Similarly, the Carnegie Council on Adolescent Development has urged that national policy must proceed beyond early education and pay more attention to continuity with middle-school youths ages 10 to 15. The Council points out that, although youths in this age range are vulnerable to failure and high-risk behavior, they are still impressionable and can be positively influenced.

Consequently, the Carnegie Council calls for federal leadership to encourage local change. Rigid class schedules should be replaced with cooperative learning in which students work together in small groups. Teams of approximately 125 students and 5 or 6 teachers should remain together throughout middle school, until students advance to high school. A core academic program should promote critical reasoning and include community service. California and Florida have begun implementing many of these changes, and the Edna McConnell Clark Foundation is funding demonstration programs to revamp middle schools. Policy planners need to follow the experience of Clark closely and build on its lessons.

■ The Comer School Development Plan

Sensitive to the Carnegie call for new local governance procedures, the Comer School Development Plan makes school a more productive, better managed environment for poor minority children. Developed by James P. Comer, Maurice Falk Professor of Child Psychiatry at the Yale University Child Study Center, the plan is a form of school-based management in which parents, teachers, and teachers' aides form a school governing team that establishes the school's curriculum, activities, attitudes, and values.

Within this management and governance framework, a parent-participation program involves parents in classroom and other school activities. A parent is hired to work in each classroom on a part-time basis. In addition to serving on the governance team, parents are encouraged to volunteer as teachers' aides, librarians, newsletter staff, and social activity organizers.

A school psychologist and other personnel reinforce work and support the process by providing direct services to children and advice to the school and parent leaders.

The academic curriculum established by the governance team is flexible. It varies from school to school, based on the priorities of the team and the needs of the children, just as successful inner-city community-based programs combine comprehensiveness with flexibility.

The Carnegie Council on Adolescent Development has urged that national policy must proceed beyond early education and pay more attention to continuity with middle-school youths ages 10 to 15.

Chapter 3

Students in two New Haven, Connecticut, elementary schools where the full program was first demonstrated between 1975 and 1980 showed improvement in attendance and academic achievement. One school ranked fourteenth in attendance among New Haven Public Schools in 1975–1976. After the program was begun, the school ranked eighth or better in all but two of the subsequent nine years. Graduates of one of the demonstrations were compared with their counterparts from another elementary school serving children of the same socioeconomic status. The Comer graduates had considerably higher language skills, math skills, and work-study skills than did the comparison youth.

As a result of the demonstrated success, the School Development Plan is now being replicated widely in inner-city schools throughout the nation. Professor Comer observes, "We haven't had a serious behavior problem in the schools where we have been involved in over a decade." He believes that the strength of his plan is its concentration on institutional change for the entire school. This also is one of the few programs evaluated as successful in inner-city locations which has significantly involved parents.

■ "I Have a Dream" and State Variations

Whereas the Comer plan seeks institutional change, the "I Have a Dream" Program created by Eugene Lang places a premium on mentoring individual youth. The program originated when Mr. Lang, a wealthy businessman and philanthropist, returned to his elementary school in East Harlem and promised to pay the college tuition of every graduating sixth-grade class member who finished high school and qualified for higher education. Today, about two-thirds of the kids in this class have received high school diplomas or general education diplomas (GEDs). More than half are enrolled at least part time in public and private colleges; only one is in prison. School dropout rates—and correlated crime—are far higher for comparable young people in East Harlem. A skeptical former deputy school superintendent said at the time of Mr. Lang's promise, "If 50% of those kids are going to college, it's a small miracle." Mr. Lang's "I Have a Dream" Foundation now is replicating the idea across the nation in tough, inner-city schools.

A promising, comprehensive elementary school plan at the state level that builds on Mr. Lang's concept is the Rhode Island Children's Crusade. The state of Rhode Island provides state college scholarships for low-income pupils, combined with academic and remedial help from third grade through high school. The only requirements are that parents allow state monitoring of report cards and that students obey the law, shun drugs, avoid early parenting, and, of course, do not drop out. Pupils are tutored and paired with mentors throughout primary and secondary school. When old enough, top performers can secure summer jobs, where they can serve as role models to others.

The Rhode Island plan, which is contingent on the state matching funds with the private sector, builds on New York State Liberty Scholarships for low-income students, but Rhode Island enrolls them at an earlier age and provides educational and social assistance.

> The state of Rhode Island provides state college scholarships for low-income pupils, combined with academic and remedial help from third grade through high school. The only requirements are that parents allow state monitoring of report cards and that students obey the law, shun drugs, avoid early parenting, and do not drop out.

The key to these and other related programs seems to be not only the assurance of a college education, but also the provision of a mentor:

> American scholars lack much verifiable data on what prevents dropouts, but the few studies attempted and the experience of nearly every educator who has ever faced a discouraged student seem to converge on a crucial point: the need for at least one adult to establish a relationship of trust with each youth, providing a secure outlet for fears and enthusiasms and living affirmation that someone cares if that student leaves school.

Public/Private Ventures is undertaking a comprehensive evaluation of "I Have a Dream." If the evaluation is positive, we endorse replication across the nation of the original Lang concept and the later state variations. We also believe that there is considerable potential for merging the institutional change goals of the Comer plan with the individualized mentoring and financial support of the Lang plan.

The need for variations on the Lang concept is all the greater given the declining rates of college enrollment for African American males.

There are a host of related initiatives being tried in schools across the nation, but few have been scientifically evaluated. For example, in Lawrence, Massachusetts, Family Service America is implementing a curriculum for seventh and eighth graders who need to improve self-esteem and assume more control over their lives. During the fall semester, adult trainers mentor them. In the spring semester, the trained students seek to display newly acquired skills by, in turn, mentoring second and third graders. Evaluations with very small test and comparison groups, using pre- and post-thematic apperception tests, among other measures, appear to show significant improvement in program kids *vis-à-vis* the comparison group. More ambitious designs are needed that include longer-run outcomes like dropouts, pregnancy, crime, and violence.

■ High School Apprenticeships

Attempts to blend high schools and job training have been unsuccessful in the United States. Only a few thousand students are currently in youth apprenticeship programs in about 20 states. What gives these programs potential, however, their advocates say, is the intensity of the training and the goal of a certifiable skill universally recognized by employers.

Probably the best model for vocational training and apprenticeship is Germany. There, approximately two-thirds of the country's students participate in a formal apprenticeship program. It offers training in 375 occupations. A social compact promises a likely job when they are finished. German students not planning to attend college usually choose their occupation as young as age 14. The dual system of work and study forms the core of career training in Germany.

The system is considered a major reason for Germany's long economic boom and a key to why Germany's high-tech workers are admired from Detroit to Tokyo. German corporations recognize the good outcomes, see the system as a pipeline for future employees, and so are willing to pay a great amount—40% of the system's cost.

Principal responsibility for overseeing the German system lies with the Federal Labor Agency, a sprawling nonprofit corporation run by representatives of business,

We believe that there is considerable potential for merging the institutional change goals of the Comer plan with the individualized mentoring and financial support of the Lang plan.

Chapter 3

labor, and government. It also is the largest employer of psychologists in Germany and offers a range of testing services devised to bring each citizen into the career where she or he will be happiest and most productive.

Much of this may not work in the United States. Here, the education system has long considered early tracking of young people to be a form of class oppression that consigns them to working class lives at an early age. General education is seen as a requirement of American democratic society.

Still, with the Clinton administration's efforts to make the American labor force more competitive, more American public officials are studying Germany's approach. And many high schools in inner-city areas do want to build closer links to businesses. In addition, there is considerable incentive right now for businesses to reach out to high schools in the United States. Based on projected demographic trends, the number of 18-year-olds in the population will not again reach present levels until the year 2003. Consequently, companies are being increasingly forced to reach out to inner-city minorities, many of whom are unskilled. Companies have an incentive to train the disadvantaged. Cities in regions that have the most success in such training will have an edge over other regions in the United States and foreign competition. Basic skills in English and math are essential. But the level of training must rise even higher—because international competition demands more skills. Even simple clerical work often requires computer knowledge.

What programs are available as guides for how high school students, particularly in inner-city neighborhoods, can acquire these basic skills and receive vocational and apprenticeship training that can lead to solid jobs?

Some of the answers appear to lie in experimental programs such as Project Prepare in Chicago and Project ProTech in Boston.

Project Prepare. Project Prepare, which began five years ago as a private, nonprofit project backed by federal funding through the Eisenhower Foundation and by state funding, is a comprehensive vocational skills training program for at-risk teenagers in three inner-city Chicago public high schools. Implemented by Youth Guidance, Inc., a citywide nonprofit community organization, the multiple-solution project offers intensive job-skills training linked to job placement and support services (such as counseling and crisis intervention). One key component of Project Prepare is an arrangement with local businesses that help train students in exchange for offering them jobs upon completion of the program.

Two hundred and seventy-two students in three schools participated in the first year of the project; another 227 students served as comparisons. (They did not receive services from the project but continued in standard vocational education courses.) Upon entry into the venture, both project youth and their comparison groups possessed similar low grade point averages, low job-readiness skills, and low class-attendance rates. The program's planned services were implemented fully in one high school, the Roberto Clemente Community Academy, and in lesser degrees at the two other schools. As might be expected, full implementation yielded stronger improvements in students' attendance, job readiness, and retention rates.

At Clemente, Hyatt Hotels Corporation built a state-of-the-art kitchen to train students in culinary arts, donated a chef from Hyatt to train them, and instituted

---

Germany's vocational training and apprenticeship program is considered a major reason for Germany's long economic boom and a key to why Germany's high-tech workers are admired from Detroit to Tokyo.

Companies are being increasingly forced to reach out to inner-city minorities, many of whom are unskilled. Companies have an incentive to train the disadvantaged.

a three-year curriculum and internship program. Students like the food vocational education program because of the high-tech equipment, serious commitment from Hyatt, and the dynamic teachers and counselors. The annual operating cost of the project, including the corporation's donation, amounts to less than $2,000 per youth.

The evaluation of the first year of the project showed that Clemente students who received Project Prepare's comprehensive services improved their job-readiness skills and attendance rates and stayed in high school longer than comparison students. These differences were statistically significant. Dropout rates at Clemente for Project Prepare students were 13% lower than for comparison students.

These evaluation findings are sufficiently promising to allow for replication. Accordingly, Project Prepare has now expanded to another inner-city high school in which the McDonald's Corporation has pledged to train and place 52 sophomores from Wells High School after they complete a three-year, intensive management and business curriculum modeled after McDonald's Hamburger University management courses. While attending the courses and finishing high school, the students are eligible for part-time jobs with local owners–operators of McDonald's restaurants. An evaluation of the replication currently is under way.

Project ProTech. A related program is Project ProTech in Boston. Members of this youth-apprenticeship program spend part of their day in high school and the rest of the day cultivating a marketable skill—in this case as a hospital technician. Students in Project ProTech are promised part-time hospital jobs during two years of high school and two years of junior college. After that, they are supposed to be certified in a skill marketable in the medical industry. Currently, students are working in areas like histology, radiology, and hematology. Part of ProTech's promise is that it centers on an expanding industry—health care—where future employment opportunities are likely to be plentiful. However, the program is very new, there is no real evaluation yet, and it is uncertain in terms of how many high-risk youth who can be employed. It also is expensive. With a federal grant of almost $1 million, the program is able to serve only 120 of Boston's 15,000 high school students. Accordingly, a comprehensive evaluation is in order, and then an assessment needs to be undertaken of the potential for replication.

■ School Desegregation Combined with Inner-City School Enrichment

We believe that investments in inner-city schools should be increased at the same time that opportunities are expanded for schools in the suburbs for inner-city youth.

Policy need not be either/or. In our democracy, the priority should be on provision of opportunity so that parents can decide locally what is best for their families.

America is resegregating. A new study by Professor Gary Orfield at Harvard University shows that about 70% of all African American and Latino children and youth are attending predominately minority schools.

The continuing reality of school segregation is like a family secret that will not stay hidden, exposing the unresolved and politically explosive issues of race, class, and poverty in American life.

Over the last 12 years, courts have moved away from ordered busing, aiming for a mix of required desegregation goals and incentives like specialized magnet schools.

Chapter 3

> Because residents in many cities carry the main burden of busing and because, when some inner-city schools are closed, principals and teachers—usually minorities—can lose their status in the system, some inner-city parents now would rather have all-minority schools they can oversee.

However, despite years of negative publicity about busing, desegregation has worked in dozens of small and middle-size cities—and some larger ones as well. For example, one model of success has been St. Louis. A court settlement there gave inner-city children the right to attend suburban schools. About one-third of those eligible, 14,000 children, have ventured into the suburbs since the mid-1980s. Because suburban parents did not have to bus their children into the inner city, they accepted the plan.

While inner-city families won the right to access suburban public schools, the St. Louis experience also illustrates the complex situation they face. Inner-city children have to brave a largely alien world. The inner-city families more likely to choose the suburban integration are better educated, more aggressive advocates for their children, and more self-confident. Children of some of the most troubled families are left behind in the worst schools. Because residents in many cities carry the main burden of busing and because, when some inner-city schools are closed, principals and teachers—usually minorities—can lose their status in the system, some inner-city parents now would rather have all-minority schools they can oversee, perhaps via the Comer School Development Plan, rather than participate in desegregation.

This dilemma illustrates the most difficult issues in desegregation—the enormous gaps in spending between the rich school districts of the "fortunate fifth" of the income distribution (see chapter 1) and the poor school districts of the truly disadvantaged, the connection between segregated housing and segregated schools, the consequences of "white flight" to better public schools in the suburbs, and a backlash against desegregation by some whites as well as African Americans.

Said one veteran desegregation lawyer, "I am more convinced than ever that if we're talking about providing real educational opportunity, then we have to confront the issue of racial *and* economic isolation."

Policy has been further complicated by what we believe to be the failure of the Supreme Court over the last 12 years to take the leadership role it should. Because the Supreme Court has refused to hear key cases, the cases have been decided in the lower courts.

> Inner-city public schools should be saved and the first priority is to lift their performance to that of the best suburban schools.

We believe that inner-city public schools should be saved and that the first priority is to lift their performance to that of the best suburban schools. We also believe that families should have the opportunity to send their children from poor inner-city public schools to wealthier public schools, usually white, if they choose to do so. Given the lack of leadership by the Supreme Court, vision now needs to be reestablished by the Clinton administration. Desegregation can be given a huge boost via the bully pulpit, by the President spreading the word on where and how desegregation has worked well, and by the Education Department allocating more funds to school systems that are prepared to replicate those desegregation successes, like St. Louis—as part of an overall inner-city public school enrichment plan like the Carnegie Foundation's National Urban Schools Program.

What about private school vouchers? Although it is important to provide inner-city families with as much choice of schools as possible, federal responsibility must focus on upgrading inner-city public schools and on the children from the most troubled homes who need the most attention. Voucher schemes that would allow low-income families to spend vouchers at either public or private schools do not provide nearly enough funds for inner-city kids to go to the top private schools. Nor do the private schools have the incentive to provide quality education for truly disadvantaged children. Vouchers for private school tuition would drain tax dollars from the public schools and weaken them further.

Crucially, public school desegregation policy must be part of a broader, multiple solution federal plan to discourage spatial segmentation. In terms of segmentation caused by income differences, the need is to reform job training and placement for inner-city residents (see chapters 4 and 5) and to make the federal income tax more progressive by taxing the richest one percent, while reducing taxes for the middle class, working class, and the poor (see chapter 7).

In terms of housing segregation, the need is to replicate fully for all those qualified the successful Gatreaux model in Chicago, which uses housing vouchers to promote suburban integration (see chapter 5). Gatreaux should be accompanied by carefully implemented plans to keep the middle class in or to bring them back to urban neighborhoods, *as long as lower income families are not pushed out and are given good employment and educational opportunities.*

Given the loss of tax bases from the central city to the suburbs in many places, the federal government needs to condition grants to states and localities on local agreements to share across the entire metropolitan area (including suburbs) the value of commercial property, as well as other elements of the area-wide tax base, for property tax purposes—following the successful plan, for example, of Minneapolis/St. Paul.

And the federal government should closely monitor the school finance plans in Michigan and other states that transition from property taxes to other forms of taxes that allow for more equitable expenditures in inner cities and the suburbs. If the Michigan-style plan works, the federal government should create incentives for all states to adopt it.

■ National Education Policy for the Inner City

Unlike Japan and many European nations, the United States makes its decisions about education locally, without mandates from a government ministry. The U.S. Department of Education does not build schools, hire teachers, write textbooks, dictate curricula, administer exams, or manage colleges and universities.

But the federal Department of Education's mission *is* to expand educational opportunity, set standards, innovate new ideas, which, if successful, can be replicated locally, undertake careful evaluation, and disseminate information.

We recommend that the Department of Education receive appropriations of up to $500 million per year to implement the proposed reforms of the Elementary and Secondary Education Act of 1965, implement the National Urban Schools Program proposed by the Carnegie Foundation and the middle-school reform proposed by the Carnegie Council, replicate the Comer Plan much more widely, replicate variations on the Lang Plan *if* comprehensive evaluation shows their worth, experiment with still unproven vocational and apprenticeship training, replicate already successful vocational and apprenticeship training (like Project Prepare), and push for more school integration based on plans like St. Louis that have worked. This level

Voucher schemes that would allow low-income families to spend vouchers at either public or private schools do not provide nearly enough funds for inner-city kids to go to the top private schools. Nor do the private schools have the incentive to provide quality education for truly disadvantaged children.

of spending should be leveraged at the rate of one new federal dollar for each eight state and local dollars, as recommended by the Carnegie Foundation for the Advancement of Teaching.

Considering the magnitude of the problem, improvements in inner-city education must be coordinated with community-based nonprofit youth investment programs, job training and placement, community-based housing and infrastructure development that will help generate the jobs, community-based banking, community-based policing, and inclusion of high-risk youth in high-tech development, these initiatives are set out in chapters 4 and 5.

Chapter 4

Creating Opportunities For Youth and Young Adults

Experience and available scientific evidence have shown that the primary institutional vehicles for a comprehensive family policy must not only be schools, but community-based nonprofit organizations and the employment training system.

Community-Based Extended-Family Sanctuaries

A good many successful initiatives for at-risk youth are extended family sanctuaries—oases and safe havens off the mean streets. They supply some of the support and discipline missing from natural families. They also reconnect parents with their youngsters.

> What people want is something that works. Most people I met care little about which party gets the credit. Indeed, such talk about partisan gains or losses disgusts and further alienates them from Washington. They want to celebrate American successes and American efforts.
> Haines Johnson
> *Divided We Fall*, 1994

Examples of Success

Over the last 25 years, despite pessimistic rhetoric that "nothing works" and in the face of 12 years of federal government disinvestment, many inner-city nonprofit extended family programs have shown encouraging success. We illustrate community-based nonprofit successes with the Argus Community in the Bronx; Centro Sister Isolina Ferre in San Juan, Puerto Rico; Delancey Street in San Francisco and other locations; the Dorchester Youth Collaborative in Boston; City Lights School in Washington, D.C.; the Door in New York City; and Project Redirection in various locations.

Most of these initiatives assemble at the grass roots community level combinations of school dropout prevention, gang prevention, crime prevention, drug prevention, child poverty reduction, self-esteem building, teen-parenting guidance, employment training and placement, economic development, and community policing. Many of these programs have been judged successful through careful scientific evaluations. Many have "bubbled up" from the grass roots, providing ownership by the disadvantaged. Often, they have evolved because traditional alternatives, like schools, have failed.

Chapter 4

■ The Argus Community

The Argus Community in the Bronx is an extended family program founded in 1968 by Elizabeth Sturz, a poet and former probation officer. Argus is a community-based center offering programs for high-risk youth and adults ages 17 to 21. Mostly these youth are African American or Puerto Rican. The center, states Ms. Sturz, provides an "alternative life program for adolescents and adults who have been on the treadmill of unemployment, underemployment, street hustling, welfare, substance abuse, crime and prison, and who saw no way out for themselves."

Through residential and nonresidential programs, Argus attempts to offer fundamental nurturing often lacking in the families and communities from which these youth come. It seeks to create an extended family of responsible adults and peers who offer warmth, nurturance, communication, and structure, while teaching productive values to disadvantaged inner-city youth. Within this extended family setting, the program offers prevocational, vocational, and academic training as well as substance-abuse treatment and aftercare while working to link participants with employers in New York City. Training in computer skills, desktop publishing, building management, weatherization, and horticultural services is offered. Basic literacy skills and GED preparation classes are delivered through an alternative school at Argus.

Over time, Argus has added programs for housing, treating, and training homeless drug-addicted men, mentally ill drug-addicted men, and drug-addicted women with children. In addition, family planning, health care, and early education are offered. These services not only provide parenting assistance for the children of teen mothers in the program but also teach the young mothers and fathers how to be good parents. Ms. Sturz believes that "angry" alienated teenagers can be pulled in, can be brought to the point where they not only do not steal and assault but have something to give to the society." Punctuality, good attendance, and self-respect are stressed in small-sized classes by teachers who come from the neighborhoods surrounding Argus.

A new Argus residential extended family and treatment center for pregnant women, mothers, and their young children is currently being built in the Mott Haven neighborhood of the South Bronx. As part of the complex, Argus hopes to create a police mini-station at which an assigned officer will actually live. The officer will become acquainted with neighborhood residents and involved with the children, parents, and community as well as help secure the neighborhood for human and economic development.

The concept is modeled on the residential police mini-station already operating at Centro Sister Isolina Ferre in San Juan, Puerto Rico.

The nonresidential Argus program, the Learning for Living Center, is designed primarily for teenagers who have a history of drug use, have dropped out of school, are victims of sexual abuse and physical abuse and neglect, and who have been involved in criminal acts. It is designed as alternative life training to prevent youth from ending up in the residential program, which is designed for older youth with more serious problems—especially drug addiction. So Argus has developed a full range of intervention services from early prevention to treatment. Some youth are referred to Argus from other neighbor-

---

Many innovative grass-roots programs have evolved because traditional alternatives, like schools, have failed.

Through residential and non-residential programs, Argus attempts to offer fundamental nurturing often lacking in the families and communities from which these youth come.

hoods throughout New York City. But most participants reside in the neighborhood. Argus youth are at higher risk than are participants in most other community-based youth agencies in New York City. Despite the multiple problems and high-risk status of participants, however, the program has been encouragingly successful.

The Eisenhower Foundation evaluated a cycle of participants in the Argus daytime, nonresidential Learning for Living Center. Youth were assessed throughout 20 weeks of training and a follow-up period. Preprogram and postprogram measures were taken nine months apart on 100 high-risk Argus youth and 100 comparable youth who did not receive training. Results indicated that Argus youth received higher salaries and more job benefits than did comparison youth. In 1992, Argus was 1 of 18 New York City programs funded by U.S. Department of Labor job-training grants to exceed all evaluation, training, and placement goals. Recent audits of the Argus job-training programs found that no students were involved in criminal activities during these training periods and that 87% were placed successfully in training-related jobs. The cost per person for the training program was $16,000. An earlier study funded by the U.S. Department of Justice also found that Argus had the best outcomes among 50 New York State programs surveyed in terms of criminal-justice involvement and drug involvement among program youth.

As with most successful programs, Argus has multiple income streams that it is able to administer well, despite the fact that funding sources, especially public-sector bureaucracies at federal, state, and local levels, often create problems and hinder solutions. In speaking of bureaucrats at funding agencies, Ms. Sturz has praised many of these bureaucrats but warned that "one compulsive neurotic or one sadist can play Russian roulette with kids' lives and set our administrative department boiling, hissing and thumping its lid."

Argus has been able to bring on tough, dedicated, and talented staff as well as install management systems to deal with the funding bureaucracies. But the time and expense for such competence is an additional demand on a nonprofit community-based organization that works with the most troubled youth in places like the South Bronx. The problem is further compounded by the fact that the Argus program is comprehensive. Yet most funders have narrow, categorical requirements for success—what Ms. Sturz calls "slivers of programs." So Argus must piece together categorical funding in innovative ways from diverse sources in order to come up with comprehensive interventions. The Argus fiscal officer must simultaneously keep track of multiple income streams, each often with complicated reporting requirements, administered by an unsympathetic contract manager. This insensitivity to the innovative, community-specific work of organizations like Argus merely serves to frustrate and complicate unnecessarily the good work they perform.

■ **Centro Sister Isolina Ferre**

Centro is an amazing multipurpose initiative that draws in the community, creates a safe haven, and generates opportunity—education and employment. It began in the LaPlaya neighborhood of Ponce, Puerto Rico, in 1968 by Sister Isolina Ferre, a graduate of Fordham University who spent years working in New York City's

Chapter 4

toughest streets. Playa de Ponce was a community of 16,000 people neglected by government and private agencies, with delinquency rates more than twice that of the rest of the city of Ponce, high unemployment, poor health conditions, no basic health care services, and "few, if any, resources." Centro began with the following premise: "If family and community could be strengthened, and meaningful employment made available," it might be possible to "make substantial progress in the struggle against neighborhood crime and violence."

With this vision, Sister Isolina initiated several programs designed to develop the competence of community youth, many of whom were gang members. One program in particular stands out—a system of youth advocates or "intercessors." These intercessors included streetwise community youth who served as mentors for youth brought before the juvenile court. The advocates would get to know the young person and his or her peers and family as well as investigate the youth's family and work situation and day-to-day behavior. They would attempt to involve the young person in a range of developmental programs, including job training, recreation, and tutoring. But their role went beyond individual counseling. The intercessor became familiar with the life experience of the youth in order to initiate work with the young person's family, peers, and school and to advocate for the young person among staff, the police, and the courts. In short, intercessors helped the community become aware of resources that could be used to help the youth develop into a healthy adult. Despite initial distrust of intercessors, the police eventually began working closely with them, often calling them first before taking a youth to court.

Centro also developed innovative educational alternatives for youth at risk of dropping out of school as well as solicited "advocate families" who took the lead in helping their neighbors with family problems. An extensive job-training program was created on the premise that "building a community without jobs for youth is like trying to build a brick wall without cement."

In *Criminal Violence, Criminal Justice*, written in the mid-1970s, Charles Silberman called Centro "the best example of community regeneration I found anywhere in the United States." LaPlaya is considered the toughest neighborhood in Ponce. Yet from 1968 to 1977, the period of initial operations of Centro, the rate of reported juvenile offenses remained fairly constant throughout Ponce, but showed a two-thirds decline in LaPlaya.

Centro replicated the original Ponce program in San Juan. The Eisenhower Foundation provided assistance. San Juan's program embraces the original education, mediation, and employment initiatives begun in Ponce while adding a family component combined with community-based, problem-oriented policing. A police mini-station has been built at the entrance to the "campus" where buildings for the other initiatives are located. This station helps secure the neighborhood and lets Centro staff undertake its work without the fear experienced by staff who worked at Project Beethoven in Chicago. A police officer lives with his wife and three children above the mini-station, the lowest floor of which has an IBM computer training and remedial education center. The equipment is protected by the police presence. For the most part, the officer does not make arrests. He works on preventive activities accompanied by other officers not in residence but on assignment during the day.

> Centro began with the following premise: "If family and community could be strengthened, and meaningful employment made available," it might be possible to "make substantial progress in the struggle against neighborhood crime and violence."

> "Building a community without jobs for youth is like trying to build a brick wall without cement."

After the first year, crime reported to the police was down 30% in the neighborhood, while it increased in San Juan as a whole. In later years, crime diminished further, until the U.S. Department of Justice stopped funding.

Sister Isolina and the other nuns who work with her face the same kinds of bureaucracy that Ms. Sturz faces in the South Bronx. Like Argus, Centro has a competent financial-management staff to handle the fragmented income streams and their diverse reporting requirements. Throughout the years, Sister Isolina has achieved near sainthood status in Puerto Rico. She has received an honorary doctorate from Yale University as well as commendations from Democratic and Republican presidents. She uses her well-earned reputation skillfully to overcome some of the bureaucratic obstacles presented by funders.

■ Delancey Street

Mimi Silbert and co-founder John Maher, an ex-felon, founded Delancey Street in 1971. It developed as a center in San Francisco for ex-offenders to become productive citizens. Delancey Street is run entirely by ex-convicts. Named for a section of New York City's lower east side where immigrants congregated at the turn of the century, Delancey Street began with four addicts in a San Francisco apartment. Its population of former convicts, drug abusers, and prostitutes quickly grew. Eventually, program participants and Dr. Silbert purchased an old mansion.

Delancey Street rules forbid the use of alcohol or drugs and prohibit violence. In two decades of operation, there has never been an arrest for a violent incident, and the few residents who have threatened violence have been thrown out. More than 10,000 women and men have passed through the program. Participants, who range from 12 to 68 years of age, are asked to promise to stay at Delancey Street for at least two years. Eighty percent have kept this pledge. In fact, the average time spent at Delancey Street is four years.

Delancey Street has never been formally evaluated by comparing program participants with a population not involved in the program. Yet hosts of participants have moved on to lives as attorneys, business people, technically skilled professionals and construction workers.

In chapter 1, we cautioned against the overpoliticization of buzz words like "self-sufficiency." But at Delancey Street self-sufficiency was a founding principle, and Dr. Silbert has made it work. Each Delancey resident is put in charge of some aspect of the organization. There are no "experts" helping to run Delancey Street. It is run by residents. All are employed to support the extended family. Delancey Street does not accept outside funds from the public or private sectors. This is Dr. Silbert's way of overcoming fragmented funding bureaucracies. Delancey has its strict rules of behavior and a self-governing system. Each resident must develop at least three marketable skills as well as earn a high school equivalency diploma and pass a core liberal arts curriculum taught in-house. Daily activities include frequent "games" held for residents to develop their interpersonal skills. After one year of residency, there are marathon sessions called "dissipations" to help residents get rid of their guilt over past failures. Before leaving, a resident must involve him- or herself in volunteer community or social work. Residents are engaged in numerous projects, from helping the elderly to working with young people in impoverished neighborhoods.

Chapter 4

One of Delancey Street's many crowning achievements to date is its new residential center, built in a choice location on the Embarcadero in San Francisco. With assistance from unions, the Embarcadero complex was constructed almost entirely by the formerly unskilled residents. More than 250 people were trained in the construction trades. The beautiful and spacious block-long and -wide development is assessed at $30 million, though it cost only half that amount to build it, because residents constructed it themselves and many building materials were contributed. A $10 million line of credit was obtained from Bank of America in what Dr. Silbert calls "good business for the bank and good business for us."

Called the Embarcadero Triangle, the complex contains 177 apartments for Delancey Street residents as well as meeting rooms, a movie theater, a swimming pool, and space for businesses, including printing, picture framing, and catering. All of the businesses are run by residents. An upscale restaurant, also operated by Delancey Street residents, is housed in the complex. Discount retail stores are being opened in partnership with major businesses. Residents have learned to run them. Business activities net $3 million per year for Delancey Street. Dr. Silbert is the only permanent staff member. No one is paid a salary; rather everyone is both a giver and receiver in an extended family atmosphere.

> At Delancey Street, each resident must develop at least three marketable skills as well as earn a high school equivalency diploma and pass a core liberal arts curriculum taught in-house.

Currently, 500 residents live in the Embarcadero Triangle complex. More than 500 other program participants are engaged in the same rigorous program in New York, North Carolina, and New Mexico. Delancey Street recently purchased a Hilton Hotel in south central Los Angeles to house an additional 500 people. Dr. Silbert's goal is to develop Delancey Street as an example for the nation. Long-term plans include the creation of a training institute that will require participants to serve an internship of several months. The model has been replicated by other ex-felon populations around the world. Dr. Silbert also is working with the Enterprise Foundation to rebuild the Sandtown neighborhood of Baltimore.

■ The Dorchester Youth Collaborative

The Dorchester Youth Collaborative (DYC) was established in the late 1970s in a low-income, rapidly changing Boston neighborhood that was racially and ethnically mixed with large Latino, black, and white populations. DYC aimed to provide nontraditional services, activities, and advocacy for local youth considered at high-risk of gang involvement, delinquency, teen pregnancy, school failure, and substance abuse. These youth, who often came from broken families, were not being adequately served by more conventional social service agencies.

> DYC's Prevention Clubs are designed to steer neighborhood youth away from the street life and toward structured activities to help them develop self-esteem, stay in school, or find other educational alternatives.

An important part of DYC's ambitious efforts is its Prevention Clubs. These clubs are designed to steer neighborhood youth away from the street life and toward structured activities to help them develop self-esteem, stay in school, or find other educational alternatives. DYC youth use the center as physical sanctuary from the streets. It provides them with an extended family of positive role models.

From the beginning, the clubs were racially integrated and bilingual; participants were approximately equally divided among whites, blacks, and Latinos. The kids learn to relate to one another. A constant flow of young people move in and out of DYC headquarters. The atmosphere is one of hugs, handshakes, amusement, and good will.

Such camaraderie represents a significant achievement in an urban community racked by frequent racial conflict among its youth. A research team from Rutgers University noted:

> The Dorchester community had a very heterogeneous racial composition and racial tensions were a major problem. Developing an integrated youth program was an important goal, rarely tried by other agencies, and an important accomplishment.

A substantial proportion of the youth were extremely high-risk street kids who not only faced severe family problems, drug abuse, and school failure, but who had also been hard to involve in structured activities of any kind in the past.

The research team that evaluated the high-risk youth who went through DYC collected considerable information on 22 young persons who participated in the program, both at intake and periodically thereafter. Nine of the youth were interviewed at length. Their findings, though frustratingly limited, are encouraging. Although a formal control group of youth proved impossible to find, comparisons among youth in Boston as a whole and Dorchester in particular provide a useful perspective from which to view the program's success. During the period in which the DYC youth cohort was tracked (1983–1987), Boston's annual school dropout rate averaged 16% (18% among blacks and Hispanics) according to the Boston Public Schools' Office of Research and Development. Among the DYC enrollees, 28% had dropped out of school before or shortly after joining the program. Program staff convinced more than half of the dropouts to return to school. Overall the dropout rate among the participants fell to 14%, slightly lower than the city's average rate—a promising finding given the especially high-risk population enrolled in the DYC.

Dorchester District Court statistics indicated that 27% of the DYC enrollees had been arrested at least once. Participants continued to have problems with the law even after joining the program, and the percentage of those arrested after joining decreased only to 23%. While this decline is somewhat disappointing, it is important to realize that during this same period, the number of juvenile arrests in the Dorchester community increased by 63 percent, from 386 in 1983 to 628 in 1987, according to the Boston Police Department.

The Rutgers researchers concluded that the program had a positive and dramatic impact on the lives of the young people:

> While we do not have an adequate comparison group, it is important to recognize that these participants entered the program in their pre- and early teens. Six already had been arrested prior to their participation. They were approaching a time when "anti-social behavior would be more likely to occur, not less likely. . . . It appears that the program provided a structured yet supportive environment during a turbulent time of life in a difficult neighborhood. Many of those interviewed talked about DYC being a family, sometimes more of a family than the people they lived with.

Importantly, building on this success, the Eisenhower Foundation funded a DYC–Boston police initiative in which young African American police served as mentors to DYC youth. Community policing also was initiated in concert with DYC

Overall the dropout rate among the DYC participants fell to 14%, slightly lower than the city's average rate—a promising finding given the especially high-risk population enrolled in the DYC.

Chapter 4

outreach workers. Crime declined over 20% in two years in the neighborhood. The decline was statistically significant, compared with the city of Boston as a whole.

■ City Lights School

City Lights School works with District of Columbia adolescents and young adults whom the educational system can't seem to teach and the judicial system can't seem to reform. Founded under the auspices of the Children's Defense Fund in 1982, the program has helped more than 850 hard-core dropouts, juvenile delinquents, teen parents, and emotionally disturbed youth become more productive citizens.

The students who attend City Lights range in age from 12 to 22. A typical student is a disadvantaged 16-year-old who has at least one charge of delinquency, reads at the third-grade level, and suffers from serious emotional problems. Many of the students have long careers as hard-core truants, and most have been either physically or sexually abused.

The school's programs are designed specifically to enable students to find employment and live independently. A computer-based curriculum allows students to learn at their own pace. A comprehensive range of clinical services—including individual therapy, crisis intervention, and family counseling—helps the youth develop coping skills. An extensive substance-abuse prevention program provides positive alternatives to the omnipresent drug culture. Career counseling, prevocational training, independent living classes, and job-placement services help students make the transition from school to the workplace.

City Lights recently moved into a newly renovated facility. The building contains a computer center, a fitness center, and an independent living center, each of which will augment the school's existing range of services. With 15,000 square feet, the building enables City Lights to expand and serve more of the district's neediest youth. Within the next few years, the school plans to add a day-care program, an in-house health clinic, an expanded vocational program, and an after-school care program for neighborhood youth.

Evaluations are currently under way. An initial random sample of 25 students has been selected, and an additional sample of 25 has been identified. Eventually the two samples will be combined. Preliminary findings indicate that members of the initial group of 25 are experiencing encouraging progress in staying out of juvenile and adult corrections after leaving the program. Only 1 member of the 25-member sample was in a correctional facility 12 months after leaving the program. Although sampling bias may have influenced the result, a 4% recidivism rate is nevertheless striking in a population 68% of whom at admission had a recent criminal offense. Twenty-five percent of these were predicted before the demonstration project began to be repeat offenders. Whether these positive changes are the result of the City Lights treatment program will be examined more closely in the future.

The high rate of students involved in school, work, or training 12 months after leaving the program was another encouraging result of this initial evaluation. Seventy-six percent of the sample was engaged in one of these activities, and 84% of these former participants were employed. This finding, which approximated the predicted rate, is encouraging, given the sluggish economy and high levels of unemployment in the Washington, D.C., African American community.

> A typical City Lights student is a disadvantaged 16-year-old who has at least one charge of delinquency, reads at the third-grade level, and suffers from serious emotional problems.

The Door—A Center of Alternatives, Inc.

The Door began 21 years ago as a single-site, multiple-solution, extended family program for youth and young adults 12 to 20 years old. Housed on three floors of a building in lower Manhattan that it owns and operates as a condominium for other nonprofit organizations, the Door offers more than 30 programs in prevention, enrichment, and remedial services to 6,000 New York City area residents each year. Ninety-four percent are African American, Latino, or Asian.

A paid staff of 145 is assisted by an equal number of volunteers to provide legal services; health, mental health, and health-education services (including substance-abuse treatment, family-planning services, prenatal care, well-baby care, HIV testing and counseling, and general primary care); career counseling; job training and placement; creative and physical arts classes; an alternative high school with a cross-cultural curriculum; GED preparation classes; on-site day care; crisis support service; youth leadership training; and hot meals. All services are provided free of charge and are confidential. The only requirement for eligibility is a desire to participate and an agreement to abide by the Door's formal code of conduct, a set of rules addressing self-discipline and respect for others. Every new client is given a full tour of the facility and an explanation of all its services; Door members participate as tour guides. One-half of all youth served by the Door were referred by friends who had used its services.

The Door, like Argus, has found that many funders provide categorical resources for youth instead of flexible resources for persons with multiple problems. Says one Door staff member, "Our society and our culture are organized in a fragmented way. And so is most public and private funding."

The Door funds its services through government contracts, more than 80 private institutions, and individual donors. Categorical funding provides monies for most of its financial base. However, the notion of comprehensive funding—multiple solutions to multiple problems—is slowly catching on, at least in New York State. In an experiment with the Door, the state consolidated seven discreetly funded contracts into one $1.4 million master contract, thus simplifying fiscal reporting requirements. Redundancies remain, however, because each state agency still requires its own separate client-data tracking forms, thus requiring Door staff to keep two sets of records—one for the master contract and one for each separate funding agency. The Door responded by developing measurable, comprehensive outcome objectives from which progress reports can be developed based on outcomes instead of process measures. "We want them to consider reading skills and job placement rates as outcomes, and not the number of times we blinked our eyes at this kid," one staff person said.

The Door has undergone several evaluations, although none has used comparison or control groups. Nonetheless, some of the changes among program youth have been so dramatic that it is difficult to conclude that the program was not responsible, at least in part, for these changes. For example, a three-year study cited in a National Institute on Drug Abuse (NIDA) monograph on model programs showed that 40% of Door participants either stopped using drugs or significantly reduced their usage. The Door's GED success rate is among New York City's highest. Further evaluations by outside evaluators have been planned.

> **Efforts to replicate The Door have failed, in part because its program design operates outside traditional funding streams available to community-based organizations.**

> **Each state agency requires its own separate client-data tracking forms, thus requiring Door staff to keep two sets of records—one for the master contract and one for each separate funding agency.**

Chapter 4

■ Lessons Learned from Promising and Innovative Programs

We have examined scores of other indigenous, nonprofit family and youth investment programs. Some, such as Argus, Centro, the Dorchester Youth Collaborative, and Project Redirection, have undergone sufficient scientific evaluation and demonstrated that they are successful. Other programs, such as Delancey Street, City Lights, and the Door, have not undergone sufficiently rigorous evaluations, although they appear to be extremely successful. Hundreds of other programs throughout the nation may also hold promise, despite the fact that they have not been formally evaluated.

In looking at the success stories that have been formally evaluated, as well as the programs that appear to be on the right track but need more rigorous evaluation, several common-sense lessons seem clear:

- There is value in organizing and implementing at the grass-roots level.
- Multiple solutions are needed for multiple problems—the "butterfly effect" applies.
- Solutions need to be flexible, and staff need to be caring and tenacious.
- Sound management must be put in place.
- A way must be found to secure at least minimal resources each year.

✦ There Is Value in Organizing and Implementing Programs at the Grass-Roots Level

Because they are in closer touch with the people they serve, successful community-based nonprofits often work better for high-risk children, youth, and families than government bureaucracies and inner-city schools. This conclusion is based on many years of experience, but very recent new support comes from the Carnegie Corporation report, A *Matter of Time: Risk and Opportunity in the Non-School Hours*, which recommends expansion of community-based youth organizations, especially in the inner city.

Because the "bottom line" of successful community nonprofits is doing what works in a comprehensive way to save children, youth, and families, they often meet those goals more completely than for-profit organizations and business-dominated coalitions, like Private Industry Councils, with leadership that has a more materialistic bottom line.

A community base allows neighborhood people, including high-risk youth, to acquire a stake in planning and implementing programs and to tailor solutions to local needs, as perhaps best demonstrated by Centro. In some successful grass-roots ventures, the result is *both* positive change for individual high-risk youth, like reduced dropout rates, and positive change for the geographically defined community—like less fear, crime, and drug dealing in the neighborhood and more business retention and economic development.

Successful programs draw staff from the community and from graduates of the programs. They are not, or not all, or not just, "professionally trained" in academically defined disciplines, like social work. They have street training and street smarts. This provides common-sense insight, an ability to easily cast aside nonsensical and narrow academic or professional school theories and ways of doing things. The result is flexibility in program design and an instinctive understanding

---

Successful community nonprofits often meet goals more completely than for-profit organizations and business-dominated coalitions, like Private Industry Councils, with leadership that has a more materialistic bottom line.

A community base allows neighborhood people, including high-risk youth, to acquire a stake in planning and implementing programs and to tailor solutions to local needs.

that the multiple problems faced by high-risk inner-city children and youth require multiple solutions that cut across traditional bureaucracies.

✦ Multiple Solutions Are Needed for Multiple Problems— The "Butterfly Effect" Applies

Vaclav Havel, President of the Czech Republic, has written about the "butterfly effect":

> It is a belief that everything in the world is so mysteriously and comprehensively interconnected that a slight, seemingly insignificant wave of a butterfly's wing in a single spot on this planet can unleash a typhoon thousands of miles away.

We are not certain about typhoons far away, but in the inner city, interconnectedness is not at all mysterious in successful programs for children, youth, and families.

Most of the successful programs that we have reviewed begin with some form of extended family "sanctuary" (a place to go) off the street. It may be residential, as with Delancey; nonresidential, as with Centro; or both, as with Argus. Paid and volunteer mentors function as "big brothers" and "big sisters"—offering both social support and discipline in these extended families.

Often, youth who need such social investments are teen parents who receive counseling in parenting skills, as in Project Redirection. In some successful programs, where feasible, mentoring and counseling also involve the parents of the youth who receive the mentoring.

Not uncommonly, a goal of the mentoring process is to keep youth in high school, as DYC, or to help them receive high school equivalency degrees, sometimes in alternative, community-based organizational settings, as Argus and City Lights. Here, too, there are many variations among successful programs. They include day care for infants of teen parents. Remedial education in community-based settings often can be pursued with the help of computer-based programs, like those developed by Robert Tagger with US Basics (see below), which allow youth to advance an entire school year through two or three months of one-on-one computer work. There are vocational incentives to stay in school, as with the Hyatt Hotel management and food preparation course run by Youth Guidance at the Roberto Clemente Community Academy in Chicago, which assures a job with Hyatt upon graduation (see chapter 3).

Some successful community nonprofit programs also link high school education either to job training or to college. When job training is undertaken, social support and discipline continue, frequently in community-based settings, as is the case with Argus. (The training–placement link is crucial because the present national job-training program for high-risk youth—the Job Training Partnership Act—does not adequately place such youth in jobs, as discussed below.) In successful programs, job placement may be in the immediate neighborhood of a sponsoring community-based organization—as in initiatives that train young workers to rehabilitate houses, such as YouthBuild U.S.A. (see chapter 5). This can help in the social and economic development of the neighborhood.

Successful programs draw staff from the community and from graduates of the programs. They have street training and street smarts.

Chapter 4

There are some promising ventures where this combination of youth, social, and economic development is assisted by community-based and problem-oriented policing, as is the case with the Centro San Juan residential police mini-station and the mentoring of DYC youth by Boston police. Such community policing can reduce crime and fear. The crime and fear reduction can help encourage businesses and the public sector to stay or build in the inner city. If this economic development is planned correctly, it can provide jobs for high-risk youth. The youth can qualify for the jobs if they have adequate job training and if they stay in school. Staying in school is made easier by big brother/big sister mentoring and extended family sanctuaries off the street.

Children can survive long enough to get into these sanctuary initiatives if they have Head Start.

What works, then, seems to embrace a multiple-solutions formula including: sanctuary, extended family, mentoring, positive peer pressure, social support, discipline, and educational innovation that motivates a youth to obtain a high school degree; job training (which continues social support and discipline) linked to job placement; feasible options for continuing on to college; employment linked to economic development; and problem-oriented policing, which is supportive of the process for youth social, community, and economic development.

Not all successes have all of these components, but multiple solutions always are evident in the formula.

Similarly, the successes tend to have multiple good outcomes. Not uncommonly, in successfully evaluated programs, these outcomes include some combination of less crime, less gang-related behavior, less drug abuse, less welfare dependency, fewer adolescent pregnancies, fewer school dropouts, more school grades completed, more successful school-to-work transitions, more employability, better parenting among targeted high-risk youth, and more stable families. The communities where young people live can have less fear, fewer drug dealers, and business, job, and economic development. Not all model programs and replications achieve all of these good outcomes. But the point is that multiple outcomes are the rule, not the exception.

✦ Solutions Need to Be Flexible Solutions and Staff Need to Be Caring and Tenacious

We have found that successful and promising community nonprofit programs understand that these multiple solutions and outcomes cannot be routine or uniform. Variation is needed to fit the individualized needs of young people. Flexibility is helped by smaller size programs and the higher staff–youth ratios—compared with overextended traditional bureaucracies in noncommunity settings.

Successful programs often devise innovative plots and schemes to tunnel under or circle around the rules and regulations of traditional bureaucracies that provide funds. Those bureaucracies tend to be narrow and categorical—so they must be manipulated if the community groups are to come up with funding for the comprehensive interventions and multiple solutions that work best.

In *Breaking the Cycle of Disadvantage*, Lisbeth Schorr concludes that not a single example of success which she could identify "was the product of normal functioning of a large system—public or private."

> **In successful programs, job placement may be in the immediate neighborhood of a sponsoring community-based organization, which can help in the social and economic development of the neighborhood.**

The extended family sanctuaries off the street characteristic of most successes help to generate a nurturing atmosphere in which staff can show their care and commitment. Youth feel they are wanted because of the supportive atmosphere, and this facilitates participation by young people and the development of leadership skills.

To fight and circumvent the bureaucracies, staff need to be dedicated and tenacious. The founders of Argus, Centro, and Delancey, for example, have been at it for a quarter century, and the financial officer at Argus seems to possess a certain god-like patience that outlasts contract officers.

✦ Competent Management Must Be Put in Place

One stereotype of inner-city community nonprofits is that they are begun by charismatic leaders who cannot manage. There is some truth to this, and many nonprofits especially in youth and related human service fields, go out of business because of poor management. When the management failures are combined with illegal activities, especially misspending of funds, there often is a great deal of media attention. This adds to the negative image of inner-city nonprofits in the minds of some Americans, even though no proof ever has been presented to us that nonprofits commit illegal acts with greater frequency than for-profits.

Yet successful and promising programs have competent comptrollers to manage grants and contracts. Some have executive vice presidents or CEOs who manage day-to-day while the leader leads. Good management helps in good performance, which attracts more funds. More funds increase the resources available for bringing on good managers. It is a two-way relationship.

In recognition of the need for improved management, the Eisenhower Foundation has begun a Management Training Institute for principal staff members of nonprofit youth-development organizations.

As we saw in Head Start, community nonprofits are almost always underpaid. As Lisbeth Schorr concludes:

> When it comes to professional status and economic compensation, the direct provision of basic services to the least powerful has little prestige. The development of better methods to accomplish such important public purposes as reaching hard-to-reach populations with effective services is also not sufficiently prized.

It is not uncommon for community workers to receive something on the order of $20,000 per year—*roughly 400 times less than the annual compensation of the* CEO *of Coca-Cola.* Should saving a young life be valued less than making a soft drink, and so much less? While not able to overturn this free-market decision on relative worth, we note that the successful and promising nonprofits nonetheless often are able to manage livable salaries for core staff.

✦ A Way Must Be Found to Secure At Least Minimal Resources Year after Year

Because they have inspired good leadership, good ideas, multiple solutions, flexibility, dedicated and tenacious staff, and competent management, successful and

Chapter 4

> **Even the most successful community-based nonprofits experience funding as a constant problem.**

promising community-based nonprofits are able to secure at least minimal funding year after year. This is "soft money." Community nonprofits rarely are endowed.

Programs like Argus do it in part through mastery of how to access the myriad public and private funders, which includes the ability to write good proposals.

Programs like The Door do it in part because one prime, long-term funder, the Ford Foundation, has the sophistication and insight to back multiple, comprehensive solutions—and not fragmented categorical grants.

Programs like Centro do it in part because its founder, Sister Isolina, a Catholic nun, creates such an elevated moral imperative which makes it difficult for funders to deny. Her skill is reminiscent of the late, dear and now legendary Monsignor Geno Baroni, HUD Assistant Secretary for Neighborhoods during the Carter administration. Father Baroni, for example, rarely wore his clerical clothes—but made sure to have them on when he made his case annually before the Office of Management and Budget.

Programs like Delancey do it by creating business-like and for-profit ventures linked to the nonprofits. Delancey is able to involve participants in business-like ventures in part because they tend not to be 13-year-olds who still need to focus on school, but young adults who, if they can be turned around, are more ready for steady employment. Other nonprofits involved with human development, like the Mid-Bronx Desperadoes Community Housing Corporation, have integrated youth programs into economic development initiatives, and have generated income streams from the economic development, for example, through housing syndication. The methods of Delancey and the Desperadoes need to be spread to other organizations.

Still, even the most successful community-based nonprofits experience funding as a constant problem and have their bad times. Much of the reason is that community-based nonprofits are not sufficiently recognized by the public as superior service providers. In turn, funding from the public and private sectors remains minuscule compared with what is needed. The situation got worse with federal disinvestment from 1981 to 1992, even though, cynically, presidential rhetoric over this period praised community-based nonprofits. And it is more fashionable for public and private funders to provide "seed" grants only. Insufficient attention is given to ongoing, operational support.

> **One way to turn around public inattention and misperception is to communicate the cost-effectiveness of successful and promising programs.**

One way to turn around public inattention and misperception is to communicate the cost-effectiveness of successful and promising programs. Because these are genuinely *preventive*, these initiatives promise to be more enduring and more attractive to the tax-paying citizen than the superficial, reactive responses that characterize too much of our public policy. For example, the annual cost per person is over $30,000 for New York state prisons but about $16,000 for Argus residents, $2,000 for Argus nonresidents, and $1,000 for Centro nonresidents.

Program Replication

In a speech before the nation's governors, President Clinton talked about "the need to make exceptions to the rule." In the private sector, he said, exceptions do become the rule quickly, if they are successful. Everyone else in the market needs to adapt or be driven out. But in the public sector, he said, it is much more difficult to make exceptions to the rule.

These are important insights. It is true that the "social technology" for replicating inner-city, community-based, nonprofit programs is rather primitive. However, as the considerable success of the replication of Centro suggests, the difficulties that must be overcome are, in the words of Lisbeth Schorr, "not insurmountable." Carnegie Corporation President David Hamburg believes that "we know enough to act and can't afford not to act." During a recent Eisenhower Foundation cosponsored delegation to France to observe successful youth programs there, a high-ranking official in Lyon stated, similar to Dr. Hamburg, "In France, we figure out the right thing to do and we do it."

■ Lessons on How to Replicate

The conclusions of observers like Schorr and Dryfoos and of replication practitioners like Public/Private Ventures (P/PV), the Manpower Demonstration Research Corporation, and the Eisenhower Foundation tend to converge on les-sons for how to replicate.

Sound evaluations are needed as a baseline first to be sure of what to replicate—that is, what seems to work.

Careful evaluations are needed of the replications themselves to show that they achieve the same consistent results. Such evaluations need to be especially sensitive to "implementation failure." That is, we can already assume to some extent that the program idea is sound— at least in the location where the initiative originally demonstrated success. But the replication may still fail because of inadequacies in the day-to-day process of implementation.

To guard against such inadequacies, replications must build on the lessons that we have been able to glean from the original successes described above. In other words, the replications, too, must be grass-roots, multiple, and flexible in the solutions, staffed with patient and dedicated people, managed well, and adequately resourced over sufficient time. Replications to date also have concurred on the need for ongoing technical assistance and quality control, including well-packaged training materials.

Most informed observers and practitioners agree that it is wrong to assume that program replication is severely limited by a dearth of "exceptional and unique leaders." Persons like Elizabeth Sturz, Mimi Silbert, and Isolina Ferre are exceptional. But Argus, Delancey, and Centro were able to find extremely competent individuals to run the replications and program spin-offs. When replications have been run by national organizations, like P/PV, rather than directed by an originating community group, competent local implementation staff were found to be widely available.

It is the replication of general principles, allowing for significant local variation, that seems to work—not detailed, "cookie cutter" copies of the original. For example, the residential police mini-station of Centro is unique to the replication site and fits the perceptions and priorities of the replication director, which were shaped by her membership—and that of San Juan police—on a delegation to Japan to observe residential police mini-stations there.

> **Most informed observers and practitioners agree that it is wrong to assume that program replication is severely limited by a dearth of "exceptional and unique leaders."**

Chapter 4

Successful replication of inner-city youth initiatives also seem to integrate "bubble up" functions by the community group—which leads in planning and development, undertakes local needs assessments, resolves local political problems, creates local consensus and manages the program—with "top down" functions by technical assistors—who help organize funding, help create nonprofit–for-profit linkages, provide access (including travel) to other programs which offer new ideas, improve management, orchestrate quality control, lead evaluations in coordination with the community, and disseminate results through the print and electronic media in ways that also help raise ongoing financial support.

There is no necessary conflict, then, between "bubble up" and "top down." Both are needed.

■ The Biggest Obstacle: The Public Bureaucracy

France has had some successes in community-based integration of services and "one-stop shopping." With a few exceptions in a few places, America has failed.

It is not surprising, then, that those who have thought about and undertaken replications at the community level tend to agree that the public sector bureaucracy—especially state and federal government—is the biggest impediment to widespread replication.

Public-sector funders have little knowledge of or experience in how to cross institutional and jurisdictional boundaries to create the multiple solutions that work. As part of this enormous bureaucratic blind spot, public agencies typically do not, given their legislative mandates, easily cover many of the functions we have articulated as key to successful replications—like the packaging of written guideline materials, technical assistance, management training, quality control, evaluation, and guidance on how to use the media.

Much of the trouble originates with the ignorance of the lawmakers who write authorizing legislation. So reform must begin with reports by, in the case of the federal government, congressional watchdog groups, the General Accounting Office, the Office of Technology Assessment, and the Congressional Budget Office on how to redraft laws to allow budget allocations for comprehensive programs and replications.

At the executive level of federal government, interagency agreements have always included considerable "turfing" among agencies, often have been dependent on the personalities of assistant secretaries, and rarely have covered the materials, quality control, management training, evaluation, and media costs necessary for success. An alternative strategy therefore would be to reorganize agencies so that a single entity could fund and oversee community-based programs with multiple solutions.

■ A National Corporation for Youth and Family Investment

Such consolidation, however, need not necessarily create a *public* entity. It might be a national nonprofit intermediary, or series of intermediaries, that would be funded with public funds and matched by private funds.

We propose here a new National Corporation for Youth and Family Investment as the nonprofit, private-sector intermediary that would do just that.

Those who have thought about and undertaken replications at the community level tend to agree that the public sector bureaucracy—especially state and federal government—is the biggest impediment to widespread replication.

Reform must begin with reports on how to redraft laws to allow budget allocations for comprehensive programs and replications.

A private, nonprofit national institution would, based on our experience, implement programs more efficiently and rapidly than a public-sector institution. It could leverage public funds against corporate and other private sector funding better than a public agency and could promote youth investment with a more business-like image. There also could be increased tax-related opportunity owing to corporate-like "packaging" of the institution. For example, it might be possible to enact a federal tax credit to corporations that provide loans and grants to such a Corporation for Youth Investment.

A private-sector entity would allow assembly of talented, dedicated private-sector staff, with private-sector salaries and a commitment to remain with the institution for a sufficient time—at least 5 to 10 years—to make a national impact. By contrast, assistant secretaries and deputy assistant secretaries in the federal bureaucracy stay on the job for an average of about 20 months. This makes it more difficult to develop a long-term program of carefully implemented and cost-effective reforms.

Based on the lessons from the street which we have just reviewed, the new corporation would facilitate grass-roots community-based nonprofit replications that yield multiple and flexible extended family solutions that are creatively led, well managed, provide adequate salaries and resources, technically assisted with careful quality control, sensitively evaluated, and well accessed to the media. Local bubble-up variations will need to emerge, with vital top-down corporation facilitation playing a supportive rather than obstructive role.

In our discussion of child poverty welfare reform in chapter 2, we concluded that the federal government should raise the money for reform, set standards, and oversee the process—but that day-to-day operations should be decentralized. However, we found little evidence that devolution should be in the public sector or to the state level. Rather, we pointed to the kind of private-sector, nonprofit successes articulated in this chapter and concluded that available evidence supported devolution to the community and neighborhood level, where Walt Whitman's "common people" operate best. A private, nonprofit National Corporation for Youth and Family Investment fits this strategy well. It can be funded and overseen by the federal government but make grants and loans directly to private, nonprofit community organizations. These groups can receive information from the Corporation on what has worked best elsewhere and be carefully evaluated by the Corporation. States have poor records in providing such technical assistance and evaluations.

Job Training Reform

William Julius Wilson has concluded:

> Both the black delay in marriage and the lower rate of remarriage, each of which is associated with high percentages of out-of-wedlock births and female-headed households, can be directly tied to the labor market status of black males . . . . We were able to document empirically that black women, especially young black women, are facing a shrinking pool of marriageable (that is, employed, economically stable) men.

We propose a new National Corporation for Youth and Family Investment that would implement programs more efficiently and rapidly than a public-sector institution.

Chapter 4

Findings such as these lead us to conclude that the top priority in developing a comprehensive family policy for the disadvantaged is a reformed and comprehensive job training and placement program for minority males.

Table 11 summarizes how the United States lags far behind its major international competitors, Germany and Japan, with regard to job training.

For example, school-to-work transitions are left mostly to chance in the United States. In Germany, 60% of workers go through high-quality apprentice programs. In Japan, there are very close relations between employers and local schools.

The United States has vocational education available in most urban areas, quality varies widely, and as we saw above, there is a need for much more demonstration and evaluation. In Germany, as discussed in chapter 3, there is near universal availability of vocational education and the quality is uniformly high. Japan has limited availability, with quality fair to good.

Most experts give the United States a moderate rating for adult education. Community colleges offer many opportunities. In Germany, adult education is scarce but growing. In Japan, it is widespread and self-study is common.

Employee training in the United States is mostly for managers and technicians. Such training is excellent at a few companies, but nonexistent at many. In Germany, high-quality employer training is widespread among all levels of employees and it is strongly supported by the government. In Japan, employer training is widespread, with very good quality and government subsidies for small companies.

■ Evaluated Models of Success

A national Corporation for Youth and Family Investment would provide one new, focused operating vehicle that, among other goals, would help expand the capacity and number of inner-city, nonprofit organizations to train and place high-risk youth in the primary labor market.

However, we believe that the major new federal vehicle for inner-city job training should be based on already existing successes, particularly Job Corps.

Job Corps. Next to Head Start, the Job Corps appears to be the second most successful, across-the-board American prevention program ever created for high-risk youth and teenage parents. Job Corps is an *intensive* multiple-solutions program that takes seriously the need to provide a supportive, structured environment for the youth it seeks to assist. Job Corps features classroom courses, which can lead to high school equivalency degrees, counseling, and hands-on job training for very high-risk youth. Hence, as in individual community-based, nonprofit programs, like Argus, Job Corps carefully links education, training, placement, and support services.

Job Corps centers are located in rural and urban settings around the country. Some of the urban settings are campus-like. Others essentially are "street-based." In the original design, a residential setting provided sanctuary away from one's home. Today, nonresidential variations are being tried, and it will be

	United States	Germany	Japan
School-to-Work Transition	Left mostly to chance	60% of workers go through high-quality apprentice programs	Close relations between employers and local schools
Vocational Education	Available in most urban areas, but quality varies widely	Near-universal availability, uniformly high quality	Limited availability, quality fair to good
Adult Education	Moderate, community colleges offer many opportunities	Limited but growing	Widespread, self-study common
Employer Training	Mostly for managers and technicians, excellent at a few companies, nonexistent at many	Widespread, very high quality, strong government support	Widespread, very good quality, government subsidies for small companies

Table 11. Job training performance, by nation.

important to compare their cost-effectiveness with the live-in design. Yet, even for the nonresidential programs, the notion of an extended family environment has been maintained.

In 1991, Job Corps trained approximately 70,000 young people 16 to 22 years of age, most of whom were at serious risk of drug abuse, delinquency, and welfare dependency. The average family income of Job Corps participants was less than $6,000 per year, two of five came from families on public assistance, and more than four of five were high school dropouts. Since Job Corps began in 1964, 1.5 million youths of this kind have entered the program, with the typical participant being an 18-year-old minority high school dropout who reads on a seventh-grade level.

Evaluations of Job Corps have been consistently positive and its performance highly cost-effective. A 1991 analysis by the Congressional Budget Office calculated that for each $10,000 invested in the average participant in the mid-1980s, society received approximately $15,000 in returns—including approximately $8,000 in "increased output of participants" and $6,000 in "reductions in the cost of crime-related activities."

Evaluations conducted during the Reagan administration found that 75% of Job Corps enrollees move on to a job or to full-time study. Graduates retain jobs longer and earn about 15% more than if they had not participated in the program. Along the same lines, a U.S. General Accounting Office study concluded that Job Corps members are far more likely to receive a high school diploma or equivalency degree than comparison group members and that the positive impact on their earnings continues after training. According to one evaluator, "Naysayers who deny that labor market problems are real and serious, that social intervention can make a difference, or that the effectiveness of public programs can be improved will find little to support their preconceptions in the experience of programs like Job Corps."

Incomprehensibly, given available scientific evidence, the Reagan Administration tried to eliminate Job Corps year after year. The Democrat-controlled Congress resisted in the 1980s.

In the 1990s, the Republican-controlled Congress attacked Job Corps. One criticism was that considerable violence, drug abuse, and truancy had been reported. For example, in 1994, there were 461 recorded assaults by youths enrolled at the nation's Job Corps centers.

This was a serious issue that needed to be dealt with. The Argus Community, discussed earlier in this chapter, has objectives similar to Job Corps, but begins with the premise that remedial education and job training can only be done in a drug-free, violence-free environment. There is no tolerance for drugs and violence. Job Corps can improve based on the Argus model. That is one reason the U.S. Department of Labor funded the Eisenhower Foundation to replicate Argus in other locations. We also agree with suggestions that there be tougher screening of applicants and more careful selection of the persons who run Job Corps centers as well as the institutions that operate the program.

Yet the drug and violence issues must be kept in perspective. Job Corps takes the toughest kids who have faced the most intense multiple problems. There were 63,000 such youth enrolled in 1994, when the 461 assaults were recorded. That was

Chapter 4

better than what happens on the street among such populations, even though violence and drugs cannot be condoned.

Another criticism had to do with Job Corps success and drop-out rates. The 1980s success rate, of about 75% of participants moving on to a job or full-time study, meant a 1980s failure rate of about 25%. Assessments by the Department of Labor Inspector General in the 1990s found higher failure rates for some centers over some time periods—up to 50% failure rates in the first six months, for example. Given that Job Corps is the most expensive job training program ($14,000 for the average 8-month residential stay and $22,000 for a full 12 months), one Capitol Hill investigator said he was "stunned by the high drop-out rates."

Such a statement, made anonymously in a newspaper, is as incomprehensible from a scientific viewpoint as the political attacks on Job Corps in the 1980s. A success rate of 75% is more than unqualified success for this population. So is a success rate of 50%. We return to Ted Williams (chapter 3). his success rate was .400—and American men thought that unbelievable. Capitol Hill staffers ought not to impose a double standard—on white male baseball stars versus minority youth.

> A year in Job Corps remains much less expensive than a year in prison, which costs up to $30,000.

As for cost, a year in Job Corps remains much less expensive than a year in prison, which costs up to $30,000. And prison recidivism rates are very high. In addition, evaluations have shown that Job Corps outlays provide a much more impressive return than do expenditures for long-term drug treatment.

Wisely, the Clinton Administration has embraced the "Job Corps 50–50 Plan," which has as its goal expansion of the program by 50% by protecting existing Job Corps sites and opening 50 new Job Corps. centers in the next decade. Approximately 600,000 youth—about one-tenth of the six million children living in poverty—are eligible for Job Corps, which should be improved and expanded to give all a chance.

In addition, 14 states and 12 cities now operate year-round Youth Corps programs that incorporate various elements of the Job Corps. Other states and communities operate summer programs. An evaluation of the California Conservation Corps found that the work of corps members generates a positive economic return. (The superficial fad of "boot camps" as diversion programs for delinquent youth in recent years incorporates some elements of Job Corps discipline but little in the way of effective remedial education, training, and placement. Success rates were much lower than those for Job Corps.)

> The Job Training Partnership Act begun in the early 1980s has failed high-risk youth and teenage parents.

The Failure of the Job Training Partnership Act. By contrast with Job Corps, the Job Training Partnership Act (JTPA) begun in the early 1980s has failed high-risk youth and teenage parents. Evaluations have shown that although the results were marginally positive for disadvantaged adults, high-risk youth in the program actually did *worse* than comparable youth not in the program. For example, men younger than age 22 who participated in the program showed earnings $854 lower than their comparison group, with significantly greater deficits for those who took on-the-job training.

JTPA provides training, not job creation. A joke that made the rounds after JTPA's passage was that, if you called the Labor Department for information, the answering machine was programmed with a six-word response: "Read the law; ask the governors."

JTPA enrolls only approximately 5% of those eligible for assistance; moreover, the 5% that are eligible are not the truly disadvantaged. A 1991 assessment by the U.S. General Accounting Office concluded that much JTPA training involves placing trainees in low-skill work rather than investing in improving their skills. Indeed, as Elliott Currie, of the University of California at Berkeley, concludes, studies of how JTPA works suggest that its main function has been to provide a stream of low-wage workers—most of whom are already comparatively "job-ready"—to private employers who would probably have hired similar people without the program.

These views are further reinforced by Harvard Kennedy School Professor John Donahue, who concludes in his book *The Privatization Decision*, "There is no compelling evidence that the JTPA system, on balance, makes much difference for the employment, earnings and productive capacity of American workers." Some observers believe that control for implementing training and placement should be taken from corporate-dominated private industry councils (PICs) and given to redesigned local entities in which indigenous, nonprofit community leaders have at least as much representation as does the for-profit sector. We concur with this recommendation.

■ The Comprehensive Competencies Program

Some JobStart sites have incorporated a computer-based individualized instruction approach to teaching basic skills developed by Robert Taggart, Director of the Office of Youth Programs in the Department of Labor from 1977 to 1981. This initiative is based on extensive research with disadvantaged youth. The franchised system includes computerized management and testing techniques and is being used in 250 schools and community-based agencies in combination with other education and job-training methods.

The package includes self-paced instructional materials that allow participants to work one-on-one with the computer without risk of the kind of embarrassment that can occur in a classroom setting. The package also integrates all modes of teaching, workbooks, and audiovisual materials. Teachers are encouraged to spend as much time as possible with individual students. Multiple evaluation studies using comparison groups have shown that participants make significant gains in reading and math after 28 hours of instruction time.

■ YouthBuild U.S.A.

YouthBuild is a paid job-training and housing-rehabilitation program for young persons 16 to 24 years old offered in many cities nationwide. Based on a concept program begun in 1978 in East Harlem, YouthBuild was formally launched in 1988. Using public and private funds, it provides hands-on training in construction skills for as many as 18 months. Approximately 500 students have been enrolled in the program thus far. Many enrollees are male African American high school dropouts and single parents.

Not only, then, does YouthBuild generate jobs that can help stabilize families, but it provides shelter for families.

One-half of the program time is spent in academic classes mastering basic literacy and mathematics skills and preparing for high school equivalency diplomas,

Control for implementing training and placement should be taken from corporate-dominated private industry councils and given to redesigned local entities in which indigenous, nonprofit community leaders have at least as much representation as does the for-profit sector.

Chapter 4

> A key part of YouthBuild is that students can build self-respect, learn leadership skills, and begin to take control of their lives for the first time.

and the other half is spent at work sites rehabilitating abandoned buildings to create affordable permanent housing for homeless and low-income inner-city residents. In conjunction with the job skills and academic instruction, participants receive individual counseling, peer support, driver's license training, and recreational and cultural activities. A key part of the program, according to founder Dorothy Stoneman, is that students can build self-respect, learn leadership skills, and begin to take control of their lives for the first time.

Upon completion of the training program, YouthBuild refers participants to construction-related unions and other apprenticeship programs or college. While in the program, a student is paid approximately $500 per month and can earn raises and bonuses for good work and good attendance.

No formal evaluations have as yet been completed of YouthBuild, although a short-term measure of attendance among YouthBuild participants at four sites appeared promising. Eighty-three percent of enrolled participants stayed with the program for at least the first five months. On average, 60% stay to the end of the program and obtain regular jobs paying an average of $16,000 annually.

An evaluation has been initiated by Massachusetts Institute of Technology's Department of Urban Studies and Planning, Harvard's Kennedy School, and P/PV. Preliminary analyses indicate that a participant's likelihood of finishing the training program is based on whether the participant had already committed him- or herself to leaving the streets. According to the evaluation, previous criminal involvement and baseline reading and math scores are not strong predictors of a participant's retention in the training program. Ronald Ferguson concluded,

> Youth who are ready for such a program will respond to the opportunity and will work hard to put their lives on the right course. These findings . . . remind us not to prejudge and write off entire classes of youth because certain of their characteristics—such as low test scores—signal past problems.

Although evaluation is ongoing, YouthBuild is now expanding to up to 30 new sites under funding from the U.S. Department of Housing and Urban Development. The program operates in conjunction with nonprofit community-development corporations.

■ The Summer Training and Education Program

The Summer Training and Education Program (STEP) research demonstration was begun by P/PV in 1984 to test the effects of remediation, work, and life-skills intervention over two summers on 14- and 15-year-olds from poor urban families who had serious academic problems.

At five locations, STEP provided youth with half-day summer jobs under the federally funded Summer Youth Employment and Training Program, combined with half-day remedial reading and math using specially designed curricula and innovative teaching approaches. A half-day each week was devoted to issues concerning decision making and responsible sexual and social behavior.

The total intervention lasted 15 months. At the beginning and the end of the program, participants received a summer of intense intervention—the remedial education and the summer job, respectively. During the regular school year,

STEP interventions were less intense and were accompanied by the regular school curriculum.

Employment and training institutions that implemented the program were local agencies of the U.S. Department of Labor, including PICs from the JTPA system, which provided jobs for the kids in day camps, day-care centers, parks and recreation programs, building and grounds-maintenance programs, and offices. Public schools served as the remedial education agencies. Indigenous community-based nonprofit organizations, such as Argus or Centro, were not used, although one large community-action agency became involved in the program.

Because implementation occurred mostly through large, impersonal public institutions rather than through smaller nonprofit organizations with individualized and multiple solution approaches, the evaluation design was able to use random assignment and formal control groups. (See chapter 3 for a discussion of how randomization and formal control groups usually are inappropriate for programs run by smaller community-based nonprofit organizations.) The impact findings, based on 5,000 youth were as follows (emphasis added):

> STEPS's summer effects were consistently and impressively positive. Reading and math test scores after the first STEP summer were about one-half grade higher for youth receiving STEP than for a control group receiving only summer jobs. STEP youth also had significantly higher scores on tests measuring knowledge about sexually responsible social and sexual behavior. STEP youth—one-third of whom had been held back in school—had high attendance rates in the program, and a high return rate (75%) for the second summer.
>
> *The impressive summer impacts did not hold up once youth left STEP and returned to their regular school and life routines. STEP youth experienced the same school dropout, college entrance, teenage pregnancy and employment rates as the control group youth. Evidently, a positive and successful experience in work, education and life skills over two summers was not sufficient to alter the life trajectories of poor urban youth.*
>
> *The problems of many of these youth—both STEP treatments and controls—persisted and grew during the follow-up period.*

These findings support the need for longer, more sustained, more intense interventions, as is typified in Job Corps. The lack of sustained impact may also reflect the inadequacies of PICs as job-implementing agencies, of JTPA as the overall implementing system, and of traditional inner-city public schools, which have not been structurally changed by Carnegie- and Comer-type reforms. Indigenous, community-based, nonprofit institutions, if managed well, would have been in a better position to sustain intervention over 15 months—and considerably longer—and to better complement classroom instruction and job placement with more intense mentoring, discipline, job training, and individualized, flexible support.

■ A New Comprehensive System

In perspective, the research on success and failure of programs suggests that the nation needs a more comprehensive federal job training and placement system

Chapter 4

Ray Marshall and Marc Tucker call for a national employment and training board composed of government officials and business, labor, and education leaders to coordinate and streamline the half-dozen overlapping training programs that are now sponsored by several government agencies.

that focuses on high-risk youth. Such a system should build on the successful efforts of Argus, Job Corps, Comprehensive Competencies, YouthBuild (if evaluations are positive), and other innovative American variations on German vocational training programs. For example, with U.S. Department of Labor funds, the Eisenhower Foundation presently is replicating Argus in Washington, D.C., and Des Moines, Iowa, with the goal of providing a model for national use that invests more per high-risk youth than JTPA but less than Job Corps.

JTPA needs to be scrapped, in our view. We need to proceed far beyond marginal reforms of JTPA by Congress. Major structural reform of the system is required. Part of the reform should be based on *Thinking for a Living*, by Ray Marshall, Secretary of Labor in the late 1970s, and Marc Tucker, head of the National Center of Education and the Economy. They call for a national employment and training board. It would be composed of government officials and business, labor, and education leaders. The board would coordinate and streamline the half-dozen overlapping training programs that are now sponsored by several government agencies.

As envisioned by Marshall and Tucker, the national board and local board counterparts would be formed from the 600 PICs established via JTPA to implement job training and placement. Currently, the PICs are made up primarily of and controlled by business leaders. Congress viewed this type of structure as being better able to make decisions affecting localities than would a government agency. It was reasoned that the private sector was more efficient than the public sector and that business leaders had better knowledge of labor market needs than did government bureaucrats.

Yet the failure of JTPA for high-risk youth also suggests the failure of business-dominated PICs to implement the program in ways that benefit high-risk youth. Accordingly, Marshall and Tucker's employment and training boards provide a way to implement a new comprehensive system at the local level. We suggest that one-third of the members of the national and local boards consist of nonprofit community organization representatives, one-third of for-profit business representatives, and one-third of public-sector representatives—so that job training and placement can be undertaken in the nonprofit, for-profit, and public sectors.

Implementation of such a system should be coordinated with the proposed Corporation for Youth and Family Investment in order to employ high-risk youth through local nonprofit organizations, target jobs on building and restoring houses in the inner city, focus on repairing the urban infrastructure, initiate community policing to help secure economic development, and provide services for social development (for example, teachers and support staff for inner-city schools modeled on the Comer and Carnegie plans and reform of the Elementary and Secondary Education Act).

■ Returning to Pre-1980 Funding Levels

In 1980, JTPA replaced the Comprehensive Employment and Training Act (CETA), which was a public service job training and placement program implemented locally through government agencies. Accusations of fraud, nepotism, and inefficiency surrounded CETA. For example, city halls hired receptionists who sat in rooms where phones never rang. Nonetheless, during the late 1970s, CETA was successful in focusing its hiring and training on the hard-core unemployed. For the first time, unemployment among African American males decreased.

In 1979, CETA was funded at almost $11 billion per year. When it was transformed to JTPA, funding was dramatically reduced as part of federal disinvestment efforts to, for example, $3 billion in 1986 (Figure 3, page 25). In the new comprehensive system proposed here, we need to return to 1979 levels—to add about $8 billion per year so that the total is again at least $11 billion per year for job training and placement in the for-profit private sector, the nonprofit private sector, and in public service and public works jobs. Safeguards against mismanagement need to be established at the same time. We need to retain the CETA focus on hard-core unemployment, but implement jobs through more cost-effective Marshall and Tucker councils, which are nonetheless not as dominated by corporate representatives as JTPA.

More specifically, of this $11 billion per year, at least $2 billion should be for Job Corps, focusing on the truly disadvantaged. This would add 50 more Job Corps centers, as part of the Job Corp 50–50 plan. About $7 billion should be for intensive job training and remedial education focused on the truly disadvantaged. This would bring the job-training system roughly back up to 1979 CETA training levels. The remaining $2 billion of Labor Department funds should be one source of funding for job placement and creation for high-risk people in the inner city. We would combine this $2 billion with at least $13 billion more per year in job placement and creation funds from other agencies, as discussed in chapter 5, to cover the salaries of the truly disadvantaged in rehabilitating and constructing inner-city homes, repairing inner-city infrastructure, securing inner-city neighborhoods through community policing, and providing other critically needed inner-city social support services—like teachers and child-care workers. This would include public works and public-service employment. As much as possible should be channeled through community-development corporations controlled by inner-city residents.

The comprehensive reform proposed here is somewhat similar to the recommendations in the Ford Foundation's report titled *The Common Good*. It builds on the excellent job-training recommendations in the William T. Grant Foundation report titled *The Forgotten Half*, although the reform proposed here advocates for more funds than does the Grant recommendation of approximately $1 billion more per year. If reforms are enacted and if the Corporation for Youth and Family Investment is funded at approximately $500 million, high-risk youth and young adults can be integrated into the job markets.

To manage the job training–placement linkages more cost-effectively; to ensure that street-level implementation of employment and training boards resembles Job Corps, Comprehensive Competencies, and other successful programs; to help streamline interagency coordination and implementation and publicize effective youth programs; and to evaluate programs that have been replicated—a federal office responsible for overall policy and direction of high-risk youth employment efforts needs to be reestablished. Such an office might be established along the lines of the short-lived Office of Youth Programs run by the Department of Labor during the late 1970s. State and local governments need similar coordination.

When CETA was transformed to JTPA, funding was dramatically reduced as part of federal disinvestment efforts.

A federal office responsible for overall policy and direction of high-risk youth employment efforts needs to be reestablished.

Chapter 4

■ The Minimum Wage

The minimum wage, which represents society's effort to establish a floor below which market forces should not be allowed to drive the living standards of workers, has declined sharply in real value after inflation during the past two decades. Persons who work full time at the minimum wage have found it increasingly difficult to support a family even at the poverty line. Simple logic suggests that inner-city poverty and the social impoverishment and isolation that accompany it cannot be overcome by providing jobs that pay below the poverty level. Recent research has shown repeatedly that too many new jobs are low paying and unstable. This trend will continue, given the large number of service-oriented jobs expected to dominate new job creation during the next decade. Such jobs cannot hold families together, build a vibrant community economy, or offer an attractive future for the disadvantaged youth, many of whom think the "good life" can be secured only through drug dealing.

A new federal policy of investing in people and reconstructing our cities must begin to raise the floor of earnings to provide the basis for dignity, self-esteem, and self-determination. Accordingly, we endorse the proposal by the Clinton administration to increase the minimum wage.

Health Care Reform

If education and employment are key to developing successful family policy for the urban poor, especially poor children, those who receive such services need good health in order to go to school and work and to perform well. Today, however, millions of working families do not have sufficient health care. Lack of health care and affordable and safe child care are among the key reasons for families returning to AFDC after having found their way out. Low-paying jobs available to the working poor usually lack such benefits. If an urgent health need arises in a family and transitional benefits have run out, returning to AFDC may be the only reasonable answer if available income cannot cover care.

As a result of reductions and limitations in Medicaid programs in many states, many of the basic preventive health care services for inner-city families have been increasingly curtailed. Today, Medicaid reaches fewer than half of those below the official poverty line. Lack of adequate health care has placed hundreds of thousands of poor children on the street with unresolved health and mental health needs, which exacerbates the alienation, volatility, and drug involvement of many inner-city youth. The infant mortality rate in the United States is considerably higher than in countries such as Japan, Germany, Canada, France, and Britain (Figure 14). The infant mortality rate for African Americans is considerably higher than it is in countries such as Cuba and Bulgaria. And the infant mortality rate for urban African Americans in cities such as Detroit and Washington, D.C., is nearly as high as that of China (where, under the "one-child" policy, many infant girls are killed at birth in the hope that the parents later will have a boy). As sad as that record is, per-capita health care spending is *far greater* in the United States than it is in Japan, Canada, Italy, and Britain.

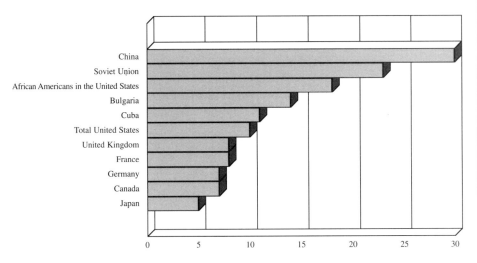

Fig. 14. Infant mortality rates, by nation.

Professionals, consumers, and advocates broadly agree that health care must be universally available and affordable and that health care systems must be restructured to be more family friendly in order to be more efficient and cost effective. Family members are, after all, the primary promoters and caregivers for the health, safety, and well-being of one another. They seek out health care services, monitor treatment, provide follow-up care, and encourage or ensure compliance with treatment regimens.

Most Americans agree that our nation's health care system needs to be reformed. Thirty-nine million people are uninsured, and a majority of those who are insured are covered for only the most basic services. Yet, health care consumes 14% of the gross domestic product. The United States is the *only* industrial country in the world that does not assure universal health care coverage to its populace.

From the perspective of poor families in the inner city, health care reform should make Medicaid available to everyone who is eligible, particularly to those who need prenatal care; provide comprehensive coverage for the working poor; create healthy quality-of-life outcomes on a par with Japan, Western Europe, and Canada; and link improved physical and mental health to improved education and job opportunities.

We should not ask how we can design a health care reform strategy that preserves the power of the insurance industry, but rather should ask how we can guarantee for our people high-quality comprehensive physical and mental health diagnosis, treatment, rehabilitation, and prevention services, with emphasis on treatment in the least restrictive setting, consistent with the patient's clinical needs and the family's ability to provide care in the most cost-effective way.

The Canadian and German national health systems work reasonably well in supplying universal coverage, allowing patients to choose their own physicians and providing high-quality prevention and treatment. Compared with the American health care system, the Canadian system, which is financed by taxes, provides quality health care for approximately one-fourth the cost per capita of the American system (Figure 15). A Canadian-style single payer system would generate considerable savings without denying people their choice of service provider.

Chapter 4

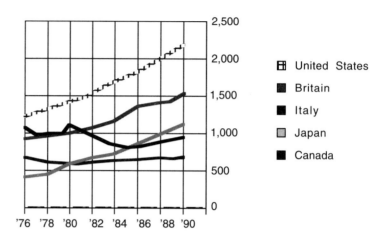

Fig. 15. Real* health care spending per capita, by nation, 1976–1990.

*Deflated by GOP deflators and adjusted by purchasing power parities

In a recent poll, 69% of Americans said they favored a Canadian-style system.

In large part because of powerful lobbies like the American Medical Association, health care reform in the United States will be incremental, and certainly not Canadian. In this volume, we have chosen not to plunge into the intricacies of the health care debate other than to lay out long-term needs that must be addressed for the truly disadvantaged. This course allows a more singular focus on the education and employment policies that we believe are the highest priority for inner-city families and for the economic development and public safety needed to generate jobs.

Chapter 5

Generating Jobs for Inner-City Families through Economic Development

The job creation that William Julius Wilson views as critical for the healthy development of families in the inner city (chapter 4) should not just be in any industry.

Rather, the employment should be generated by and for sectors whose development complements the needs of poor families. Like Robert Kennedy, we speak of employment of the truly disadvantaged in rehabilitating housing for poor families, repairing the urban infrastructure, and economically developing the inner city. Since Kennedy, the need has deepened.

We have many examples of what already works, based on years of experience. We need to expand them to scale so that there is significant change across the entire nation.

> Our cities are in dire need of rebuilding, especially at the core. Our public facilities are in similar need of repair. In the coming years, these needs will multiply almost beyond measure. If we begin now to repair the decay of the past and meet the needs of the future, we can create hundreds of thousands of new jobs directly, and indirectly, millions more.
> Robert F. Kennedy
> *To Seek a Newer World*, 1967

Community Enterprise by Private Nonprofit Community Organizations Funded by the Federal Government

From 1981 to 1992, federal disinvestment accelerated the decline of urban America:

- From 1981 to 1992, federal aid to the cities was cut by 60%, after adjusting for inflation.
- Appropriations for the subsidized housing programs operated by HUD decreased by more than 80% (inflation adjusted) between 1978 and 1991. Housing assistance for rural families provided by the Farmers' Home Administration also dropped sharply (72%).
- By 1989 (the last year for which figures are available) two-thirds of all poverty-level renter households poor enough to qualify for federal aid received no government housing assistance to help meet high rental burdens.
- Homelessness is not abating. In a survey of 28 major cities conducted annually by the U.S. Conference of Mayors, city officials reported that demands by peo-

Chapter 5

ple seeking emergency food and housing escalated substantially in 1991—in addition to similar increases in prior years. Requests for food grew by an average of 26% in the surveyed cities in 1991; shelter needs rose 13%.

■ The supply of inexpensive rental housing continues to dwindle, even as the number of poor seeking such housing swells. By 1989, there were more than 4 million more poor households seeking apartments with low rents than there were units available in a price range they could afford.

■ Rent burdens continue to place tremendous strain on lower-income households. Today, almost 60% of the nation's poor renters pay at least half of their meager earnings for shelter.

■ For hard-pressed local governments, deep cuts in housing and other assistance programs are the rule. Many states became far more active in the housing arena during the late 1980s, but today, tight budgets have forced many cutbacks. An ever-increasing share of state resources deals with the consequences of poverty and distress—not with the prevention of problems. Today, prison building is the second most rapidly growing category of state spending.

■ Building on LISC and the Enterprise Foundation

Because of this vast federal disinvestment, we now need federal reinvestment on an equal scale. As with investments in children, youth, and families, only the federal government has enough resources and the capacity for leadership to revitalize our depressed urban areas. Based on what has worked, from 1981 to 1992, we believe that the first priority for a new policy should be a federally funded program in which HUD funds national, private, nonprofit-sector intermediaries. In turn, these intermediaries should fund local, private, nonprofit community-development corporations.

The national Corporation for Youth and Family Investment proposed in chapter 4 is based in part on the Local Initiatives Support Corporation (LISC) and James Rouse's Enterprise Foundation. These two organizations help frame our vision of community economic development as discussed in this chapter. We recommend HUD's direct funding of LISC, the Enterprise Foundation, and new national economic development intermediaries like them. However, funding should be done so that private-sector nonprofit intermediaries can continue efficient and successful rehabilitation of housing without being burdened by bureaucratic red tape. The federal government needs to provide oversight, of course. Nevertheless, HUD bureaucrats should not meddle in what has been a small miracle over the last decade in revitalizing urban neighborhoods.

LISC and the Enterprise Foundation support local, grass-roots, nonprofit entrepreneurs who operate via community-development corporations to rehabilitate abandoned houses, build new houses, create commercial enterprises, and organize social services. Their objective is to succeed where federal programs have mostly failed, that is, to create inner-city jobs for high-risk youth and teen parents, provide decent and affordable housing for the poor and homeless, create vital neighborhood business districts, promote within the community, and foster strong community-based and community-owned institutions in which residents participate.

Today, almost 60% of the nation's poor renters pay at least half of their meager earnings for shelter.

Generating Jobs
For Inner-City Families

The community-development corporation concept originated with Robert Kennedy after his famous walk through New York's Bedford-Stuyvesant neighborhoods; the ensuing legislation was sponsored jointly by Senators Kennedy and Javits in 1966. These first-generation community-development corporations were funded by the Ford Foundation and the Office of Economic Opportunity. They included the Bedford-Stuyvesant Restoration Corporation in Brooklyn, New York; the East Los Angeles Community Union in Los Angeles; the Woodlawn Organization in Chicago; and the Delta Foundation/Mississippi Action for Community Development.

Initially, 15 such community-development corporations were formed in distressed urban and rural communities. Today, 2,000 community-development organizations exist, although some of these organizations are one-person enterprises. In the next decade, we need to mature and expand the existing "mom and pop" operations to establish 2,000 well-managed new community-development corporations in the most deteriorated urban and rural neighborhoods across America.

Since the early 1980s, LISC and Enterprise Foundation loans and grants had a dramatic impact on pockets of urban America. For example, they helped restore the Liberty City section of Miami after the riots in the early 1980s. They replaced graffiti and rubble in five square miles of the South Bronx in New York with new homes and parks.

As a result of such success, combined with the withdrawal of federal investment in low-income housing during the past 12 years, community-development corporations are currently the biggest developers of low-income housing in the United States.

Community-development corporations have survived as a result of resourceful and dynamic leadership. Today, however, we need national leadership from the White House and from HUD, Health and Human Services, Labor, and Commerce to fund and expand these model programs.

To develop additional funding as well as create a system of checks and balances to minimize bureaucratic red tape, HUD monies should be matched by funding from private-sector foundations and corporations. For example, LISC was created by the Ford Foundation and six corporations in 1979. In 1991, the community-development corporation movement was accelerated when LISC and the Enterprise Foundation received a commitment for more than $62 million from the Prudential Insurance Company, the Rockefeller Foundation, the Lilly Endowment and five other major private-sector foundations to pump loans into 20 cities for housing primarily and for day care and other community facilities. Local corporations, governments, and foundations have supplied matching funds, and the entire plan exceeds $500 million over a five-year span.

In 1994, the secretary of HUD took the lead, creating an $88 million National Community Development Initiative with $20 million from HUD, $15 million from the Rockefeller Foundation, $15 million from the Prudential Insurance Company, $12 million from J. P. Morgan, and smaller amounts from other foundations. The initiative allows community-development organizations to obtain an additional $750 million from other public and private programs, which often require a local contribution. These monies are being lent to 23 cities, and the loans are overseen by the Enterprise Foundation and LISC.

In the next decade, we need to establish 2,000 well-managed new community-development corporations in the most deteriorated urban and rural neighborhoods across America.

To develop additional funding as well as create a system of checks and balances to minimize bureaucratic red tape, HUD monies should be matched by funding from private-sector foundations and corporations.

Chapter 5

As part of the expansion of national nonprofit intermediaries and local community-development corporations, management training needs to be expanded to local organizations. Today, various national and local organizations train nonprofit organizations in the community economic-development field. The preeminent organization is the Development Training Institute in Baltimore. Principal staff of community-development corporations participate in three training sessions in a year's time. Between training sessions, they work in their local communities. Some of this time is spent doing their usual work with their local community-development corporation; other time is spent on assignments for the Development Training Institute. The capacity of the Institute needs to be expanded significantly to train more community-development corporations. In addition, other organizations like the Institute need to be created.

■ The Kind of Local Community Development Corporation That Needs to Be Expanded

The New Community Corporation in Newark, New Jersey, illustrates what is needed when we advocate for a process through which HUD funds LISC and Enterprise Foundation-type intermediaries provide grants and loans to existing and new community development organizations as part of a comprehensive national family—and home—policy.

Shortly after the Newark riot in 1967, a Roman Catholic parish priest and a few neighborhood volunteers in the Central Ward of Newark founded a nonprofit agency called the New Community Corporation (NCC). Its mission was to help residents "improve the quality of their lives to reflect individual dignity and personal achievement." Twenty-five years later, NCC is an $80-million-per-year enterprise, housing more than 6,000 people in ten well-maintained properties, caring for 600 children in six day-care centers, providing 2,800 meals daily, and employing 1,200 people from the neighborhood. The NCC has become New Jersey's largest nonprofit housing operation and one of the largest in the country. Monsignor William Linder, the founder of NCC, was honored by President Clinton during inauguration week in 1993. Monsignor Linder describes NCC as a "network of care," a safe haven for those residents who have never shared in the downtown area's economic boom. Many NCC staffers began there as high school dropouts but now have master's degrees. In honor of his work, Monsignor Linder received a grant from the John D. and Catherine T. MacArthur Foundation.

The secret to NCC's funding operations was based on savvy and independence. A $7 million loan from the Prudential Foundation helped NCC to build a Pathmark supermarket—one of only two full-sized supermarkets in all of Newark. The loan also established a credit union with $1.6 million in assets, a donut shop, a restaurant, medical offices, a spa, and St. Joseph's Plaza—a $2.5 million project to renovate the shell of a 120-year-old Gothic-style church, which houses the corporation's headquarters. Most of the funds were obtained through long-term loans from government organizations such as New Jersey's Housing and Mortgage Finance Agency; HUD funds—for example, Community Development Block Grants—also were used. The NCC leveraged state and federal monies against private-sector monies until aid to cities was cut during the 1981–1992 period.

As part of the expansion of national nonprofit intermediaries and local community-development corporations, management training needs to be expanded to local organizations.

The problem with public funds, NCC officials say, is that city governments try to bargain favors for votes, and state and federal governments attempt to dictate conditions of aid. Yet private companies are no better because they invest in operations that take money out of communities, instead of reinvesting it in communities. As part of the package it negotiated with the Pathmark supermarket chain, NCC reaps two-thirds of the profits from the store. Those profits go back into the community to support other projects.

Although no evaluations of NCC have been completed, a multimethod assessment of its effects on NCC residents is currently being conducted by the New School for Social Research's Community Development Research Center. As part of the assessment, an ethnographer is living at NCC, and community surveys of NCC and a comparison community are assessing residents' satisfaction, personal efficacy, and community engagement.

■ Housing as a Human Right, Not a Commodity

How does an innovative, nonprofit delivery system that enables community organizations to rehabilitate and build housing for the poor as part of a national family policy relate to the existing housing-development system? In the current system, real-estate developers, builders, mortgage lenders, investors, and landlords seek to draw a profit from housing commodities. The private housing sector adds costs to housing, from land development through every stage of construction or rehabilitation to the final sale. The Institute for Policy Analysis in Washington, D.C., has recommended a national housing program that treats housing as a human and family right as opposed to a commodity from which large profits can be made. The Institute's proposed delivery system transfers the development, construction, rehabilitation, and management of housing from the for-profit to the nonprofit sector.

Details of this nonprofit-sector housing development and rehabilitation plan, which we endorse, have been introduced in Congress. The plan provides a legislative point of departure from current federal policy, which, in effect, "bribes" for-profit developers to build low-income homes.

It will take more than a decade to develop enough new nonprofit organizations to address the housing needs of the poor. Lobbyists for the for-profit developers will exert tremendous pressure on developers to keep HUD money flowing to them. So we do not recommend dramatic increases in housing rehabilitation and building by nonprofit community development corporations in the immediate future. Instead, we recommend a program through which HUD can expand the nonprofit sector's capacity to become involved in housing over the next decade. As success is demonstrated, the nonprofit constituency will be further developed. Ideally, more leaders like Monsignor Linder and more organizations like the NCC will gain significantly more clout.

If HUD cannot assume this role, then an alternative institutional mechanism will need to nurture nonprofit housing development.

For such a program to work, it is important to negotiate U.S. mayors' acceptance of a delivery system in which HUD, or an alternative institution, funds national nonprofit intermediaries to make loans and grants to local community-development corporations. Such support can be gained by continuing to channel some

Chapter 5

HUD funds to mayors via housing grants and community-development block grants. However, mayors should be required to use most of this funding for loans and grants to nonprofit community-development corporations in low-income neighborhoods. Federal funds should not be transferred to mayors for downtown-improvement projects such as shopping malls and hotels, as was done with the Urban Development Action Grant program, which thrived in the late 1970s. These grants enriched for-profit developers, did little for impoverished neighborhoods, supplied few high-quality jobs for high-risk youth, and for the most part failed to support inner-city nonprofit organizations.

■ Nonprofit and For-Profit Linkages: More Homes for Families

At the national level, the nonprofit Enterprise Foundation has a for-profit subsidiary that feeds revenues into the Foundation's nonprofit component. Similarly, community-based organizations such as Delancey Street and NCC are nonprofit organizations that have created for-profit subsidiary businesses. We recommend that HUD require all federally financed local nonprofit housing and community-development corporations to create for-profit subsidiaries that feed revenues into the parent organization. Such requirements would help achieve a balance between tapping entrepreneurial potential and ensuring that inner-city development is not used simply to benefit the affluent. The goal should be to create job opportunities for high-risk youth. Up to now, HUD has done little to recognize formally the vast potential of physical development, including housing and commercial revitalization, as a way of investing in high-risk youth.

HUD needs to create an atmosphere that allows interchange between nonprofit and for-profit activities. For example, although housing rehabilitation should be initiated through nonprofit community-development corporations, HUD should build on successes such as the TELESIS Corporation—a for-profit economic-development organization that has demonstrated cost-effectiveness as well as social-development wisdom.

TELESIS has renovated Paradise at Parkside, a northeast Washington, D.C., apartment complex with 600 apartments. One of the most attractive features of the $20 million Paradise at Parkside rehabilitation effort is the creative way in which TELESIS has brought financing partners together. One funding source, the AFL–CIO Housing Investment Trust, invested $10 million in return for a guarantee that all construction workers would be union members. Other financing includes $6 million from Consumers United, $3 million from the Washington, D.C., Department of Housing and Community Development, $4.5 million from HUD, and $500,000 from HHS. The Federal and National Mortgage Association (FNMA) is providing financial services.

Renovation costs average approximately $30,500 per apartment—an amount in sharp contrast with the $130,000 per-unit cost to the federal government and the District of Columbia government to renovate the nearby Kenilworth-Parkside public housing complex, which was held up by HUD from 1988 to 1992 as perhaps the best federal example of tenant management and ownership. A group called the Paradise Cooperative hopes eventually to convert the complex to cooperative ownership by residents.

> **HUD needs to create an atmosphere that allows interchange between nonprofit and for-profit activities.**

The founder of TELESIS, Marilyn Melkonian, a Deputy Assistant Secretary at HUD in the late 1970s, is a savvy, nontraditional developer who works with politicians with understated sophistication. TELESIS has been able to integrate social development with physical development to create solutions to multiple problems experienced by the inner-city poor. Employment training and classes on life skills, such as budgeting and home ownership, are conducted by the greater Washington Mutual Housing Association. A day-care center and after-school tutoring for children are available to residents. Some Paradise residents work at construction and property-management jobs at the development. A youth organization founded by Paradise teenagers provides tutoring for kids. Of the 60 members in the youth-tutoring group, 22 are graduating high school students headed to college. A Japanese-style police mini-station has been opened. Three full-time D.C. metropolitan police officers have been assigned to the mini-station, which is located in an apartment unit near the community center. This mini-station is modeled after the Centro program in San Juan, which the Eisenhower Foundation scientifically evaluated as successful and which reduced crime by 30% in its first year (chapter 4). Following San Juan, the Paradise koban includes young-adult "advocates" who act as buffers between police and youth on the verge of trouble.

■ Capitalization of Community-Development Banks

Sound community-based family policy needs sound community-based banking to help finance economic development to generate jobs.

A network of community-development banks needs to be capitalized through national private-sector intermediaries. The banks should be owned by inner-city community partners and should reinforce the creation of local for-profit–nonprofit linkages.

The South Shore Bank in Chicago is an excellent example of this kind of initiative. During the past 20 years, South Shore has proven that a determined lender can reverse the process of urban decay and simultaneously make a profit. The process began with the purchase of a local bank. The founders of South Shore created a for-profit real-estate-development company and a nonprofit community-development corporation to work closely with the bank. The bank provided an opportunity for people to support social goals without risk by investing in federally insured deposits. The real-estate company offered the possibility of profits, with some risks. The community-development corporation sought government and private grants.

The South Shore neighborhood of Chicago consists of 250 square blocks in which approximately 78,000 people live not far from Lake Michigan. South Shore has provided financing for approximately one-third of the area's housing stock. A key ingredient in South Shore's success has been its ability to attract deposits from outside the bank's neighborhood and then to invest in the neighborhood. This reverses the pattern typical of many banks—to collect deposits in poor communities and then to invest outside those neighborhoods. As a result of its initial success, South Shore has expanded to other locations. For example, in Southern Arkansas, the Winthrop Rockefeller Foundation asked South Shore to organize a community-development banking company, which led to the creation of the Southern Development Bank Corporation. Instead of concentrating on real estate, the main business in the residential neighborhood that South Shore serves, the Southern Development Bank

Chapter 5

Corporation concentrates on creating businesses and jobs to replace the factory jobs lost around Arkadelphia and Pinebluff, Arkansas, in the 1980s.

Both the South Shore Bank and its Arkansas replication have found it difficult to finance small for-profit businesses. Many such businesses fail in low- and middle-income locations. Problems include lack of markets, management expertise, and community infrastructure. As a result of the many failures with small business, South Shore has cut back on business lending that is vulnerable to loss. To compensate, it has increased loans guaranteed by the Small Business Administration. In 1991, South Shore made $8 million of small business loans, more loans than any bank in Chicago. At Southern Development Bank Corporation in Arkansas, the company has continued with its business-lending program. Since the 1980s, it has issued almost $11 million of loans to borrowers who would not otherwise have obtained credit.

> **In 1991, South Shore made $8 million of small business loans, more loans than any bank in Chicago.**

The founders of South Shore are cautious about replicating the program in devastated neighborhoods such as south central Los Angeles. We are somewhat more optimistic, believing that community-based banks could be located initially on the margins of devastated inner-city communities. Based in neighborhoods where some infrastructure remains, community banks could be gradually moved into neighborhoods with poorer infrastructure.

Local community-development banks need to assist entrepreneurs and expand infrastructure by establishing small-business development centers to help provide auditing services, automated inventory-control business planning, and accounting-control systems. Community development banks should encourage loans to established grocery stores, bank branches, clothing stores, pharmacies, and other retail services. Such services not only are convenient for shoppers, but reinforce a sense of community. These businesses provide jobs and opportunity for entrepreneurship for inner-city residents.

> **Community-based banks could be located initially on the margins of devastated inner-city communities, then gradually moved into neighborhoods with poorer infrastructure.**

As a source of capital for community-development banks, consideration should be given to proposals to tap public pension funds. Currently, public pension funds maintain approximately $600 billion in assets. Public pension funds are invested in both stocks and bonds. One plan is to use a small portion of these funds—10%—to reinvest in the inner city. Federally guaranteed securities could serve to secure the funds, similar to Fannie Mae or Ginnie Mae bonds. Pension funds could buy and sell these federal securities, and pension funds would provide both security and a market return on investments. Federal guarantees would insure that pensioners are not at risk. As part of a community-development banking system, pension-fund investment managers could develop expertise with these new federally guaranteed securities. The Secretary of HUD has begun pension-fund financing in cooperation with the AFL–CIO Housing Investment Trust, and we applaud this breakthrough.

The capitalization of community-development banks should be linked to tougher enforcement by HUD of the Community Reinvestment Act of 1977, which requires banks to invest in their communities. To date, despite lack of enforcement by federal regulators, the Community Reinvestment Act has been successfully used by local governments and community organizations to attract bank financing for housing development and homeowner mortgages. It also has been used to pressure banks to open branches in inner cities. In addition, it should be recognized that commercial loans can be as important to neighborhood strength as are home mortgages. That is why the Community Reinvestment Act should be strengthened—to allow for evaluation of the lending performance of banks, based on commercial loans issued. Insurance companies should be added to Community Reinvestment Act jurisdiction as well because insurance coverage plays an important role in the success or failure of neighborhood business districts.

At the same time, all efforts by Congress to weaken the Community Reinvestment Act, in the name of supply-side, trickle-down economics, should be strongly resisted.

Establishing a traditional federal agency to run these programs might impose too much bureaucratic red tape on a community-development banking system. However, a new institution may be needed—a National Community Development Bank. A partial model for such an institution is the National Cooperative Bank (though without the power struggles that revolved around its creation). Federal legislation should allow for a one-time appropriation of funds, with a time limit for the entity to become self-sustaining and independent of the federal system. Included in a legislative package should be authority for the National Community Development Bank to mandate cooperation from agencies like HUD, the Small Business Administration, and the Economic Development Administration.

New community-banking initiatives should move cautiously by funding a few local development banks at first. Only a small pool of trained and experienced development bankers are available to train new staff. Development banking requires patience. It will not yield immediate and dramatic results. The risk of mistakes is increased if the number of banks outstrips the capacity to maintain quality control. Executives from the South Shore Bank, LISC, TELESIS, and the Enterprise Foundation should be among those who help develop and guide the initiative.

■ Housing Desegregation Combined with Inner-City Housing Rehabilitation

In chapter 3, we argued for increasing investments in inner-city schools at the same time that opportunities are expanded in the suburbs for inner-city youth.

The consistent and parallel policy is to rehabilitate inner-city housing by and for poor families at the same time that opportunities are expanded for those families to live in the suburbs.

In both cases, we believe that policy should provide sufficient opportunity to let families decide for themselves. That is democracy and free-market choice.

For housing, the proven success is the Chicago Gautreaux program, which uses housing vouchers to promote suburban integration. Poor inner-city families receive housing allowances along with one-time assistance in locating housing in integrated or predominantly white neighborhoods. This program has been a success for 15 years and has not aroused opposition from suburban neighborhoods. Gautreaux families have experienced significant long-term gains in education, employment, and economic well-being.

We encourage replication of this model initiative by HUD to all eligible households nationally. The Clinton administration plan to expand Gatreaux by $234 million over five years is a good first step in eventual replication at the scale that is needed.

Full implementation of Gatreaux should be part of a comprehensive policy that attacks spatial segmentation. Gatreaux should be accompanied by carefully imple-

> **Insurance companies should be added to Community Reinvestment Act jurisdiction because insurance coverage plays an important role in the success or failure of neighborhood business districts.**

Chapter 5

mented plans to keep the middle class in or bring it back to urban neighborhoods, *as long as lower income families are not pushed out and are given employment and educational opportunity*. Improved transportation should allow people from city centers easier access to the suburbs and vice versa.

For spatial segmentation caused by school segregation, we need to open suburban schools to inner-city residents, following the St. Louis plan, at the same time that the Elementary and Secondary Education Act reforms, the Carnegie National Urban Schools Program, and the Comer School Development Plan are implemented to restore inner-city schools (see chapter 3).

In terms of segmentation caused by income disparity, the need is to reform job training and placement for inner-city residents and to assure that jobs are permanent, primary legal labor-market employment (see chapter 4), and to make the federal income tax more progressive (see chapter 7).

For spacial segmentation caused by loss of tax bases from the central city to the suburbs, the federal government needs to condition grants to states and localities on local agreements to share across the entire metropolitan area (including the suburbs) the value of commercial property, as well as other elements of the area-wide tax base, for property tax purposes. This follows the successful model, for example, of Minneapolis/St. Paul. We also need to carefully evaluate new initiatives in states like Michigan, where property taxes for school financing are giving way to taxes more equitable to poor families.

■ Public Housing

Our emphasis on delivering services through nonprofit community-based entities also should be applied to public housing, which is administered by HUD. HUD makes annual subsidies to public housing authorities.

Public housing represents less than 2% of the nation's housing supply. But it looms large in the national debate about housing policy because public housing facilities concentrate welfare dependency, high unemployment, teenage pregnancy, single parenthood, serious crime, drugs, and other problems. This was illustrated by the Pruitt-Igo project in St. Louis, which eventually was dynamited by the city because it was unlivable. Today, one of the best examples of this concentration is in Robert Taylor Homes in Chicago, where, as we saw in chapter 3, Project Beethoven has had limited but still commendable success with teen mothers, their infants, and children.

We believe that public housing should not be scrapped. There are many horror stories. However, when public housing is well managed, as is the case with the New York City Housing Authority, for example, it should remain as one of several options for housing the poor. Today, there are 1.3 million public housing apartments and about 800,000 families on waiting lists at the nation's public housing authorities.

■ Resident Management

Resident management of public housing properties is the key to making public housing work. In public housing where tenants are well organized and exercise real power, conditions improve. Tenant-managed developments save money in the long run because tenants have a greater stake in their homes and therefore are less tolerant of destructive and costly behavior.

> **Public housing facilities concentrate welfare dependency, high unemployment, teenage pregnancy, single parenthood, serious crime, drugs, and other problems.**

During the 1980s tenant management and "empowerment" were much talked about. Little action was taken, however. Although few exemplary programs were touted, they had little national impact. As mentioned earlier, Kenilworth-Parkside in Washington, D.C., cost HUD and the District government $130,000 per unit to repair, whereas it cost TELESIS, a private-sector organization, only $30,500 per unit to repair Paradise at Parkside.

To expand tenant management, adequate funds need to be allocated by HUD to public housing authorities *and* to tenants so that they can be trained to manage their own housing projects. Such training might serve as a first step toward tenant-owned developments. The goal should be to create resident-run community development and management corporations. Tenant managers and owners should receive adequate subsidies for repair and maintenance. Developments should be sold as limited-equity cooperatives in order to guarantee that public housing will continue to be available to long-term residents after the initial owners have left.

When the Clinton administration took over, approximately $7 billion was stuck in the HUD pipeline from the previous administration, $3 billion of which was targeted for public housing. Thus funds to expand these initiatives are available. We must make sure that these funds are well managed by HUD and local public housing authorities.

To its credit, the Clinton administration is expanding tenant initiatives. But tenant management, especially home ownership by families, will be successful only if it is combined with resident access to preschool, child-care, education, job training, and job placement. With such multiple-purpose invesments, tenants are more likely to achieve economic independence, based on initiatives that already have succeeded.

■ Funding HUD at Pre-1980 Levels

Legislation and regulations can be implemented, at present spending levels, to reorganize the HUD Offices of Housing, Public Housing, and Community Planning and Development in order to create a nonprofit housing rehabilitation and construction-delivery system modeled after LISC and the Enterprise Foundation, for-profit delivery systems modeled after TELESIS, a community-development banking system modeled after the South Shore Bank, and expanded public housing tenant management and home ownership.

Such initiatives would help overcome longstanding problems. But we must also face the reality that housing is expensive and that more low-income housing is needed—as is demonstrated by the homelessness problem in the United States.

Appropriations for HUD-subsidized housing fell by more than 80% (inflation adjusted) between 1978 and 1991. Well in excess of $10 billion is needed to approximate pre-1980 levels and so address the housing deficits that exist. Funding for housing and community development must increase annually over coming years. Inner-city residents should be employed in such development, the role of nonprofit community development organizations expanded, the capacity of existing successful models expanded, and management training of nonprofit executives enhanced.

Attempts by Congress to further decrease funding must be resisted, as must attempts to replace the "bubble up" economic development of community nonprofit organizations with more failed trickle-down, supply-side quick fixes.

> **To expand tenant management, adequate funds need to be allocated by HUD to public housing authorities and to tenants so that they can be trained to manage their own housing projects.**

Chapter 5

Our recommendations on HUD are consistent with proposals for devolution in which HUD would operate through block grants for which private nonprofit community organizations could compete with public-sector entities, like public housing authorities. Under such a new vision for HUD, the Department would set standards, measure performance, evaluate for success, and weed out nonperforming agencies. However, such decentralization should not be used, in our view, to hide a reduction in the level of federal support—which, as we have said, should be significantly increased.

The Investment Gap, Productivity, and High-Risk Families

Reducing the investment gap that exists between the United States and its major competitors—Germany and Japan—is a primary goal of the Clinton administration. Inner-city residents should not be excluded from national policy designed to reduce the investment gap and to increase productivity.

Many economists believe that the success and failure of America's economic policies in the coming years will be measured best by productivity. To increase our productivity, experts believe, we must invest in education and job training as well as in the public infrastructure. Little disagreement exists across the political spectrum that well-targeted investment in infrastructure—especially in maintenance of existing public facilities—is well worth the up-front costs.

The United States is the only major industrial society that is not currently reviewing and ex-panding its infrastructure. Figures 16 and 17 show the dramatic reduction in American infrastructure development over the 1980s and how this reduction relates to U.S. productivity compared with countries such as Japan, Germany, and France. Elliott Currie points out that, while we allow our public capital to wither away, other countries have moved ahead of America. The Japanese,

Inner-city residents should not be excluded from national policy designed to reduce the investment gap and to increase productivity.

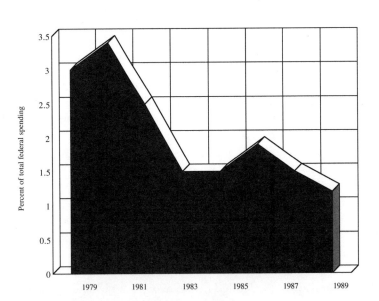

Figure 16. Public infrastructure investment in the United States between 1979–1989.

for example, have initiated a $60 billion public-works project. The French have committed $100 billion to the development of high-speed rail systems. The Germans are spending even more to rebuild and modernize the industrial base of the former East Germany.

According to the U.S. House of Representatives Public Works and Transportation Committee, 40% of the nation's bridges are structurally deficient. More than 28 million Americans are served by inadequate sewage-treatment plants. By the year 2005, traffic delays resulting from inadequate roads may cost the nation $50 billion annually in wasted fuel and lost wages. The Federal Aviation Administration estimates that 58 airports—including those in Newark and Los Angeles—will be overly congested by the year 2000, causing delays for 74% of the nation's passengers.

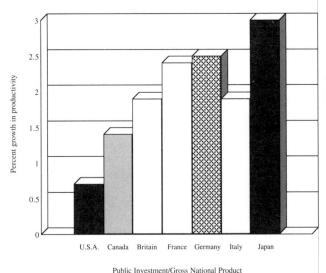

Figure 17. Public infrastructure spending and growth in productivity, by nation.

The reason for this erosion during the recent quarter century is a steady decline in federal spending on public infrastructure. For example, in 1980, more than 4% of all federal outlays were for infrastructure. By 1990, that share had fallen to 2.5%. Countries such as Germany, France, and Japan, which spend a higher percentage of their gross domestic product on infrastructure, show greater growth in productivity than does the United States.

■ Investing in Public Infrastructure

Each $1 billion spent on infrastructure translates into 40,000 to 50,000 new public- and private-sector jobs. In the 1992 report, *Ready to Go*, the U.S. Conference of Mayors identified more than 7,000 public works projects that are on hold because cities lack the funds to implement them. These projects would create more than 400,000 construction jobs and more than one million jobs within a year. The Department of Transportation estimates that between $30 billion and $40 billion will be needed to refurbish deteriorating bridges.

New York City investment banker Felix Rohatyn has proposed a $500 billion investment in infrastructure over the next decade. The Rohatyn plan, which we believe deserves careful review, would finance this outlay through a new federal trust that sold bonds to pension funds and individuals. The debt would be serviced by increasing federal gasoline tax by 50 cents a gallon, which would be phased in over a 10-year period.

Each $1 billion spent on infrastructure translates into 40,000 to 50,000 new public- and private-sector jobs.

Chapter 5

> Linking a national program to build and maintain the infrastructure with a national youth-employment policy, in particular, makes sense from every point of view.

> Whenever possible, public works and public service employment should be channeled through community-development corporations.

It is difficult to argue against the need for infrastructure development. Some critics, however, will caution about public sector investment misspending, and we agree. Improved oversight will be needed from expanded Inspector General offices in implementing agencies. At the same time, the deregulated savings and loan industry is a reminder of how badly *private* industry has failed in the last decade.

We endorse public sector jobs for both public works and public service, tied to reform of the failed JTPA system. Whatever the level of expenditure on public works—and, we hope, on public service—the goal should be to employ a substantial number of high-risk youth, parents, persons on a two-years-and-out child poverty welfare reform plan, and family members in low-income communities. In addition to such employment, and in addition to the more targeted employment in housing rehabilitation and construction discussed earlier in this chapter, we believe that the federal government should ensure that all eligible, high-risk youth and present welfare recipients are placed in jobs. As Elliott Currie concludes:

> Linking a national program to build and maintain the infrastructure with a national youth-employment policy, in particular, makes sense from every point of view. With both in place, we could employ tens of thousands of young people now condemned to the margins of the economy and train them in work that helps rebuild their communities and enhances the indispensable physical foundation of the country. The work would be challenging, often physically demanding, and visibly useful; it could help transform bleak and depressed communities into places residents could be proud of—all at considerable benefit to the larger economy.

Whenever possible, public works and public service employment should be channeled through private-sector, nonprofit community-development corporations, in our experience. We must be aware that however great the pent-up need for infrastructure repair, construction jobs generated as part of an economic stimulus plan will only last for the length of the project, especially for those at the bottom of the income ladder. With community-development corporations, which care about people in their neighborhoods, as the delivery agents, the odds at least increase that workers can be transitioned to other employment after specific initial projects are completed. This is the kind of thing Father Linder has done with NCC. Channeling public works and public service employment through private-sector community-based nonprofits also enhances the capacity of the grass-roots institution closest to the people.

The Davis-Bacon Act limits community-development corporations from employing high-risk young people at low initial wages to repair and construct housing and to work on infrastructure repair contracts because the act requires that workers be paid union wages. But organizations such as YouthBuild and Delancey Street have been able to negotiate agreements with unions to hire high-risk youth to work on relatively small projects. To expand the role of high-risk young people in the repair and construction of housing, community-development organizations must be allowed to build on the YouthBuild and Delancey Street experience. The Department of Labor needs to negotiate union waivers that allow community-development corporations to place at-risk youth and young-adult workers in entry-level construction jobs. Although such negotiations will not be easy to accomplish, unions need to recognize the importance of providing opportunities to young people in the inner city.

■ Military Conversion and High-Tech Investment

Infrastructure development is related to the post-Cold War military conversion process. To make conversion work better, an entity outside the Pentagon bureaucracy needs to be established to coordinate planning.

Conversion and retraining should consider the need for a high-tech infrastructure; national fiber optics; computer networks; as well as research, development, and implementation of smart roads, high-speed and magnetic-levitation trains, biotechnology, ceramics, advanced composites, sensors, photonics, electronic digital imaging, artificial intelligence, robotics, and computer-aided manufacturing.

New technologies to reduce environmental deterioration and pollution, for example, through research on natural gas and renewable sources of energy, should be explored.

If America's manufacturing industries are rebuilt using environmentally and ecologically safe production technologies, the economic possibilities for the next century are great. New industries to supply these technologies would be developed and established industries that adopted these technologies would have a competitive advantage in environmentally sensitive world markets. Between 10% and 20% of the $76 billion Pentagon research budget should be earmarked for civil-technology development.

It is critical that high-risk inner-city youth, teen parents, and persons moving off the AFDC *be included in training and employment opportunities generated by military conversion and technological research.* Partial models to make this happen already exist. If high-risk young people are channeled into university education through the "I Have A Dream" and related programs, their chances of employment in high-tech industries are greatly improved. But even for persons with a high school equivalency degree, national family policy and industrial policy must involve them in high-tech industries. For example, in Lille, France, a computer-maintenance training program, CIRFTEN, operates for high-risk and foreign-born youth without previous work experience. The program was formed in partnership with a corporation that deals with computer maintenance and computer networking services.

New Jobs and Overall Funding

We recommend an increase in appropriations of $15 billion per year for a minimum of 10 years to repair and construct new housing for the poor via for-profit organizations such as TELESIS and intermediaries such as LISC and the Enterprise Foundation that fund local private-sector community-development corporations. These appropriations should cover capitalization of a National Community Development Bank, expansion of the Gatreaux program, expansion of public housing tenant management, and training and placement of inner-city young people in housing repair and construction, urban infrastructure repair, and public service

It is critical that high-risk inner-city youth, teen parents, and persons moving off the welfare roles be included in training and employment opportunities generated by military conversion and technological research.

Chapter 5

> **We recommend an increase in appropriations of $15 billion per year for a minimum of 10 years to repair and construct new housing for the poor via for-profit organizations.**

> **New housing is a tangible and observable commodity that may help to secure ongoing political support and therefore additional funding for employment over the long term.**

jobs—for example, teaching in inner-city schools and meeting, at adequate salaries, the alarming need for quality child care for working parents.

Such funding would generate approximately 150,000 public-service jobs and 234,000 housing-repair, housing-construction, and public-works jobs per year. The cost of one entry-level public-service job per year is estimated at $22,000 for salary, benefits, supervision, and administration. Accordingly, 150,000 jobs would cost $3.3 billion. The estimated cost of job creation in housing, community development, and transportation projects as reported by the U.S. Conference of Mayors survey of 470 cities and approximately 4,400 urban transportation and community development projects is $50,000 per year for one entry-level job. This cost covers salary, benefits, supervision, administration, materials, supplies, and tools. The $234,000 cost for such jobs equals $11.7 billion. Thus, we recommend that a total of $15 billion be targeted toward job creation in housing and public works.

Because the need for housing is desperate, we believe that housing-repair and housing-construction jobs should initially take precedence over public-works jobs. New housing is a tangible and observable commodity that may help to secure ongoing political support and therefore additional funding for employment over the long term. It also may be easier for inner-city youth and young adults to secure private-sector jobs with construction skills than with skills in human services (even though such skills are in great demand in inner cities).

To the extent possible, these jobs should be channeled through national private-sector nonprofit intermediaries such as LISC and the Enterprise Foundation as well as similar newly created national entities. As a conservative estimate, we project that these intermediaries can leverage $1 in private funds for each $1 in public funds channeled through them. (Their historical leveraging ratios have been much higher.) If this leveraging ratio holds, then the 384,000 public service and public works jobs we propose would be doubled to 768,000. The 384,000 additional jobs generated by private funds would be based in the private sector.

The channeling of funds to private-sector community-development corporations would, over time, expand the capacities of existing community-development corporations and help finance new ones. Increased capacities of community-development corporations would, in turn, help qualify them for loans from our proposed National Community Development Bank to start, for example, subsidiary for-profit operations. Because community-development corporations are controlled by local inner-city residents, private ownership for such operations would be increased with the infusion of publicly originated and privately matched funds. Initially, community-development corporations will not have the capacity to implement all of the public-works jobs recommended here. Therefore, municipal public-works agencies will need to administer some of the job creation. It is critical, however, that such agencies target disadvantaged inner-city residents.

The National Community Development Bank, too, should be able to leverage at least $1 in private funds for each $1 of public funds. Again, this figure represents a conservative estimate. These funds would be loaned not only to private nonprofit community-development corporations, but also to for-profit businesses, especially small businesses in the inner city, to generate private-sector jobs. With National Community Development Bank capitalization of $1 billion by the federal government matched by at least $1 billion more in private funds, a substantial number of private-sector jobs could be created.

The mission of a national Corporation for Youth and Family Investment recommended in chapter 4 would be to replicate comprehensive youth programs—some of which would in turn generate a mix of private for-profit and private nonprofit jobs in the inner city. Community-development block grants, tenant management, and employment initiatives recommended in this chapter would add more jobs. (In addition, the $1 billion in capitalization for a National Community Development Bank is a one-time first-year cost. For each succeeding year of our 10-year plan, we recommend that the $1 billion be used to stimulate more housing, public-works, and public-service jobs.)

The new job-training system we propose in chapter 4 would provide intensive remedial education and job training drawing on the successes of Argus, YouthBuild USA, and Job Corps. Compared with the ineffective and inefficient JTPA system, high-risk youth trained in the new system we propose will have a much better chance to secure a job in the private for-profit sector.

Similarly, the development of high school vocational and apprenticeship training models proposed in chapter 3 would create more jobs for the disadvantaged inner-city residents in the private for-profit sector, thus displacing the need for public-sector job placement.

We also recommend that an appropriate number of high-risk youth and young adults be employed in jobs generated by federal high-tech investment. Although such efforts presently are designed primarily to assist the middle class as part of economic and military-conversion policies, federal guidelines should require that some portion of new private-sector high-tech jobs resulting from federal government stimulus be targeted to inner-city youth and other urban disadvantaged populations.

We have been discussing new spending. But the same logic applies to existing spending. For example, existing HUD funds for rehabilitating and constructing housing for the poor should be channeled through national, private-sector nonprofit intermediaries to be leveraged against private-sector for-profit funds.

In sum, we conservatively estimate that $15 billion per year for 340,000 public-service and public-works jobs can be leveraged over time to create 750,000 to 800,000 jobs per year for disadvantaged inner-city residents.

■ Total Jobs Needed

The U.S. Department of Labor estimates that approximately 1,750,000 African Americans, Latinos, and other minorities eligible for the labor force are currently unemployed in the central cities of major metropolitan areas. This estimate, which includes persons of all ages, is difficult to make in that many people have given up trying to obtain work. Better estimates are needed. Since studies by the Kerner Riot Commission in the late 1960s, little work on obtaining good estimates has been done. While we therefore take the estimate of 1,750,000 with a grain of salt, if it is at all reasonable, it means that our plan could immediately finance jobs for perhaps up to half of the hard core inner-city unemployed.

So the plan proposed here falls short of full employment. But this proposal nevertheless represents a dramatic shift from the policies of the 1980s. The level of

The mission of a national Corporation for Youth and Family Investment would be to replicate comprehensive youth programs—some of which would in turn generate a mix of private for-profit and nonprofit jobs in the inner city.

employment for the inner-city poor that we hope to generate initially—750,000 to 800,000 jobs—is at or above CETA peak levels in the late 1970s. Compared with CETA, the policy initiatives proposed here will incorporate better training, more safeguards against fraud and abuse, and a better mix of private nonprofit, for-profit, and public employment.

■ Empowerment Zones

The Clinton administration's empowerment zone program is creating linkages among economic development, housing rehabilitation by community-development organizations, transportation, job training and placement, youth development, and community-based policing. The overall program is funded at $3.5 billion. Six urban empowerment zones—Atlanta, Baltimore, Chicago, Detroit, New York, and Philadelphia–Camden, New Jersey—are funded at $100 million each, in addition to tax breaks to business to settle in the zones. The funds are being distributed over 10 years. Two "supplemental" urban empowerment zones—Los Angeles and Cleveland—will receive $125 million and $90 million, respectively. The enterprise zones proposed in the 1981–1992 period only had trickle-down supply-side tax breaks. The tax-break-only enterprise zones of the 1980s failed, based on evaluations by the U.S. General Accounting Office, the Urban Institute, and others (see chapter 1). The Clinton empowerment zones acknowledge the failures of the zones of the 1980s, retain the business tax breaks, and add multiple solutions to multiple problem investments, which the earlier evaluations suggested were critical for success in poor neighborhoods with high-risk populations.

The new empowerment zones also will need to be evaluated, of course. Will community policing be used to secure the development process? If so, will it include training to hire officers who live in the inner-city neighborhoods that they patrol and will it provide funding for enough officers to make a difference in the zone? Will private-sector community-based nonprofits play a significant role in implementing empowerment zones? Do the zones represent another limited "demonstration" project or will they be expanded to a scale equal to the dimensions of the problem?

As part of the $3.5 billion initiative, a smaller package of benefits is targeted to 65 urban and 30 rural "enterprise communities," which we believe are less likely to succeed because they are more subject to the problems and concerns with which the U.S. General Accounting Office and Urban Institute evaluations found fault (see chapter 1).

The new national service program may complement empowerment zones and enterprise communities by involving young people in neighborhood-based cleanups, housing repair, and related services. To be truly effective, however, community service workers must be recruited from the inner-city communities where they live.

Chapter 6

Increasing Public Safety to Secure Economic Development And Jobs for Families

During the past two decades, and especially among politicians seeking reelection, crime and drug policy has been framed in terms of more prisons, tougher and longer sentences, expanded use of the death penalty, more hardware, and more spending on the criminal-justice system.

This policy has failed. For example, as the graphs in chapter 2 show, we tripled our prison capacity from 1981 to 1992, *yet violent crime among minority youth increased dramatically over the same period.* The United States has the highest rates of incarceration among industrialized nations—so shouldn't the taxpayer expect low crime compared with other nations if prison-building politicians are to be believed? But *the truth is that America also has the highest rate of crime in the industrialized world.*

The cost of such failure is great—as much as $100,000 in New York to build a new prison cell and up to $30,000 per year to keep someone (disproportionately minority males) in it.

Sen. John C. Danforth (R-Mo.), a former state attorney general, consulted his own experience and concluded: "What I liked most in (the crime bill of 1994) was the prevention. What I liked most in this legislation was that which was so casually labeled pork." And, taking dead aim at derision of "midnight basketball" as emblematic of the social froth in the bill, Danforth asked, "What is wrong with basketball for kids" if it keeps them out of trouble?
Helen Dewar
Washington Post
August 27, 1994

Multiple Solutions

Given such failures, in chapter 6, we reason that a policy more helpful to inner-city children, youth, and families should be based on expanding programs that do work. This leads back to the multiple solutions discussed in chapters 2, 3, and 4. In addition, much of what works to reduce crime and drugs, we believe, should be viewed not just as a criminal justice *end* but as a *means* to stabilize economic development that generates jobs for inner-city families. Expanding what works to prevent and treat for drugs also makes some inner-city parents more capable of holding those jobs.

Chapters 3 and 4 discussed how grass-roots inner-city programs reduce crime, drugs, and child poverty while increasing the number of school grades completed, employability, and family stability. Accordingly, the most cost-effective means to reduce crime and drugs is to expand Head Start for all eligible children; reform JTPA along the lines of the Argus Community, YouthBuild USA, and Job Corps; create new jobs; and develop a national Corporation for Youth and Family Investment to replicate successful private, nonprofit, community-based programs such as Centro and boys and girls club safe havens. At the federal level, we need to understand that successful crime and drug policies require the coordinated efforts of the Departments of Labor, Health and Human Services, Education, and Justice. In other words, multiple problems require interagency cooperation to create multiple solutions.

■ Fairview Homes

A good example of a successful program that coordinates funding from various agencies to combat crime in this way is the Fairview Homes Crime Prevention Program, which was begun in Charlotte, North Carolina, public housing in 1979 as part of the Carter administration's national urban policy. The Charlotte Public Housing Authority received $450,000 from four federal departments—HUD, Health and Human Services, Labor, and Justice. The monies were used primarily to hire staff to run demonstration programs at Fairview Homes during a two-year period. Program staff included professionals, adult public-housing residents who were "natural leaders," and high-risk youth who lived in the project. With the assistance of the Fairview tenant organization, a staff of 16 adult residents and former residents was hired, and jobs also were given to 48 high-risk youth, 16 to 19 years of age.

The program provided residents with job training and work opportunities in money management, employment, health, and antidrug services. Residents were also trained in ombudsperson and advocacy skills so that they might leverage resources to continue the program after the initial funding ended. Employment opportunities were designed to nurture personal growth, skill development, and control over one's environment and life.

Crime rates in Fairview Homes, as measured by police statistics, declined throughout the duration of the program; crime in the remainder of the census tract and within the city of Charlotte rose. Police data indicated that the most dramatic decreases in crime at Fairview Homes occurred among serious assault, robbery, and burglary. Crime rates, based on interviews with residents, also decreased. Among the high-risk youth employed between the early 1980s and the late 1980s, only 3 of the 48 youth were arrested for a serious crime (drug dealing and assault), based on housing authority and police records.

The Fairview program was founded on the assumption that public-housing residents were able to deal with their own problems. The program evaluation observed:

> In those areas in which the commitment to involving residents as working partners in program development and implementation was achieved, the greatest amount of success was experienced. Where residents were involved as partners with professional staff and management [of the public housing authority], the program reached and exceeded the goals. When the residents played only menial or limited roles, only a partial achievement of goals could be found. . . . Rather than talking to and for the residents of low-

income communities, programs seeking to serve these communities should begin to talk and plan with the residents for the services that will be offered.

After the initial two-year period (1979–1981), Fairview Homes fought severe fiscal constraints. Federal funding cutbacks during the 1980s undermined the drug and alcohol program just as it was beginning to make gains. Nevertheless, funding from private foundations, local government, and other sources has kept the program alive and it has even been extended to other housing properties within the Charlotte Housing Authority.

■ Boys and Girls Clubs

An evaluation study conducted by Columbia University from 1987 to 1990 in California, Florida, Illinois, New York, and Texas compared housing projects that had boys and girls clubs with housing projects without boys and girls clubs. The study found that housing projects with boys and girls clubs showed a 13% drop in arrests for juvenile crime, a 22% decrease in reported drug activity, and 25% decrease in reports of the presence of crack cocaine. The evaluation also reported reduced alcohol use, a decline in graffiti on the walls of housing units, and a drop in requests for repairs for vandalism damage. The schools that served the young people who lived in public housing properties with boys and girls clubs reported fewer school absences, better grades, and a lower school-failure rate when compared with students who lived in public-housing properties without boys and girls clubs.

Police Reform and Economic Development

When it is designed to reduce crime in a geographic area, as well as among specific high-risk youth, such crime prevention can also help stabilize the community. Increased stability, less crime, and less fear can be used to encourage public and private investment in the community. Investment generates economic development. If planned right, the economic development generates jobs—which can be filled by high-risk youth and teen parents, if they receive sufficient training through a reformed JTPA.

In this context, community-based and problem-oriented policing can be viewed as demand-side prevention even more than supply-side law enforcement. Such policing can be linked to prevention by community-based nonprofit citizen organizations to better secure economic development—and therefore jobs and family stability.

■ Problem-Oriented Policing

What do we mean by innovative policing? Most promising is what has been called problem-oriented policing. The idea is not to react to crime after it occurs, which is what most American police do, but to prevent crime before it occurs by dealing with some of the problems that cause crime.

For example, in a comparison group demonstration program by the Police Executive Research Forum in Newport News, Virginia, the burglary rate in high-crime public housing was reduced by 35% during a two-year period. This was done not

Chapter 6

through making more arrests after crimes had occurred, but rather by improving maintenance of public-housing properties, among other preventive strategies.

■ Community-Based Policing

In addition to problem-oriented policing, community-based policing also holds promise. Community-based policing means getting officers out of cars and onto foot patrols. On foot, police can interact better with neighborhood residents, become their friends, report suspicious events, and sometimes build on friendships to pursue problem-oriented policing.

There is little scientific evaluation evidence that community-based policing in the form of foot patrols reduces crime *per se*. Evaluations by the Police Foundation and others in Flint, Michigan; Kansas City, Missouri; Newark, New Jersey; Houston, Texas; and New York City all point to this conclusion. Some findings indicate a reduction in residents' *fear* of crime as a result of police foot patrols. This fear reduction occurs mostly in middle-class urban neighborhoods, not inner-city locations. Hence, we are not suggesting that an increased police presence can by itself effectively attack crime and drug problems in low-income communities. But it can help the community deal with them.

> Over a one-year period, violent crime reported to police dropped by 15% in community-policing areas.

Wherever it is tried, community policing is popular with citizens. A police show of force can at least keep drug dealers on the move and help protect the operations of inner-city, nonprofit-based youth- and economic-development efforts. Existing businesses and public institutions can be persuaded to stay. New businesses and new public investments can be encouraged.

Along similar lines, programs like Project Beethoven in Robert Taylor Homes in Chicago can be better secured. The gangs in Robert Taylor Homes told program directors to close down once a month to allow for gang activity. If there were sufficient and appropriate community-based and problem-oriented policing, gangs might be driven out of the public housing community—so that the social development of Project Beethoven, including prenatal care, preschool, child care, and remedial education for the mothers could better proceed.

■ Police Mini-Stations

But police innovation in support of inner-city social and economic development includes many other possibilities beyond foot patrols. We believe that there is, for example, tremendous potential for the implementation of police mini-stations, as pioneered by the Japanese. Some of the mini-stations in Japan are residential. A police officer lives above the mini-station with his wife and family. (As of yet, there are no female officers so assigned to residential mini-stations.) Family members of police become neighbors to others in the community.

The Eisenhower Foundation has already shown that this notion can be developed in U.S. territories and on the mainland. For example, the Centro Sister Isolina Ferre residential mini-station in the Caimito neighborhood of San Juan (chapter 4) has experienced a police-reported crime drop of over 30% in the 1980s and a further 10% drop in the 1990s while comparison neighborhoods have not experienced anything close to this decline. The differences were statistically significant. The Japanese also have nonresidential mini-stations. These have been tried with great success in communities such as the Logan neighborhood in North Philadelphia, where crime decreased 24% in two years in a demonstration supported by the Eisenhower Foundation, while crime decreased only 6% in the police district where the Logan neighborhood is located and 10% in Philadelphia as a whole.

Residential or nonresidential, the mini-stations serve as a point where police, family, and community can better relate to one another. *They are physical locations that can help anchor economic development by offering the presence of police.* They are the physical points of departure for community foot patrols and problem-oriented policing.

There are still more variations on these themes. For example, instead of a separate mini-station, police can drop in at youth development organizations on a regular basis. At the Dorchester Youth Collaborative in Boston, such a drop-in program reduced crime by over 20% in two years (chapter 4). The drop was statistically significant. Figure 18 summarizes the evaluation findings from Boston—as well as from similar efforts by the Eisenhower Foundation to marry community policing with youth development—in San Juan, Philadelphia, and Chicago.

Along similar lines, in Alexandria, Virginia, single male police officers are being housed at little or no cost in public housing. In Columbia, South Carolina, the city offers low-interest mortgages to police officers who purchase homes in low-income inner-city neighborhoods. Similar plans now are spreading from Newark to Milwaukee.

In Newark, the Japanese notion of home visits also is being tried. Once or twice a year, an officer visits each home in his or her patrol area. The officer sits with the homeowners and inquires about experiences related to crime. Police give tips on crime prevention. When this notion was first introduced to American police chiefs by the Eisenhower Foundation on a delegation to Japan in 1988, the police chiefs were skeptical. They thought that, in tough inner-city neighborhoods especially, families would not trust police to enter their homes. This has proven not to be the case in Newark, where families have accepted police visits.

■ **Police Training**

Police training needs to be vastly improved. In the United States, police typically are trained for perhaps five to eight months before they begin work. In Japan, police cadets with college degrees go through 12 months of training, and cadets with high school diplomas are trained for approximately 18 months. In Japan, police are taught English and receive computer training. When the delegation of police chiefs went to Japan in 1988, the chiefs observed police cadets at the training academies taking courses in tea ceremony and flower arrangement. The Americans were amused. However, when they learned that such training helped Japanese police develop awareness of and appreciation for Japanese culture, some of the Americans concluded that American police officers would benefit from cultural training.

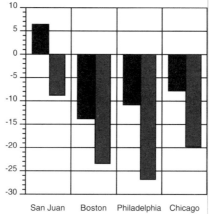

Residential or nonresidential mini-stations serve as a point where police, family, and community can better relate to one another.

Fig. 18. Changes in crime in neighborhoods evaluated between 1990 and 1993 as a result of prevention by nonprofit community groups in partnership with police.

Chapter 6

Programs that support problem-oriented and community-based policing, including home visits, residential and nonresidential mini-stations, and improved training, increase the public's sense of safety and security. Despite the rhetoric surrounding volunteerism and self-sufficiency in the 1980s, it is unrealistic and unreasonable to expect groups of ordinary citizens, who are not trained to cope with dangerous situations, to take the lead in public safety. Citizens pay taxes to support public agencies established to train and deploy people to handle dangerous situations.

Handgun Control

Improvements in public safety, fear reduction, neighborhood stability, and social and economic development can be further accelerated by strong legislation to control handguns, as advocated by many police chiefs who have lobbied through national organizations against the National Rifle Association (NRA). More teenage inner-city males die from gunshots than from all natural causes combined. This malignancy of handguns in urban America is likely to continue unabated because of the lobbying power of the NRA.

The relationship between handgun control and handgun homicides is clear. In 1990, for example, more than 10,000 homicides were committed with handguns, compared with 68 in Canada and 22 in the United Kingdom—countries with strict handgun laws. In 1967, the Katzenbach Crime Commission recommended federal and state legislation regulating the purchase, transportation, sale, and possession of firearms. In 1968, the Kerner Commission endorsed this recommendation, adding that "federal legislation is essential in order to make state and local laws fully effective, and to regulate areas beyond the reach of state government." Shortly thereafter, the Reverend Martin Luther King and Senator Robert Kennedy were assassinated, which stimulated the development of the National Commission on the Causes and Prevention of Violence, chaired by the late Milton Eisenhower. In 1969, the Eisenhower Violence Commission concluded that "the United States still does not have an effective national firearms policy."

> We recommend federal legislation to encourage the establishment of state licensing systems for handguns. The federal legislation would introduce a federal system of handgun licensing, applicable only to those states which within a four-year period fail to enact a state law that (1) established a standard for determining an individual's need for a handgun and for the licensing of an individual who shows such a need and (2) prohibits all others from possessing handguns or buying handgun ammunition.

The Eisenhower Violence Commission argued that removal of handguns would certainly not diminish the motivation and desire of people to do harm to others. However, if firearms were not so readily available, the outcomes of attacks by people on other people would be less serious. In the nearly 25 years since the Eisenhower Violence Commission, no evidence has been presented to counter this research-based conclusion.

Despite the rhetoric surrounding volunteerism and self-sufficiency in the 1980s, it is unrealistic and unreasonable to expect groups of ordinary citizens, who are not trained to cope with dangerous situations, to take the lead in public safety.

We still do not have an effective national firearms policy, despite the fact that public opinion polls show that 95% of Americans support some form of gun control.

Increasing Public Safety

Congress has passed the Brady Bill, which requires a seven-day waiting period between purchase and delivery of a handgun, and has enacted a ban (with loopholes) on assault weapons. But we still do not have an effective national firearms policy, despite the fact that public opinion polls show that 95% of Americans support some form of gun control. At least 26 states and scores of cities and counties have supported the recommendations of American police chiefs in their battle against the NRA by imposing waiting periods on some gun purchases, by banning the sale of assault rifle weapons, or both.

The NRA is perhaps the most powerful and feared lobbying group on Capitol Hill. The NRA has 2.6 million members, four hundred employees, assets of $128 million, and an annual anti–gun-control lobbying budget of more than $18 million a year. It contributes millions of dollars to congressional candidates.

The NRA is to gun manufacturers what the Tobacco Institute is to cigarette companies. In many ways, the NRA's latest marketing strategy to persuade women to buy guns (as prevention against rape) and to persuade minorities and inner-city residents to buy guns as part of a fear-based marketing campaign puts the tobacco companies' marketing efforts to shame. In contrast, many police on the front lines of our communities find the NRA's positions absurd. To quote former Washington, D.C., Police Chief Isaac Fulwood, "If we are serious, let's do something about guns. Let's say to America, hey, the day of the Wild West is over. Because anybody can get a gun. Anybody." The litany of unpopular issues that the NRA defends, for example, "cop killer" bullets, plastic "terrorist special" handguns, and assault weapons, make the NRA increasingly out of touch with American opinion polls and police departments throughout the nation. As with tobacco, firearms should be considered a broad-based public health problem and should be treated as such by government officials. A new public health campaign, such as that launched by Surgeon General Koop against smoking, must focus on the virtually unregulated distribution of handguns. Interestingly, all products sold in America are regulated by a specific federal agency to assure safety for Americans. Guns are a notable exception. We support the conclusions of Josh Sugarmann in his recent book, NRA: *Money-Firepower-Fear*:

> The ultimate solution to America's firearms crisis lies in implementing a comprehensive regulatory scheme that gives a federal agency real power to control the design, manufacture, distribution and sale of firearms and ammunition. Each category of firearm and type of ammunition would be subjected to a risk–benefit analysis to weed out those products whose potential harm outweighs any possible benefits. Manufacture and distribution would be tightly controlled, with compliance actively monitored. And the number of licensed manufacturers, dealers, and importers would be severely curtailed. The implementation of such standards would most likely result in an immediate ban on the future production and sale of handguns and assault weapons because of their limited utility and high risk. The granting of federal regulatory power would also act as a check on the industry from developing products it knows it would never be allowed to market.

Truly effective handgun control promises not just to drop the homicide rate by reducing access to lethal weapons. It can also help reduce fear in inner-city neigh-

The NRA's latest marketing strategy to persuade women to buy guns (as prevention against rape) and to persuade minorities and inner-city residents to buy guns as part of a fear-based marketing campaign puts the tobacco companies' marketing efforts to shame.

Truly effective handgun control can help reduce fear in inner-city neighborhoods, increase the feelings of security, and so promote public and private investment.

Chapter 6

borhoods, increase the feelings of security, and so promote public and private investment—which can generate services and jobs for youth at-risk and more family stability. No small part of the trauma experienced by the families in Project Beethoven in Chicago's Robert Taylor Homes (see chapter 3) is related to the brutal day-to-day experience of fear through firearms.

Drug Prevention, Education, and Treatment

For child poverty welfare reform and job-training reform to work, high-risk young people and teen parents who are being given real employment opportunity must be drug free.

In the inner city, drug policy affects family members of many ages. Preschoolers are being killed in cross-fires among dealers. Middle-school children are drug runners. Peer pressure to experiment with alcohol and drugs begins early. Teen mothers give birth to crack babies. Addiction makes it impossible for young parents to succeed in Job Corps, YouthBuild, Project Redirection, and other community-based multiple solutions.

We urge tough laws, effective police action, severe sentences, and prison space, however expensive, for dealers. At the same time, the nation must change the spending formula of 1981–1992, in which 70% of the $12 billion-plus annual antidrug budget was spent on supply-side law enforcement and interdiction and only 30% on demand-side prevention and treatment. We need a policy of 30% on the supply-side and 70% on the demand-side, like France.

Here is a real opportunity for political leadership. Despite scientific evaluations that show that community-based, demand-side initiatives—like the Argus Community and boys and girls clubs—work best, many members of Congress erroneously conclude that a vote for more prevention and treatment will be regarded by voters as a soft-on-crime position. As Congressman John Conyers, Jr., has observed, "When these proposals come up in Congress, most members want to know, before they vote, which one is the toughest. It's sort of, 'I don't know if this is going to work, but nobody is going to blame me for not being tough.'"

Similarly, in 1991, when Herbert D. Kleber, director for demand-side programs, resigned from the drug czar's office, he concluded that treatment and prevention were failures: "Clearly, if the President would stake his reputation and say, 'I'm determined to spend "x" million on treatment,' it would make it much harder for Congress to turn him down."

With the Clinton administration, the time for priority on prevention, education, and treatment should be at hand, in spite of prison-building rhetoric on Capitol Hill. To its credit, the administration changed the formula in its initial budgets—from 70/30 to 60/40.

We also applaud giving cabinet rank to the director of the national antidrug policy, but the drug czar now must be given adequate staff and reasonable control over the policies of the operating agencies to which antidrug monies is appropriated by Congress.

> **The time for priority on prevention, education, and treatment should be at hand, in spite of prison-building rhetoric on Capitol Hill.**

■ Prevention and Education

The Congressional Budget Office summed up the case for drug prevention and treatment:

> Although enforcement has undoubtedly made it more difficult and more costly to grow, process, import, and distribute illegal drugs, no hard evidence exists that intensified efforts have kept them away from users or pushed prices up to levels that, in the long run, appreciably reduced the amount of drugs purchased. The difficulty in effectively controlling street supply and price stems from competition among producers and distributors, the large markup from wholesale to retail prices, and the ability to maintain an affordable end price by diluting the drug. Those conditions, critics argue, make it almost impossible to curb drugs by means of supply controls and related activities.

With many drugs, of course, use is higher in the white suburbs than in the inner city, where the real issue is drug dealing by youth. Terry Williams of the City College of New York stated that where there are few legal labor market options—as in East Harlem, with an unemployment rate of over 16%—the drug economy can be perceived as "an equal opportunity employer." Despite the violence and brutality of the business, drug dealing may raise self-esteem, according to one East Harlem observer, more than "being exploited by the white man" or working as a supermarket bagger. Even if you are scared and want out of the drug business, peer and gang pressure can keep you in it.

The community-based programs described in this report have been successful precisely because they respond to these economic realities of the street. The mentors and big brothers in these programs expose the lies promoting big money to be made in crack dealing. Remedial education, job training, and job placement in a supportive setting combine to provide viable options that make sense to many young people.

The nation's first priority should be to support community-based inner-city nonprofit organizations' efforts to deliver multiple-solution drug prevention and education. Our second priority should be to support inner-city schools as a service-delivery vehicle. Unfortunately, despite the substantial federal monies spent each year on drug prevention and education in schools, the federal government provides little guidance about what works best. Much research on drug prevention and education is incomprehensible and inaccessible. Accordingly, bewildered school administrators often select the best packaged, most eye-catching programs, even though such programs offer little scientific evidence of their success.

America's schools need more federal guidance written in common-sense English on how and why school-based drug education initiatives appear to work. But inner-city educators need to listen just as much to Richard Price, who in his recent novel, *Clockers*, describing inner-city drug trade, states,

> This one drug dealer said to me, "The scariest thing to a kid out here on the streets is not drugs, AIDS, guns, jail, death. It's words on a page. Because if a 15-year old kid could handle words on a page, he'd be home doing his homework instead of selling dope with me."

Chapter 6

The point is that, in the inner city, drug education also is synonymous with learning basic reading and math skills—and that can be done best through the multiple solutions articulated in this report.

■ Treatment

Successful drug-treatment initiatives need to be expanded to the point where all addicted inner-city family members can obtain help, especially as part of a comprehensive job-training and job-placement program.

Each year, approximately 700,000 addicts are unable to secure treatment. According to the National Association of State Alcohol and Drug Abuse Directors, each dollar spent for treatment saves $11.54 in costs for prisons and lost job productivity. A study financed by the National Institute on Drug Abuse (NIDA) of 10,000 individuals in residential, outpatient, and methadone programs found that such treatment methods significantly reduced heroin and cocaine use. Up to five years after treatment, less than 20% of the clients were using any drug, excluding marijuana, and the proportion of clients committing predatory crimes had been reduced by more than 50%.

But more treatment is not enough; we need better treatment. Too often, conventional drug treatment represents little more than a revolving door through which addicts enter programs, then return to communities that remain essentially unchanged. Many addicts feel alienated by most existing treatments and do their best to avoid them.

✦ Therapeutic Communities

Therapeutic communities have a role to play in a comprehensive national treatment policy. The term therapeutic community describes residential programs that serve a wide spectrum of drug and alcohol abusers. In comparison with other methods of drug treatment, therapeutic communities coordinate multiple solutions in a single setting—vocational counseling; work therapy; education; recreation; group, family, and individual therapy; and medical, legal, and social services. Mentors, staff, and peers serve as role models for successful personal change. The treatment process involves initial orientation, primary treatment during which participants progress from junior status to role models, and gradual reentry into society.

The residential program at the Argus Community (see chapter 4) is a therapeutic community that merits close examination.

Other examples of promising therapeutic communities include Abraxis in Philadelphia; Daytop Village in New York; Gateway House in Chicago; Phoenix House in New York; Amity in Tucson; Second Genesis in Washington, D.C.; and Stay'n Out in New York. All of these programs were created as heroin-treatment programs and all of them now offer cocaine treatment as well.

According to Mathea Falco, in *The Making of a Drug Free America*, residential therapeutic communities such as Phoenix House offer physically and psychologically rigorous programs. In fact, fewer than one of six clients completes the one- to two-year course of treatment. However, those who do complete the program remain drug free far longer than those who drop out.

> **Too often, conventional drug treatment represents little more than a revolving door through which addicts enter programs, then return to communities that remain essentially unchanged.**

Less confrontational, more user-friendly residential centers like Amity in Tucson have shown better success in keeping people in treatment. Amity emphasizes the importance of work and learning and holds frequent group meetings led by staff members, half of whom are Amity graduates, serving as role models. Overcoming denial is the critical first step to recovery. At Amity peers become a surrogate family that helps residents learn to face their own anger and shame.

Therapeutic communities operating within prisons, for example, Stay'n Out, which has treated more than 1,500 inmates in two New York State prisons, offer great hope for drug offenders, particularly if they receive aftercare services to help them find employment, obtain education, and continue their treatment. Recovery rates are generally twice as high among addicts who have families, jobs, and friends. Treatment programs that offer strong alternatives to drug use—vocational training, help finding jobs, new opportunities and friendships—work best. Many of the elements that we have identified as common among successful inner-city *prevention* programs also appear to underlie therapeutic communities established for *treatment*.

✦ Need and Consensus for Drug Treatment

Still, the surface has barely been scratched with regard to treatment innovations in the United States. There exist 5,000 treatment centers of all kinds; most are short-term, outpatient programs, with little scientific evidence of their benefits with regard to costs. Many drug-treatment programs are too expensive, insufficiently evaluated, poorly staffed, and not oriented toward integrating the drug abuser into a productive life in a functioning community.

Little coordination exists for channeling the estimated four million addicts into treatment programs. Most treatment slots are still designated for heroin users. Today, however, heroin users are outnumbered by cocaine addicts and multiple abusers, who require different treatment strategies. Insufficient attention is focused on the special needs of disadvantaged persons and women. And some models, developed primarily for adult addicts, are less relevant to the drug problems of high-risk youth. We need to learn more about how best to provide effective treatment for inner-city youth and other family members—including the relative merits of residential versus day treatment—and how to remove the barriers that now keep many youths away from available treatment. *We do know this: Something close to a consensus has emerged that significantly more funding is required to close the gap between treatment need and availability among the disadvantaged. Without it, hard drugs will continue to ravage families and communities in the inner city; drug-related violence will continue at levels that place many neighborhoods in a state of siege.*

Unless we begin to reverse that situation, it will undermine all of our other efforts to develop the inner city economically and socially and so stabilize inner-city families.

Expanded drug-abuse treatment, intensive outreach, and aftercare need to be linked closely with youth-enterprise development, family supports, intensive remedial education, and other services. As a high official at NIDA observed, "For many addicts, it's not rehabilitation; it's habilitation. They don't know how to read or look for work, let alone beat their addictions."

Chapter 6

Stop Doing What Doesn't Work

In spite of substantial scientific evidence, Congress is pursuing what doesn't work, like prisons and boot camps, and cutting what does work, like community-based partnerships between youth development organizations and police. The current mood on Capitol Hill is *déjà vu* all over again. It is reminiscent of funding under what was called the New Federalism in the 1970s—when, for example, the Law Enforcement Assistance Administration made a grant to San Diego, California, for a submarine and to Mobile, Alabama, for three tanks. Every effort must be made to organize a new citizen revolt, this time for the 1996 elections, to reverse such misdirection that merely throws money at the problem. Simultaneously, we need to encourage proposals, like that of Governor George Pataki of New York, which provide alternatives to prison for low-level drug offenders.

Chapter 7

Investing In Inner-City Families To Scale: Finding the Money

The financing of a national family policy for the inner city requires only a modest shift in priorities. If we can find hundreds of billions of dollars to bail out the savings and loan industry, we should be able to set aside a small percent of that amount per year to invest in at-risk families. We must ask pointed questions: How can appropriations for housing poor families decline by 80% while Federal Housing Administration losses alone amounted to nearly $7 billion as part of a 1980s HUD scandal in which the Federal Housing Commissioner pled guilty to conspiracy? Will the federal government continue to spend billions on Star Wars and the space program but not invest sufficiently in crack-addition treatment for pregnant mothers to reduce, for example, a District of Columbia infant mortality rate that is three times the national average and far higher than the rates in Cuba and Bulgaria?

> **[In 1994] taxpayers will spend $51B in direct subsidies to businesses and lose another $53.3B in tax breaks for corporations, according to the Office of Management and Budget and the Joint Committee on Taxation. Those who want welfare recipients to work as a condition of public assistance should expand their efforts to cover corporations dependent on federal largesse.**
> **James P. Donahue**
> *The Washington Post*
> **March 6, 1994**

Common sense dictates that we invest in families and reconstruct our communities. To do so, we must use those programs that already have been proven successful in the public sector and private sector. We must encourage and support public–private ventures. We must realize that private-sector human and economic development is generally more successful when run by nonprofit inner-city organizations.

The nation's family-policy priority should be to replicate to scale multiple-solution, private, nonprofit, community-based programs such as Argus, Centro, Delancey Street, and the New Community Corporation as well as innovative for-profit community-oriented ventures such as TELESIS. These replications should be coordinated with expanded public-sector initiatives in public school reform, YouthBuild USA-inspired job training linked to job replacement and economic development, community banking, infrastructure and high-tech development, and problem-oriented community-based policing.

This comprehensive family package should be financed primarily at the federal level, but leveraged with private resources and state and local public resources. However, we must be reasonable in the burdens we place on state and local governments and not require them to come up with resources they obviously do not possess, as was the case with federal disinvestment from 1981 to 1992.

Chapter 7

Public and private institutions at the city rather than state level are good vehicles for initiating changes.

Neighborhood-Based Program Implementation

Federal financing should not be combined with federal program implementation. Programs should be initiated and managed at the community level. The most cost-effective, least bureaucratic way to create urban change is to design and run programs to meet local needs. When people have a true stake in designing and planning a program, they will work harder to ensure that it is successful. Private-sector inner-city nonprofit organizations typically are more in touch with community problems and needs than is the federal government. The community organizations are much better than the government in encouraging participatory democracy. Well-managed community organizations are able to deliver multiple services to combat multiple problems. Community-based and street-savvy for-profit programs such as TELESIS also engage genuine grass-roots participation.

Public and private institutions at the city rather than state level also are good vehicles for initiating change. Such programs, when they are based in neighborhood offices or centers, are more efficient and cost-effective than is a diverse and broadly scattered network of services. The French coordinate services in this way much more so than the United States.

Local and State Investment

The suburbs hold great potential resources for financing services to the inner city. Secretary of Labor Robert Reich has spoken of the "fortunate fifth," those citizens who have "escaped" to the suburbs and thus eroded the tax base of the nation's central cities. The federal government needs to open the tax bases of suburban communities to the needs of disadvantaged persons who remain in our inner cities by attaching tax-sharing requirements to federal grants provided to states and communities. The Urban Institute recommends that grants from federal and state governments be allocated in such a way that requires recipients to share the value of commercial property as well as other elements of the local tax base for property-tax purposes. The Minneapolis/St. Paul area, for example, has implemented a state-mandated policy requiring neighborhood sharing of taxes based on a proportion of the growth in metropolitan area revenues.

Although some Americans view tax-base sharing as extreme, it is not from an international perspective. "Few other countries permit the degree of local fiscal separateness that has become common in urban America," the Urban Institute concluded. In this vein, we should evaluate carefully recent reforms in states like Michigan, where property taxes for school financing have been replaced by alternative taxes spread across the state.

Federalism Revisited

The far-reaching reforms advocated in this report will require more resources than state and local governments are able to provide. Only the federal government has enough resources and, potentially, the moral authority to reverse the forces that are destroying inner-city families.

But how do we move federal dollars into our inner cities? We suggest an array of mechanisms: federal grants and loans to nonprofit intermediaries that grant and loan monies to private, nonprofit neighborhood organizations; federal grants and loans to city governments with the stipulation that monies be made available to private neighborhood nonprofit organizations; and federal grants and loans made directly to nonprofit organizations.

Federal funds for high-risk families should not, for the most part, be targeted through the states. The reasons are given in detail in chapter 2.

New Levels of Investment

To sustain family policy at a scale equal to the dimensions of the problem, an additional $15 billion in annual appropriations is needed. Such funding would allow implementation of the reforms discussed in chapters 3 and 4. This increase includes providing adequate prenatal care among poor inner-city mothers and adequate developmental care of infants and toddlers; funding three years of Head Start for all eligible three-, four-, and five-year-olds (and some two-year-olds); replicating nonprofit, community-based organizations through a new national Corporation for Youth and Family Investment; replacing JTPA with a new job-training and -placement system based on community successes like Argus, YouthBuild USA, and Job Corps; and refocusing anticrime and antidrug initiatives onto prevention and treatment. It also covers implementing public school reforms, including refinement of Chapter I of the Elementary and Secondary Education Act of 1965; implementing recommendations from several Carnegie reports; replicating the Comer plan; replicating programs such as "I Have A Dream" if evaluations indicate that they are successful; expanding vocational and apprenticeship programs such as Project Prepare and Project ProTech; and extending school desegregation initiatives based on the success of St. Louis and many smaller cities. The prime federal funding agencies for these ventures are the Departments of Labor, Health and Human Services, and Education.

Additional funding at the $15-billion-per-year level for 10 years is needed for the reconstruction of inner-city neighborhoods and the closing of the investment and productivity gaps between the central city and the suburbs. Much of this funding should be targeted at employing the inner-city unemployed in housing construction. Part of this funding must support the efforts of nonprofit and for-profit organizations (for example, TELESIS) to integrate multiple-solution youth-development initiatives into economic development. Training and placing inner-city residents in youth-investment occupations such as teaching and providing child care should be included. This funding should cover, as well, repair of the urban infrastructure through the employment of inner-city residents, creation of community-development banks in the inner city, expansion of tenant management in public housing, more community and problem-oriented police, and expansion of the successful Gatreaux housing desegregation program to all eligible inner-city

Chapter 7

residents. Federal initiatives to encourage private-sector high-tech investments should stipulate that a significant proportion of the jobs generated be slotted for poor inner-city residents. The primary federal funding agencies for these programs are Labor, Housing and Urban Development, Transportation, Commerce, and Justice as well as a new, independent National Community Development Bank.

We would begin, then, to approach funding equal to the dimensions of the problem with $150 billion in total appropriations for children, youth, and families over one decade and $150 billion in total appropriations for coordinated housing, security, infrastructure, and high-tech investment over the same decade. With the exception of funding Head Start for all eligible children, the proposed $300 billion over 10 years returns funding levels to levels similar to the late 1970s. Our proposal limits new funds to programs that have been proven successful.

This funding is targeted toward inner-city, disadvantaged families. It does not cover impoverished rural areas, although such areas also have great needs. Our funding does not necessarily cover all the costs of AFDC reform, though it concentrates on the prime cost—job training and placement for mothers and fathers in AFDC families. Nor does our budget include the costs of health care reform. A reformed health-care system will make multiple solutions far easier to implement in the inner city, for example, adequate drug treatment linked to drug prevention. Our budget assumes that matching corporate, foundation, state, and local funding would provide significant opportunities for high-risk youth and families.

The National Debt and Other Competing Priorities

A policy to finance what works on a scale equal to the problem must, in today's political and economic climate, be accompanied by a plan to reduce the national debt.

Federal tax policy in the 1980s promised substantial tax relief without reduction of services. The political rationale for this policy—the trickle-down, supply-side economics that President Bush called "voodoo economics,"—stated that by cutting taxes on the wealthy, economic growth would be generated. Tax revenues would not decline; they might even increase. Through this trickle-down mechanism, it was argued, the deficit would be reduced.

But voodoo economics did not work. Tax revenues declined. Throughout the 1980s, government officials quoted Thomas Jefferson's views on taxation while ignoring his view that debt was the "greatest of dangers" to be feared. Meanwhile, the national debt skyrocketed. In 1980, the federal deficit was $59 billion and the national debt was $914 billion. In 1992, the annual deficit was more than $300 billion and the national debt was more than $3 trillion. During this period, domestic programs were cut sharply, while the military budget was greatly increased.

By 1992, for the first time since the late 1950s, the national debt was more than half the size of the entire economy. The cost of interest on the debt, nearly $200 billion in fiscal year 1992, currently exceeds combined federal spending for education, science, law enforcement, transportation, housing, food stamps, and AFDC. By 1992, the debt was growing faster than the economy, and costs of servicing the debt were consuming larger and larger portions of the government's resources. The ratio

Throughout the 1980s, government officials quoted Thomas Jefferson's views on taxation while ignoring his view that debt was the "greatest of dangers" to be feared.

of public debt to economic output is higher in the United States than it is in Germany, France, or Britain.

Trickle-down, supply-side theory asserted that tax cuts would not increase the deficit. However, when the deficit began to rise, many supporters of supply-side economics were not greatly troubled. In fact, some began to see a clear advantage in the skyrocketing debt. Allen Brinkley concludes that the supply-side fiscal crisis opened "a back door for doing what many on the right had been unable to achieve with their frontal assaults in the 1950s and 1960s. It undercut support for starting new government programs, and even for sustaining old ones, less by discrediting the programs than by pinning them against a need to reduce a huge and growing national debt."

This strategy, however, has had a devastating effect on inner-city families. The Clinton administration seeks reform, for example, in AFDC. But reform is crippled by the argument that we can't afford it because of the debt. In addition, because of the debt, Congress has required that new expenditures be accompanied by new revenues or by equivalent reductions in related programs. Hence, AFDC reform, according to current rules, must be financed by cuts in domestic programs, which creates a kind of "social cannibalism."

Yet Congressional rules do not allow financing new domestic expenditures from reductions in military and foreign-aid budgets. This is absurd.

Jeff Faux of the Economic Policy Institute states that administrations that attempt to implement domestic reforms are limited to a "pilot program presidency." Even though we know a lot about programs that do work, we lack resources to replicate such programs at a scale equal to the dimensions of the problem. So administrations are able to implement only modest, experimental, pilot demonstration programs.

Federal reform today is also imprisoned by public attitudes. In 1981, voters believed the ridiculous promise that government could simultaneously cut taxes, sustain services, and reduce the deficit. Instead of taking responsibility for their mistake, voters have become more cynical toward government.

Given these circumstances, the best strategy may be to begin with incremental reform based on what works. At the same time, the electorate needs to be reminded about the origins of the national debt and the results of funding cutbacks for domestic programs. If incremental reforms show promise, modest victories can be claimed and programs can be expanded. A knowledgeable electorate will lead to voter pressure on Congress to pass more significant reform.

Source of Funds

How do we find the money for initiating the reforms presented here? Avoiding lengthy talk of budgets and projections for years to come, the following sections give broad categories from which monies can be drawn to finance reforms as well as meet other funding needs. The categories include revenues redirected from existing federal domestic programs, revenues resulting from reduced military and foreign-aid budgets, revenues from reduced entitlements to the wealthy and corporations, and revenues from increased taxes on the wealthy, alcohol, and tobacco.

The cost of interest on the debt currently exceeds combined federal spending for education, science, law enforcement, transportation, housing, food stamps, and AFDC.

The electorate needs to be reminded about the origins of the national debt and the results of funding cutbacks for domestic programs.

Chapter 7

■ Revenues from Existing Federal Domestic Programs

Monies should be redirected from the existing JTPA into the job training and placement initiatives recommended in chapter 4. Such reform should be linked to welfare-reform initiatives and a program to fund nonprofit organizations to facilitate the building and rehabilitating of housing for and by the poor.

Perhaps the most significant change here is our proposal to change from the 70/30 ratio of supply-side to demand-side programs. The ratio is that of France: 30/70. In other words, 70% prevention, education, and treatment and 30% law enforcement. To its credit, the Clinton administration has begun to change the ratio in this direction.

Other domestic programs might be reduced, eliminated, or more cost-effectively managed at great savings to the taxpayer if we garner the political will to overcome powerful lobbyists. To cite just a few examples, we could eliminate the National Helium Reserve (which was created for World War I blimps), the Interstate Commerce Commission (which produces a great deal of paperwork but very little benefit for consumers), the space station (which represents a luxury during a period of massive social and economic deficits), the "weed and seed" program (which is heavy on law-enforcement weeding but provides little new revenues for educational and employment seeding), and the "McGruff" crime dog program (which a recent Justice Department study has shown not to reduce crime).

These are very modest suggestions. Other reports like *Mandate for Change* by the Progressive Policy Institute have far longer lists of programs with far more reductions and eliminations. These lists should be carefully examined. For example, the Institute lists domestic and international programs that provide federal subsidies for special interests that could be phased out as part of a plan to control lobbyists (see chapter 8). Savings of approximately $7 billion could be achieved in the first year and approximately $35 billion over four years.

The House Government Operations Committee has issued a report specifying nearly $15 billion in potential annual savings in the near term if administrative or legislative changes were made in programs ranging from student loans to timber sales.

■ Military Spending

The Cold War is over, yet decreases in the military budget have been relatively small. The congressional rule preventing reallocating military and foreign-aid monies to domestic budgets should be overturned.

The best way to reduce the defense budget is to define defense needs, then build a budget to meet those needs. As former Secretary of Defense Robert McNamara concluded:

> You go to ground zero. This is a new era. It's the post-Cold War world. You start with a blank sheet of paper. You begin with a statement of our foreign policy objectives, you examine the threats necessary to overcome to achieve those objectives. You consider the military strategy, the force structure required to address those threats, and that's your budget.

Many well-qualified experts across the political spectrum support significant cuts in military spending. Reductions in the Strategic Defense Initiative are high

The congressional rule preventing reallocating military and foreign-aid monies to domestic budgets should be overturned.

on many lists. William W. Kaufman, a defense analyst for several U.S. defense secretaries, concluded in a Brookings Institution study that the United States can reduce its defense budget to less than $200 billion per year over the next 10 years without undermining its post-Cold War global commitments or its position in arms-control negotiations. Three past chairmen of the Joint Chiefs of Staff have testified before Congress that the United States does not need to deploy outmoded missile systems. Former Reagan administration defense official Lawrence J. Korb has a plan to contract the armed forces "in recognition of the political–fiscal realities" of a changing world. *Business Week* points to 20 stultifying pages of Pentagon details necessary for procurements of underwear, hand towels, and hot chocolate. It observes, "In a $4T economy with a $1T federal budget there is surely room for some shifts in spending"—including a shift "away from guns and toward people." The conservative British *Economist* has argued that the United States can do without more aircraft carriers. A recent Senate Budget Committee report stated that the Pentagon has stockpiled at least $30 billion of spare parts, uniforms, and other equipment that it does not need. The report also found that the Department of Defense has orders in for $1.8 billion in supplies that its own auditors say should be canceled. A Harvard Business School study has concluded that $40 billion a year could be saved through improved Defense Department management and quality control.

Common Cause has identified "tons" of congressional military pork. For example, $20 million per year is used to install new gasoline engines in army trucks—despite a 10-year surplus of engines and plans to convert the trucks to other fuels. Another $238 million has been appropriated for 12 more Marine Corps amphibious barges, which propel equipment from ship to shore. Yet as these monies were appropriated, funds for supply ships to carry the barges were cut. In each case, the appropriations passed because a member of Congress was in a position to demand and obtain local pork.

The federal government currently spends approximately one-sixteenth as much on all employment and training activities as it does on military procurement alone. Community-based extended family programs must hold bake sales to help finance drug-abuse prevention programs. Funded at $500 million per year, the Corporation for Youth and Family Investment which we propose costs five-sixths of one B-2 stealth bomber.

Powerful lobbyists and members of Congress seeking pork for their constituents offer great resistance to reductions in military expenditures. However, a well-planned military-conversion program can overcome some of this resistance. The rest depends on presidential and congressional leadership and courage. We agree with the Kaufman plan. The Cold War is over. Our military budget ought to reflect it. We believe that military reductions must be in terms of actual outlays, not merely smaller increases in future expenditures.

■ Agency for International Development

The end of the Cold War has diminished political and popular support of American foreign aid administered by the Agency for International Development (AID), a semiautonomous agency under the general policy direction of the State

Chapter 7

Department. As the war and atrocities in the former Yugoslavia and in other areas of the world demonstrate, new foreign policy challenges are emerging. But the role of foreign aid in meeting these new challenges is unclear. A General Accounting Office (GAO) report concluded that AID does not have a strategic mission for carrying out its role, pointing to a complicated and incoherent set of objectives with no specific priorities in place. The agency has been buffeted by the agendas of other competing federal agencies, by the active role that Congress has taken in programming its decisions, and by the lobbying of special-interest groups.

Beyond strategic goals, the GAO report concluded that AID was mismanaged in the 1980s. For example, the agency did not emphasize the evaluation of program results during this time and did not collect baseline and outcome data needed for scientific assessment. In addition, according to the GAO report, AID had serious accounting and financial reporting problems that prevented the agency from determining reliably the status of appropriated funds, whether property on hand was paid for, and resources used to achieve program results. For example, in 1992, AID had $418 million in disbursements unmatched with corresponding obligations, some for as long as 10 years.

> New foreign policy challenges are emerging, but the role of foreign aid in meeting these new challenges is unclear.

Annual appropriations for AID have been in the $6 billion to $7 billion range. Yet throughout the 1980s, lack of strategic direction and sound management created a pipeline of obligated but unspent funds exceeding $6 billion.

The Clinton administration has implemented much needed reform, and we do see the need for foreign economic aid—as long as it is well managed, targeted on strategic objectives that have been redesigned for the post–Cold War world, and promotes democracy. Expanded aid to South Africa, for example, fits these priorities. But the present need to focus on the economic development of the underdeveloped world *within the United States* is greater. Given the current new priority on American economic development, particularly in terms of investment in human capital, we believe that there should be a substantial reduction in the size of the AID budget for the foreseeable future. Over each of the next 10 years, we believe that $2 billion to $4 billion per year of our plan for children, youth, families, and the inner city should be financed by cutting the AID budget in half. The AID pipeline of obligated but unspent funds should be reduced.

> We see the need for foreign economic aid—as long as it is well managed, targeted on strategic objectives that have been redesigned for the post–Cold War world, and promotes democracy.

The same kind of comprehensive reassessment, accompanied by reduced funding that is reallocated to U.S domestic policy, is needed when it comes to U.S. contributions to the World Bank and International Monetary Fund.

■ Reducing Entitlements to the Rich

Entitlement programs benefit primarily middle-class and poor families. Social Security, unemployment insurance, and tax deductions for mortgage interest are especially important to the middle class. In addition, the poor receive entitlements such as AFDC, Medicaid, food stamps, and eligibility for child-nutrition programs.

Some current proposals have asked to place a ceiling on total entitlement program costs. Under such plans, for example, during any year in which projected entitlement costs surpassed the ceiling, congressional committees with jurisdiction over entitlements would need to pass legislation to reduce costs. If legislation was not enacted, according to such plans, across-the-board cuts in entitlement programs would occur. Usually such proposals exempt across-the-board cuts for programs relevant to the middle class, such as Social Security and unemployment insurance. However, such proposals usually do not exempt entitlements for the poor, such as AFDC, Medicaid, food stamps, and child nutrition.

We agree that total entitlement costs are growing rapidly, threatening to increase the national debt even more. But entitlement costs are growing primarily in the area of health care. Figure 15 (see chapter 4) compares per-capita health care spending among the United States, Japan, European countries, and Canada. Even though U.S. health care insurance is not as comprehensive as in these countries, our costs are higher. So we do not recommend a ceiling on total entitlement costs or any sequester that is biased against poor families. A more equitable strategy is to reform the health care system and to impose tough cost constraints on it.

As part of the political rhetoric from 1981 to 1992, entitlements have been associated with the poor. Yet, over this period, there has been a tremendous increase in what can be called entitlements for the rich—mainly tax breaks.

■ Corporate Entitlements and Welfare

Ignoring the cost of corporate entitlements and welfare distorts the debate on AFDC. Most taxpayers do not realize that, in 1994, they spent $51 billion in direct subsidies to businesses and another $53.3 billion in tax breaks to corporations.

In 1994, the most costly form of corporate welfare consisted of $29 billion in subsidies for agribusiness. By comparison, the 1994 cost of food stamps was $25 billion and of AFDC was $15 billion. The U.S. Bureau of Land Management (BLM) is a case in point:

> The BLM rents out public lands to ranchers for cattle grazing. In 1992 the BLM's annual grazing fee was $1.92 per animal, according to the National Wildlife Federation. But private landowners charge their grazing customers, on average, $9.26 per animal. The low grazing fees amount to a food stamp program for livestock belonging to wealthy ranchers. In 1992, the government's below-market rates cost the taxpayers an estimated $55 million in revenues.

A typical beneficiary of this subsidy is J. R. Simplot of Grandview, Idaho. He paid the government $87,430 for the privilege to graze cattle on public land, according to the National Wildlife Federation. If the government had billed Mr. Simplot at free-market prices he would have had to pay $410,524. It is not as if Mr. Simplot is going to suffer without public assistance. He is on the Forbes' 400 list of richest Americans with an estimated net worth of over $500 million.

Agricultural corporate welfare extends into many other areas. Why, for example, are there tobacco subsidies when cigarette smoking causes cancer? Why does the Agriculture Department annually give away to Sunkist, E. & J. Gallo Winery, Campbell's Soup, McDonald's and the manufacturers of M & Ms $100 million for foreign advertising?

Most taxpayers do not realize that, in 1994, they spent $51 billion in direct subsidies to businesses and another $53.3 billion in tax breaks to corporations.

Chapter 7

Beyond agriculture subsidies, American taxpayers spend billions more on subsidizing timber (to bail out loggers), oil companies (to drill hard-to-reach wells), utility companies that serve rural areas (long after electrification of those areas), and mining companies.

Although powerful lobbyists will be in opposition, we are confident that the majority of American taxpayers would support repeal of the virtually unlimited deduction for interest on corporate debt and elimination of tax subsidies for companies that eliminate jobs in the U.S. and create jobs offshore.

Billions of dollars in taxes are owed by foreign-controlled companies that do business in the United States. Laws governing taxation of foreign-owned companies that do business in the United States need to be enforced. Estimates of lost revenues range widely from $3 billion per year to $30 billion per year.

■ Increasing Income Taxes on the Rich

In chapter 1, we discussed how personal income taxes increased for poor and middle-class families and decreased for the wealthy throughout the 1980s. For example, the incomes of the wealthiest 1% increased by more than 120% from 1977 to 1988. During this period, the highest individual tax rate was reduced from approximately 70% to 28%, and the income tax became much less progressive. *Countries such as France, Germany, Italy, and Japan have much wider gaps in tax rates between the wealthy and the poor.* Among the 24 wealthiest nations, only Turkey collects a lower percentage of gross domestic product in taxes than does the United States. The Paris-based Organization for Economic Cooperation and Development concluded that the United States "would remain among the least taxed even if taxes were raised sufficiently to balance the federal budget."

Using another comparison, to finance the integration of East Germany, Germany increased taxes. However, even if the United States were to match the old, lower level of German taxes, according to Elliott Currie, we would generate an astonishing $400 billion more per year in revenues:

> And German taxes are in the middle of the European range. The Scandinavian countries, France, Holland, and Austria tax much higher. Their relatively higher tax burdens have apparently not hurt their ability to complete in the international economic arena.

We believe that a significant increase in taxes should be instituted for the wealthiest 1% in the United States. Raising the tax rate for the richest Americans to approximately 40% would put the United States in line with Great Britain but still keep the United States far below rates in France (57%), Germany (56%), Italy (50%), and Japan (50%).

How much new revenue would be generated by significantly increasing taxes on the rich? The Congressional Budget Office estimates that such an increase might yield, at a maximum, $40 billion over four years. The rich, however, have considerable flexibility in terms of exposing income to taxation. For example, if the income tax is raised but the capital-gains tax remains the same, the rich can convert ordinary income into capital gains income. So the capital-gains tax must be raised in tandem with personal income tax.

Considering how voodoo economics in the 1980s hurt the middle class and the poor, they should receive tax decreases at the same time that taxes are increased on the rich. The goal should be a net increase in revenue to the government.

■ Taxes on Alcohol and Tobacco

Several billion dollars per year in revenues could be raised by increasing excise taxes on alcoholic beverages and cigarettes with the added benefit of decreasing alcohol- and tobacco-related health costs as well as the complex social costs associated with their consumption. In real terms, taxes on these items have decreased sharply in recent decades. Adjusted for inflation, taxes on alcohol are only approximately 25% of taxes in the early 1950s; taxes on cigarettes are closer to 50%. Doubling these taxes would raise approximately $10 billion a year. New findings from the Environmental Protection Agency showing that second-hand cigarette smoke is a human carcinogen may make raising cigarette taxes more feasible politically.

Public and Political Support

In 1992, before the Los Angeles riots, a *New York Times* national poll asked: "If the U.S. saves a lot of money on defense spending in the next few years, what should most of the money be used for?" Possible answers were reducing the deficit, domestic needs, and tax cuts. Seventy-two percent of respondents chose "domestic needs," 14% chose "deficit reduction," and 8% chose "tax cuts." These priorities held among Republicans, Democrats, and independents. In 1992, immediately after the Los Angeles riots, the *New York Times* and CBS asked in a nationwide poll (Figure 19): "Are we spending too much money, too little money, or about the right amount of money on problems of the big cities, on improving the conditions of blacks, and on the poor?" Sixty percent of the respondents stated that too little was being spent on problems of the big cities, 61% said that too little was being spent on improving the condition of African Americans, and 64% said that too little was being spent on problems of the poor. The pollsters also asked, "To reduce racial tension and prevent riots, would more jobs and job training help a lot, help a little or not make much difference?" Seventy-eight percent of the respondents said that more jobs and job training would help a lot.

In 1993, a citizens' jury representative of voters throughout the nation voted for $70 billion in tax increases, including $20 billion in "sin taxes" on cigarettes and alcohol and $30 billion in income tax increases on Americans who earn more than $200,000 per year.

Politically, the list of corporations that have funded or otherwise supported nonprofit community-based economic development organizations such as those discussed here reads like the *Fortune* 500. The recent bipartisan National Commission on Children, chaired by Senator Jay Rockefeller, called for implementation of Head Start for all eligible children and for increased support of Job Corps. The corporate executive officers on the Committee for Economic Development have endorsed Head Start as the most cost-effective prevention plan yet devised. The Fairview Homes public housing program was begun in 1979 as a Carter administra-

Chapter 7

tion urban initiative and received awards as a national model program in 1985 and 1987. Moreover, most of these initiatives, or their underlying concepts, have been embraced by reports issued by the Carnegie Corporation and the William T. Grant Foundation.

To us, all of this is proof that political support exists for doing what works. The 1994 elections signified an impatience by the citizenry for solutions.

Opinions on how much is being spent on . . .

- Too much
- Too little
- Just right
- Don't know

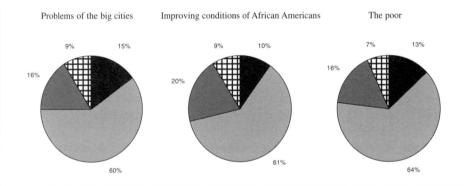

Opinions on whether or not racial tension and riots could be reduced or prevented by . . .

- Very helpful
- Somewhat helpful
- No difference

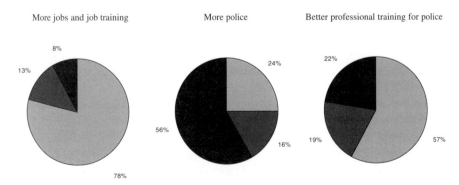

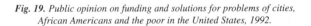

Fig. 19. Public opinion on funding and solutions for problems of cities, African Americans and the poor in the United States, 1992.

130

Chapter 8

Mobilizing Citizens and Families to Reform Congress And the Media

To a considerable extent, we know what doesn't work, what does work, and the technical solutions to finance effective policies and programs at a scale equal to the dimensions of the domestic problem. But inner-city family policy will not be refomed until the political process is reformed. Articulating policy and financing reform is meaningless if we fail to identify and overcome the political obstacles that hinder reform.

This chapter summarizes the political changes most needed: controlling lobbyists, diminishing the impact of powerful interest groups, imposing term limits while reforming campaign financing, and making Congress more honest, efficient, and capable of legislating family-friendly policies for the inner city.

> Rehabilitating democracy will require citizens to devote themselves first to challenging the status quo, disrupting the contours of power and opening the way to renewal. [Common citizens must engage their environments and] question the conflict between what they are told and what they see and experience.
> **William Greider**
> *Who Will Tell The People*

Congress may have neither the ability nor the will to reform itself. Like Walt Whitman, then, we must put our faith in the common people. Aided by private-sector foundation support, grass-roots nonprofit organizations must assume a leadership role in fighting for political reform, advocating for effective inner-city programs, and reforming the media establishment.

Controlling Lobbyists

In *Who Will Tell the People: The Betrayal of American Democracy*, William Greider concluded, "Organized money is ascendant and organized people are inert, because money has learned how to do modern politics more effectively than anyone else." In presidential campaigns and congressional campaigns, the notion of "one person, one vote" does not hold true in America today. Big money distorts decisions on family policy, tax policy, defense spending, bank reform, health care reform, housing reform, education reform, and gun control to the detriment of the poor and the cities.

Chapter 8

Health-insurance companies have blocked universal coverage financed by employers. Throughout the 1980s, Congress allowed itself to be bullied by the banking industry, resulting in deregulation, the savings-and-loan scandal, and a bailout costing taxpayers more than $400 billion. Lobbyists, wealthy individuals, and corporations fund election campaigns. Presidential campaigns now cost more than $100 million. The winner of a Senate race spends approximately $4 million. House races cost more than $300,000. Most of this money is spent on media coverage, particularly television advertising. As a result, members of Congress must spend so much time on fund-raising activities that they have insufficient time to think through effective policies. Congress normally does not schedule voting on Mondays and Fridays so that members can raise money at home and in Washington, D.C.

As playwright Arthur Miller concluded:

> We can do away with hypocrisy by making Congress a private enterprise. Let each representative and senator openly represent, and have his salary paid by, whatever business group wishes to buy his vote. Then, with no excuses, we will really have the best representative system money can buy. No longer will absurdly expensive election campaigns be necessary. Anyone wanting the job of Congressional representative of, say, the drug industry could make an appointment with the council of that industry and make his pitch. . . .
>
> Possible objections: the abstract idea of justice would disapear under a system that takes only private economic interests into account. Secondly, the corporate state, which this resembles, was Mussolini's concept and resulted in the looting of the public by private interests empowered by the state.
>
> Objections to the objections: we already have a corporate state. All privatization would do would be to recognize it as a fact.

■ Campaign Finance Reform for Presidential Races

For national campaigns, federal rules seem clear enough. Individuals can donate up to $20,000 to political parties for the support of national candidates. Corporations and labor unions cannot donate anything. However, in practice, the rules have been interpreted so as to allow a large loophole, often called the "sewer money" loophole. That is, donations of any amount can be made if the money is placed into a separate account for administrative costs or for party activities such as voter-registration drives. Of course, this "soft money" frees up more "hard money" for the national candidates.

This is not the way things are supposed to be. After the Watergate scandal, campaign laws were passed to curb the influence of big-money donations. Laws stated that Republican and Democratic nominees were to run their full campaigns exclusively on public funds, which amounted to $55 million for each party in the 1992 campaign.

The loophole, however, has allowed the two major presidential parties to seek funds from wealthy individuals, labor unions, and corporations. The two national parties have raised over $135 million in sewer and soft monies since 1981.

> **Members of Congress must spend so much time on fund-raising activities that they have insufficient time to think through effective policies.**

Mobilizing Citizens
And Families

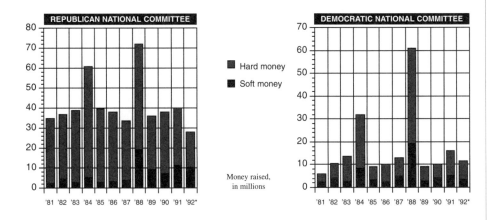

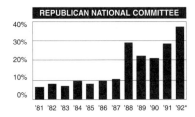 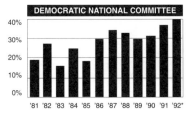

Top soft money donors to National Republican Party
Committees, 1988–June 1992.

1.	Archer Daniels Midland	$1,157,000
2.	American Financial Corp.	$965,000
3.	Atlantic Richfield Co.	$862,000
4.	RJR Nabisco	$802,000
5.	International Marketing Bureau	$574,000
6.	U.S. Tobacco Co.	$568,000
7.	Henry Kravis, George Roberts, Paul Raither, and Robert I. MacDonnell of Kohlberg, Kravis, Roberts	$530,000
8.	Nicholas and Theodore Forstmann and William Brian Little of Forstmann Little & Co.	$488,000
9.	Merrill Lynch & Co.	$452,000
10.	Philip Morris	$383,000

Top soft money donors to National Democratic Party
Committees, 1988–June 1992.

1.	United Steelworkers of America	$757,000
2.	National Education Association	$582,000
3.	American Federation of State, County and Municipal Employees	$517,000
4.	United Auto Workers	$418,000
5.	Frederick W. and Susie Field, Los Angeles, film and record producer	$403,000
6.	Alida Rockefeller Messenger, Minneapolis, philanthropist	$400,000
7.	Sheet Metal Workers union	$388,000
8.	Richard J. Dennis, Chicago, commodities broker	$366,000
9.	RJR Nabisco	$320,000
10.	American Federation of Teachers	$296,000

Fig. 20. *The size of "soft money" or "sewer money" loophole in the United States campaign contributions, 1981–1992.*

The Republican National Committee has raised more of these soft monies than has the Democratic National Committee. But such monies are more important to the success of Democrats in that they account for 29% of the Democratic National Committee's resources, which is twice the percentage for the Republicans. Figure 20 shows the size of the sewer money loophole and lists some of its major contributors. We and many others recommend that this loophole be closed for national campaigns.

Chapter 8

■ Campaign Finance Reform for Congressional Races

The best way for Congress to reduce the influence of money is to limit the amount of cash raised and spent in a campaign. However, the U.S. Supreme Court has ruled that campaign spending is constitutionally protected. Consequently, congressional campaign spending can only be capped by following the current procedures for presidential campaigns, whereby candidates are offered public financing in exchange for voluntary limits on outlays. Under this plan, once an office seeker for Congress raises enough private money to reach a specified threshold, government funding kicks in. For example, under one proposal, candidates would qualify for matching funds by winning a primary and by raising either $250,000 or 10% of a general election ceiling, whichever is less.

Beyond public financing of congressional elections, candidates need to be given free broadcast time. Strict ceilings should be placed on the amounts that congressional candidates can raise in an election campaign. Equally explicit ceilings should be placed on the amount that individuals can donate to the candidates, campaign contributions from political-action committees should be forbidden, mass mailings and computer-generated letters by incumbents that actually function as campaign literature should be eliminated, and the Federal Election Commission should be replaced with an agency with enough clout to institute criminal sanctions instead of token fines when rules are broken. In addition, we need far shorter presidential and congressional campaigns.

Thanks to the work of the Common Cause anticorruption campaign, a substantial majority of the House and Senate members are publicly on record in favor of most of these campaign reforms. They now need to act on their promises. Nonprofit citizen groups must remind them of their promises.

■ Other Controls on Lobbyists

Hill and Knowlton, the huge Manhattan-based lobbying shop with major operations in Washington, D.C., is perhaps the most notorious lobbyist for hire, accepting some of the world's most unsavory clients: the People's Republic of China to enhance its image after the Tiananmen Square massacre, the brutal Duvalier dictatorship in Haiti, and the scandal-plagued bank of Credit and Commercial International. The daily activities of such lobbyists need to be placed under tighter control. Their clients and activities should be made public. A congressional bill requiring disclosure of embarrassing activities might inhibit a member of Congress from accepting expensive meals, exotic vacations, and other perks from lobbyists.

We endorse the Progressive Policy Institute's recommendation that a bipartisan commission be established by the President to reassess all programs that provide federal subsidies for special interest groups. With such a commission, special tax breaks for industries could be phased out as being unproductive entitlements to the wealthy.

Controlling the power of monied interests would help create a more level playing field for minorities and disadvantaged families as well as potentially raise new funding for inner-city families.

Mobilizing Citizens And Families

Reforming Congress

To eliminate gridlock, Congress must be reformed. Reform initiatives should include passing campaign fund reform, pressing Congress to institute policies that support long-term solutions for multiproblem families, and imposing term limits.

■ Campaign Reform

Campaign finance reform is not just the best way to control lobbyists; it also is the most effective way to keep Congress honest. The executive branch and citizen groups cannot allow Congress, and particularly the leadership of Congress on both sides of aisle, to back pedal on campaign-finance reforms proposed by Common Cause. Leaders of both parties in Congress may fear that such reform will lessen their power and thwart their personal and partisan ambitions. Every effort must be made by citizen groups to seal off corrupt special-interest monies away from Congress. Members of Congress who sell themselves to such lobbyists should be targeted by public-interest citizens groups.

■ Pressing Congress to Take a Long-Term View

Politicians generally take a short-term approach to community and national problems, seeking quick solutions to complex problems so they can claim political credit for responding to immediate needs while pacifying powerful interest groups. But fragmented solutions to multiple problems rarely work in the long term. Legislators need to be educated about the long-term benefits of comprehensive legislative packages that confront multiple problems. The General Accounting Office, the Congressional Budget Office, and the Office of Technology Assessment can help in this task by publicizing reports on the failure of most legislation to include program-evaluation monies to support replication of programs that work. Great presidents like Lincoln and Roosevelt were able to articulate a long-term national vision that engaged citizens and forced the political system to respond. By defining and communicating the crises of their times, they were able to garner the political and public support needed to initiate comprehensive and long-term solutions to problems. Nonprofit organizations must help educate the public and politicians about solutions and programs that work and support leaders with a broad vision of the problems confronting the nation.

■ Term Limits—Only If Accompanied by Campaign Finance Reform

In a recent ABC/*Washington Post* poll, 83% of respondents said that their congressional representative was more interested in getting elected than in getting something done. Throughout the 1980s, Congress allowed funding for job training and placement for the poor to drop from $11 billion to $3 billion, housing appropriations for poor families to be cut by 80% while prison building tripled, and cumulative Star Wars spending to exceed $30 billion by the early 1990s. In 1994, despite the numerous polls indicating the desire of citizens to reform the health care system and to institute gun control, members of Congress from the minority side of the aisle, backed by the monied interests of the health-insurance industry and the

> Politicians generally take a short-term approach to community and national problems, seeking quick solutions to complex problems so they can claim political credit for responding to immediate needs while pacifying powerful interest groups.

Chapter 8

NRA, were able to block health care reform and nearly remove the ban on assault weapons from the 1994 crime bill.

After congressional debate on the 1994 crime bill, many voters in an informal *New York Times* survey concluded that the problems of governance in America are rooted in the institutions of Washington itself—from politicians, whose convictions shift with the latest polls, to lobbyists, whose contributions are the lifeblood of campaigns, to the news media, which thrive on conflict.

In the 1992 elections, term-limit proposals were on the ballot in 14 states; each proposal passed decisively. Strong antiincumbent feelings continued in the 1993 and 1994 elections. But we need to impose uniform federal term limits. Some states now have limits of 6 years; others have limits of 8 or 12 years. Without uniform limits states without term limitations have an advantage in Congress.

The long-term success of federal term limits in Congress depends on unelected staff people and consultants being cycled out of positions of power and influence. They should leave with the elected officials who appointed them so that they do not become a permanent bureaucratic ruling elite. Because term limits do not necessarily militate against electing new members of Congress who are also influenced by campaign money from special interest groups or who are wealthy enough to take off time from a career to campaign, campaign-finance reform must be linked to federal term limits. The goal should be to give more Americans the opportunity to run for Congress. Lack of personal wealth should not be a barrier.

Promoting Grass-Roots Leadership by Citizens

To reverse the political betrayals of the American family, and democracy itself, we need national leaders who are courageous, lobbyists who are controlled, and legislatures that are honest and efficient. In the words of William Greider, "Rehabilitating democracy will require citizens to devote themselves first to challenging the status quo, disrupting the contours of power and opening the way to renewal." Common citizens must engage their environments and "question the conflict between what they are told and what they see and experience." Organizations such as Family Service America, the Children's Defense Fund, Common Cause, Congress Watch, the Center on Budget and Policy Priorities, and many others need to be supported in their work for family and policy reforms. Such organizations need funding to expand their activities, and other organizations like them need to be created and developed. These organizations serve as watchdogs on the federal process. The foundation community in the United States needs to significantly increase its financial support of these watchdog organizations.

■ Organizing to Replicate What Works

The Children's Defense Fund is a good example of grass-roots organizing in support of family priorities. Over recent years, the Children's Defense Fund has lobbied for and won more than a 10% increase in Head Start funding. The public-interest lobby for reform of the Job Training Partnership Act is not nearly as strong as is the children's lobby; it deserves more support from foundations. The public-

> Organizations such as Family Service America, the Children's Defense Fund, Common Cause, Congress Watch, the Center on Budget and Policy Priorities, and many others need to be supported in their work for family and policy reforms.

interest lobby for changing the delivery of new and rehabilitated housing for the poor is emerging more rapidly as a result of the success of LISC and the Enterprise Foundation during the past decade. Currently, there is no significantly strong public-interest lobby for private-sector nonprofit organizations for children, youth, and family development nonprofits—such as Argus, Centro, and Delancey Street. The Corporation for Youth and Family Investment proposed here could become that lobby. However, if it were financed through federal funds, the lobbying work would need to be placed into a separate organization funded by foundations and individuals, which would have the advantage of focusing on advocacy of multiple-solutions approaches to multiple problems.

■ Organizing to Reform the Political Process

The Common Cause Anticorruption Campaign is a prime example of a nonprofit organization working to reform the political process. Its efforts should be reinforced and expanded via increased foundation support.

Organizations such as Congress Watch also need support, for example, to remind citizens that, despite talk of reform by new members of Congress in 1993, a congressional committee in great demand for membership was the House Public Works Committee—the committee with the most pork to distribute.

Other less well known nonprofits show how citizens are improving the work of our democracy. In Oregon, Project Vote Smart satisfies voter demand for impartial and factual information about people seeking office in their states. During the most recent presidential campaign, the project answered more than 200,000 calls requesting information on the policy position, backgrounds, and financiers of congressional and presidential candidates. Project Vote Smart's budget was approximately $1.5 million, that is, approximately what a presidential candidate raises in a single fund raiser. The money came from foundations and membership funds.

Similarly, in Pennsylvania in 1992, the Citizens Jury Project assembled "juries" representative of population mixes in various parts of Pennsylvania. Each jury examined rivals in the U.S. Senate race, reviewing issues such as education, health care, and the economy. The jury then rendered a "verdict" on the candidates. The project also has begun juries on reducing federal expenditures and increasing taxes.

■ Increasing Voter Registration

Ideally, anticorruption and voter-education projects will increase voter registration and turnout at the polls. The United States has the lowest level of voter turnout of any major democracy. The 55% turnout in the 1992 Presidential election was the largest in nearly 30 years. Typically, fewer than half of all eligible voters come to the polls in a presidential election year. The least likely groups to register and to vote are poor and minority voters in large cities. Here registration is the major barrier; when the poor are registered, more than two-thirds of them vote.

How, then, do we increase voter registration among the poor and disadvantaged? The Canadian system offers some guidelines. When an election is called, a complete national registration is carried out in a matter of weeks by an agency called Election Canada. More than 70% of eligible voters go to the polls in Canada.

The United States has the lowest level of voter turnout of any major democracy.

Chapter 8

Reforming the Media

After the 1992 Los Angeles riot, a national New York Times/CBS News poll asked Americans to identify the biggest obstacle to urban reform. Fifty-two percent said "a lack of knowledge" (see Figure 21). This opinion may result in part from the effectiveness of well-financed lobbies, which during the past 30 years have successfully conveyed through the media the message that little works in the public sector. For example, the Heritage Foundation in Washington, D.C., the largest and best-financed foundation promoting this message, has a television studio on its premises. Nonprofit initiatives are needed to train a new generation of media specialists who can articulate programs and policies that do work. For better or worse, the electronic media will continue to affect the opinions and attitudes of American citizens.

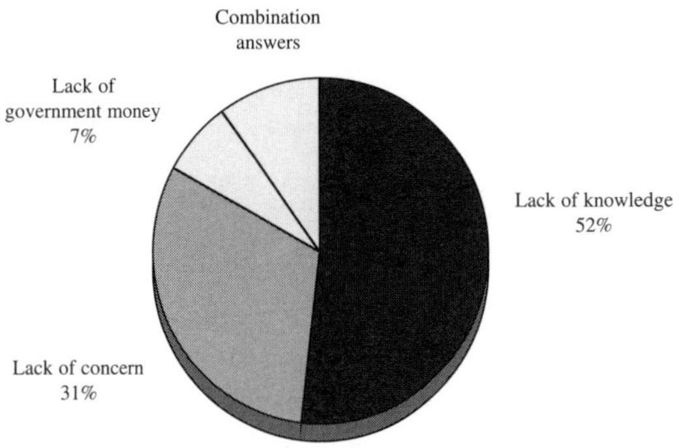

Fig. 21. Responses to a 1992 New York Times/CBS News survey question seeking public opinion with regard to the greatest difficulty facing any money-spending effort to solve problems of cities.

Former Senate Majority Leader George Mitchell observed, "What is not controversial is not news." Proponents of innovative programs and policies must learn to combat the media's tendency to create conflict and controversy. Television interviewers and news reporters seek conflict and opposition because they perceive controversy in terms of ratings and profits. Advocates for inner-city families need to learn how not to respond to loaded questions and to promote their views within a framework in which they feel comfortable. Good television can promote consensus building.

Coalitions of national nonprofit organizations must push television networks and local stations to expand public announcements and provide coverage of policies and programs that work. We envision Patrick Ewing describing the Argus Community in New York, former Surgeon General Antonio Novello showing how Puerto Rico's Centro Isolina Ferre has benefited the community, Bill Cosby talking to program directors at the Challengers Boys and Girls Club in south central Los Angeles, Maya Angelou exploring Family Service America's Families Together with Schools program, Michael Jordan hanging out with Youth Development members in Chicago, and the President and First Lady informing the public about the City Lights School in Washington, D.C. Such well-known public figures would help provide credibility for leaders of successful inner-city programs. As Neal Peirce asks in the National Journal:

> Where in films and television are some of the real heroes of today's urban America? What about the amazing civic entrepreneurs who head community development corporations or the dedicated, fervent citizens who work

Nonprofit initiatives are needed to train a new generation of media specialists who can articulate programs and policies that do work.

to make homeless shelters homey, havens for battered women humane, and health clinics caring?

The purpose of such public service advertising should not be to make the poor less likely to have babies or commit crime or more likely to stay in school or stick with job training. Rather, the purpose should be to convince citizens that we do know what works and teach them how to press their political representatives to pass legislation in support of such programs and policies.

We should not fund establishment organizations to produce public-service messages that, in effect, seek to impose their own values on minority families. We need to fund more minority producers to generate public-service ads. Currently many national and local nonprofit organizations are capable of producing effective messages. For example, the Dorchester Youth Collaborative (see chapter 4) has the technical ability to produce and market videos containing public-service messages.

Public-opinion experts estimate that it takes up to 10 years between the introduction and public acceptance of a new idea. The problems of inner-city families have been decades and generations in the making. Ten years is a relatively short period for changing attitudes on how such problems might be resolved.

The media have also failed to communicate clearly programs and policies that don't work. For example, there has been little media coverage comparing welfare dependency of the poor with government welfare entitlements to corporations. During the debate on the 1994 crime bill, little coverage was focused on the fact that prison building and boot camps don't work, based on available scientific evidence. The press bungled the savings-and-loan fiasco. Reporter Howard Kunz concluded that "in the 1980s, most reporters and most editors . . . didn't want to challenge the government on a lot of fundamental stuff. . . . No news media organization wanted to question authority." And similarly, in her exposé of lobbyist Robert Gray, Susan Trento concluded,

> Nothing seems to get cleaned up. From Watergate to Koreagate to Debategate to the Sex and Drug investigation to Iran-Contra to the Savings and Loan and HUD scandals to BCCI, it seems that the same people are doing the same things over and over, and never getting punished—and no one seems to care. *The triangle—the media, the government, and the lobbying and PR firms—protect each other* [emphasis added].

Nonprofit organizations must expose this "triangle" as well as pressure the media to report on policies that don't.

Some indications of responsible media behavior are evident. The *Charlotte Observer*, for example, initiated the "Your Vote in '92" project in North Carolina. Before the political campaign began, the newspaper polled readers on the issues that they cared most about—a kind of needs assessment. The *Observer* then oriented its coverage to the public's greatest needs and concerns. Articles outlined alternative solutions to problems, and positions taken by the candidates on those solutions were assessed. As a result, voter turnout increased by nearly one-third from 1988 to 1992 in the area where the paper is based.

Public-opinion experts estimate that it takes up to 10 years between the introduction and public acceptance of a new idea.

Chapter 8

Other newspapers around the nation have also improved their coverage of important local and national issues. For example, "Ad Watch" boxes that analyze and evaluate the content and honesty of candidate advertisements became more common in newspapers across the nation. Even some radio and television coverage became more substantive in the 1992 campaign. National Public Radio continued its stellar coverage of campaign issues, and MTV's "Rock the Vote" initiative attempted to draw young people to the ballot box.

Perhaps the most salient electronic media campaign contribution to the 1992 election occurred during the series of presidential and vice presidential debates in October 1992. The four debates allowed considerable time for the media to cover issues. Ross Perot, the independent candidate, was allowed to debate, which added a fresh perspective on issues. The decision to allow, at least in one debate, the candidates to meet and interact with the audience, if they wished, in a town-hall-type setting proved immensely popular with the voters and provided new insights into the candidates. It is important to note that such coverage was the result of the bipartisan Commission on Presidential Debates, a nonprofit entity supported by private funding. Given the success of this commission, we urge private funders to address the public's hunger for substantive policy initiatives that emerged during the debates.

The Challenges Within

As John Gardner warned, grass-roots organizations and citizen-action groups must be prepared to make sacrifices. Throughout the 1980s, America consumed too much and saved too little. Quick fixes were substituted for public responsibility. The trillion-dollar debt represents a tax on our children. Americans must have the intelligence, willingness, courage, and strength to face hard realities. We must resist congressional reversions to the voodoo economics and prison building of the 1980s—and to cuts in the most successful programs like Head Start and remedial education linked to job training and placement for high-risk youth. We must acknowledge the need for long-term solutions based on what works. To paraphrase Vaclav Havel, we must rediscover within ourselves a deeper sense of responsibility toward the world.

This young nation's most serious challenges to date have been external. Serious external dangers remain, but the graver threats to America, and to the American and inner family, are internal. The political climate in Washington, D.C., today reflects internal decay. The greatness and durability of most civilizations has been finally determined by how they have responded to these challenges from within. Ours will be no exception.

> **The greatness and durability of most civilizations has been finally determined by how they have responded to challenges from within.**

Sources

Chapter One

Abramowitz (1989), Barringer (1992), Center on Budget and Policy Priorities (1988), Children's Defense Fund (1994), Chira (1994), Cohn and Vobejda (1993), Cunningham (1991), Curtis (1991, 1994), DeParle (1991, 1993a), *Economist* (1989a), Edelman (1987), F.B.I. (1992), Furlong (1992), Greenfeld (1992), Guskind (1990), Levitan, Gallo, and Shapiro (1993), Mauer (1990, 1992), McAllister (1990), McFate and Reed (1992), National Advisory Commission on Civil Disorders (1968), National Commission on the Causes and Prevention of Violence (1969), National Commission on Children (1993), Phillips (1990), Scruggs (1993a, 1993b), Sentencing Project (1992), Shapiro and Greenstein (1991), Toner (1992), Vobejda (1989, 1992a), Youth Indicators (1991), Zuckerman (1992).

Chapter Two

Alexander (1995), Allen (1994), Apple (1995), Associated Press (1994), Baker (1995), Balz and Haveman (1995), Birdsong (1989), Brinkley (1994), Califano (1995), Center on Budget and Policy Priorities (1994), DeParle (1994a, 1994b, 1994c), Dowd (1994), Edelman (1986), Ford Foundation (1989, 1992), Gibbs (1994), Gifford (1993), Gueron and Pauly (1991), Ifill (1993), Jencks (1992), Kuttner (1994), Lurie (1992), Marcus (1993), McFate, (1991), *Milwaukee Journal* (1994), *New York Times* (February 22, 1994; June 17, 1994; June 19, 1994; December 12, 1994; January 9, 1995; January 15, 1995), Pear (1995a, 1995b), Poliat et al. (1988), Rich (1993), Schorr (1988), Vobejda (1994a, 1994b, 1994c, 1994d, 1995a, 1995b), *Washington Post* (January 7, 1993; May 2, 1994; July 31, 1994; December 18, 1994; January 10, 1995), Wilkins (1995).

Chapter Three

The section on preschool is based on the following works: "Funds Available for New Englanders . . . " (1991), Berrueta-Clement et al. (1984), Chira (1994), Children's Defense Fund (1994), Hamburg (1987), Harris (1987, 1990), Smolow (1992), Teitelbaum (1993), *Washington Post* (April 8, 1994; July 31, 1994).

The section on inner-city school system innovation is based on the following works: Berger (1989), Carnegie Corporation (1992), Carnegie Council on Adolescent Development (1989), Carnegie Foundation for the Advancement of Teaching (1988), Fisher (1992), Fiske (1989, 1990), Hoffman and Broder (1989), Kinzer (1993), Milton S. Eisenhower Foundation (1993), Poliat et al. (1988), Schorr (1988), Schwartz (1993).

Chapter Four

The section on community-based extended family sanctuaries is based on the following works: Currie (1993), Curtis (1985, 1993a, 1993b, 1994), Dryfoos (1990), Ferre (1987), Fink et al. (1983), Freedman (1991), Kohn (1989), Mecs (1993), Milton S. Eisenhower Foundation (1990, 1993, 1995), *New York Times* (February 23, 1976), Schorr (1988), Silberman (1978), Silbert (1984), Sturz (1983, 1992), Whittemore (1992).

The section on job training reform is based on the following works: Auspos et al. (1989), Donahue (1989), Fisher (1992), Gross (1993), Karr (1992), Kaslow (1995), Killborn (1990), Levitan and Gallo (1992), Levitan et al. (1993), Mallar (1982), McFate (1991), Milton S. Eisenhower Foundation (1993), *New York Times* (February 17, 1992), Reich (1991), Rich (1992), Sklar (1989), Taggart (1981), USA Basics (1989), Youth Policy Institute (July 1989).

The section on health care reform is based on the following works: Blanksteen (1992), Field (personal communication, December 16, 1994), Himmelstein and Woolhandler (1992), *New York Times* (February 22, 1994), Pear (1993a, 1993b), Priest (1992a, 1992b, 1993a, 1993b, 1994), *Washington Post* (January 21, 1993).

Chapter Five

The section on community enterprise via nonprofit organizations funded by the federal government is based on the following works: Apgar et al. (1991), Atlas and Dreier (1992b), Chira (1993), Dreier (1991, 1992, 1993), Galster (1991), Gifford (1993), Gugliotta (1995), Kennedy (1968), Lehman (1992), Mariano (1991, 1992), Milton S. Eisenhower Foundation (1993), National Housing Task Force (1988), *National Journal* (1992), Peirce and Steinbach (1987), Quint (1992), Steinbach (1992), Struyk et al. (1989), Turner (1992), Turner et al. (1992), Urban Institute (1992), *Washington Post* (January 7, 1993; January 27, 1993), Wienk (1992), Youth Policy Institute (July 19, 1989; November 29, 1992), Zdenek (1989).

The sections on the investment gap, productivity, overall funding, and high-risk families are based on the following works: Bernstein (1993), Bernstein et al. (1993), Bolionis (1993), Borrus (1992), Broad (1992), Brotman (1993), Currie (1985, 1993), Garland and Delvare (1993), *Japan Times* (1992), Kuttner (1992a, 1992b), Leonard and Greenstein (1990), Levitan and Gallo (1992), Levitan et al. (1993), Lohr (1993), Madrick (1993), Marshall and Schram (1993), Milton S. Eisenhower Foundation (1993), National Advisory Commission on Civil Disorders (1968), Olson (1992), Passell (1992), Pearlstein (1992), Prestowitz (1990), Reich (1991, 1992), U.S. Conference of Mayors (1993).

Chapter Six

The sections on crime prevention, economic development, and police are based on the following works: Argus Community (1993), Bayley (1992), Clines (1992), Cuomo (1992), Currie (1985, 1993), Curtis (1985, 1992), Elliott (1991), Harrell and Peterson (1992), Hayes (1982), Matthews (1991), Mauer (1990), Milton S. Eisenhower Foundation (1990, 1993, 1995), National Commission on the Causes and Prevention of Violence (1969), Pate et al. (1986), Shinke et al. (1991), Skolnick and Bayley (1986), Spilette et al. (1991), *USA Today* (1992b), Youth Policy Institute (December 19, 1989c), Zedleski (1985).

The section on handgun control is based on the following works: Currie (1985, 1993), Curtis (1985), Milton S. Eisenhower Foundation (1993), National Commission on the Causes and Prevention of Violence (1969), *New York Times* (February 4, 1993), Sugarman (1992), *Washington Post* (July 1, 1991).

The section on drug prevention and treatment is based on the following works: Berke (1989), Bourgois (1989), Broder (1989), Currie (1985, 1993), Curtis (1989a, 1993b), DeLeon (1988), Eck and Spelman (1987), Isikoff (1992, 1993), Kolata (1989), Malcolm (1989), Rua (1990), Russell (1992), Treaster (1992a, 1992b, 1993), Williams (1989).

Sources

The section on the current politics of crime is based on the following works: Anderson (1994), Curtis (1985, 1994), Dewar (1994), Ifill (1994), Johnson and Dirk (1994) Marquand (1995), Seelye (1995), Treaster (1995).

Chapter Seven

The sections on neighborhood-based implementation, local and state investment, and the debt are based on the following works: Barr (1993), Brinkley (1994), Broder (1994b), National Advisory Commission on Civil Disorders (1968), *New York Times* (February 28, 1991), Peterson and Iver (1993), Rich (1993), Tolchin (1993).

The section on sources of funds is based on the following works: Alexander (1995), Atkinson (1989), Clymer (1992, 1993), Congressional Budget Office (1992), Currie (1993), Donahue (1994), *Economist* (1991), Friedman (1993a, 1993b), Gordon (1989a, 1989b), Hoffmann & Seidman (1990), Kelly (1992), Kinsley (1993), Kuttner (1995), *Manchester Guardian Weekly* (1989), Mann (1988a, 1988b), Marshall and Schram (1993), McNamara (1992), Mufson (1993a, 1993b, 1993c), Mufson and Priest (1992), Nasar (1992), National Advisory Commission on Civil Disorders (1968), *New York Times* (February 4, 1990; March 8, 1990; March 9, 1990; June 14, 1992; November 10, 1992; November 30, 1992; January 17, 1995), Nunn (1990), Oreskes (1990), Pear (1993b), Rayburn (1993), Rosenbaum (1993), Rowen (1990), Schmitt (1992), Sciolino (1990), Shapiro and Greenstein (1989, 1991), Smith (1990), Taylor (1990), Tidwell (1992), Tylar (1989), Uchitelle (1990), USA *Today* (1992a), U.S. House of Representatives (1992), U.S. General Accounting Office (1992a, 1992b, 1992c), *Wall Street Journal* (1992), Wynes (1992), Youth Policy Institute (December 19, 1989a; December 19, 1989b).

The section on timing of a reform scenario and political feasibility is based on the following works: Applebone (1992), Johnson and Haynes (1994), Milton S. Eisenhower Foundation (1993), National Commission on Children (1993), Toner (1992).

Chapter Eight

The sections on controlling lobbyists and reforming Congress are based on the following works: "Alert!" (1992), Applebone (1992), Babcock (1992), Berke (1993), Broder (1992, 1993), Califano (1993), Cohen (1991, 1992), Committee for Economic Development (1987), Denny (1992a, 1992b), deTocqueville (1969 edition), Devroy (1993), *Economist* (1993), Egan (1993), Greider (1992), Ifill (1990), Johnson and Haynes (1994), *Los Angeles Times* (1992), Mann and Ornstein (1992), Marshall and Schram (1993), Mufson (1993c), *New York Times* (January 24, 1993; January 31, 1993; February 8, 1993; February 10, 1993; February 21, 1993), Nisbet (1992), Oreskes (1989b), Overby (1992), Pear (1993a), Rose (1994), Rotunda (1993), Sheilds (1994), *Washington Post* (January 6, 1993; February 7, 1993), Will (1993), Young (1992).

The sections on promoting grass-roots leadership by citizens and challenges are based on the following works: Belton and Coleman (1994), Broder (1992c), Children's Defense Fund (1994), Clairborne (1993), Greider (1992), Harrison (1993), Havel (1992), Johnson and Haynes (1994), Kennedy (1987), Kurtz (1992), Matthews (1992), Milton S. Eisenhower Foundation (1993), Moyers (1989), National Advisory Commission on Civil Disorders (1968), National Commission on the Causes and Prevention of Violence (1969), Royko (1993), Shapiro and Greenstein (1989), Shapiro and Greenstein (1991), Trento (1992).

Tables & Figures

Table 1 Source: Joint Center for Political and Economic Studies	18
Table 2	19
Table 3	19
Table 4	20
Table 5	20
Table 6	20
Table 7	21
Table 8 Source: Joint Center for Political and Economic Studies	21
Table 9 Sources: Organization for Economic Cooperation & Development; *Time*	48
Table 10 Sources: Educational Testing Service; Organization for Economic Cooperation & Development; *Business Week*	51
Table 11 Source: Office of Technology Assessment; *Business Week*	78
Figure 1 Source: Congressional Budget Office	23
Figure 2 Source: Organization for Economic Cooperation and Development; *New York Times*	24
Figure 3 Sources: Federation of American Scientists; Levitan, Gallo and Shapiro (1993)	25
Figure 4 Sources: Congressional Budget Office; Department of Commerce; Office of Management and Budget	25

Figure 5 26
Sources: Congressional Budget Office; New York Times

Figure 6 26
Sources: Internal Revenue Service; Federal Revenue Board; Barlett and Steele (1992)

Figure 7 27
Sources: The Sentencing Project; Penal Reform International

Figure 8 27
Source: New York Times

Figure 9 28
Sources: Center on Budget and Policy Priorities; Congressional Budget Office

Figure 10 30
Sources: U.S. Department of Justice; USA Today

Figure 11 31
Source: New York Times

Figure 12 31
Source: Van Dijk, et al. (1990)

Figure 13 46
Source: Berrueta, et al. (1984)

Figure 14 87
Sources: Unicef; Children's Defense Fund

Figure 15 88
Source: Organization for Economic Cooperation & Development

Figure 16 100
Sources: Congressional Budget Office; Business Week

Figure 17 101
Sources: Congressional Budget Office; Business Week

Figure 18 111
Source: Milton S. Eisenhower Foundation, Community Policing and Youth Development, May 1995

Figure 19 130
Source: New York Times/CBS News National Poll, May 1992

Figure 20 133
Sources: Center for Responsive Politics; Republican National Committee; Democratic National Committee; Washington Post

Figure 21 138
Source: New York Times/CBS News National Poll, May 1992

Bibliography

Abramowitz, Michael. "Infant Mortality Soars Here." *Washington Post*, September 30, 1989, p. l.

Allen, Jeanne. "Benefits of Choice." *New York Times*, November 8, 1993, p. A18.

Allen, Jodie T. "South Bronx Cheer: A Miracle Grows amid the Rubble." *Washington Post*, July 19, 1992, p. C3.

_____. "Welfare Terminator II." *Washington Post*, June 19, 1994, p. C1.

"Alert!" *Common Cause Magazine*, Fall 1992, p. 39.

Alexander, Richard. "First Reform Welfare for Corporations." *New York Times*, January 13, 1995, p. A30.

Ambrose, Stephen E. "Clinton Should Take a Cure from Roosevelt's Conservation Corps." *International Herald Tribune*, December 1, 1992, p. 4.

American Drug and Alcohol Survey. *Drug and Alcohol Use among Boston Public School Sixth through Eighth Graders*. Ft. Collins, CO: Author, 1988.

Anderson, David C. "The Criminal Funnel." *New York Times Magazine*, June 12, 1994, pp. 56–58.

Apgar, William C., et al. *The State of the Nation's Housing*. Cambridge, MA: Harvard University Press, 1991.

Apple, R. W., Jr. "You Say You Want a Devolution." *New York Times*, January 29, 1995, p. E1.

Applebone, Peter. "From Riots of the 60's, a Report for a Nation with Will and Way for Healing." *New York Times*, May 8, 1992, p. A19.

Argus Community. "Plan for a Residential Koban." Bronx, NY: Author, 1993.

Associated Press. "GAO Criticizes Welfare Training Effort." *Washington Post*, December 19, 1994, p. A8.

Atkinson, Rick. "Stealth: From Eighteen Inch Model to 70B Muddle." *Washington Post*, October 8, 1989, p. 1.

Atlas, John, and Peter Dreier. "From 'Projects' to Communities: How to Redeem Public Housing." *American Prospect*, Summer 1992a, p. 74.

_____, and Peter Dreier. *A National Housing Agenda for the 1990s*. Washington, DC: National Housing Institute, December 1992b.

Auspos, Patricia, George Cave, Fred Doolittle, and Gregory Hoerz. *Implementating Job Start: A Demonstration for School Dropouts in the JTPA System*. New York: Manpower Demonstration Research Corporation, June 1989.

Babcock, Charles R. "Both Parties Raise Millions in 'Soft Money.'" *Washington Post*, July 26, 1992, p. A1.

Baker, Russell. "Those Vital Papers." *New York Times*, January 17, 1995, p. A19.

Balz, Dan. "Studying the Mistakes of Carter's Presidency." *Washington Post*, November 29, 1992, p. A1.

_____, and Judith Havemann. "Governors Pushing Welfare Flexibility." *Washington Post*, January 30, 1995, p. A1.

Barlett, Donald L., and James B. Steele. *America: What Went Wrong?* New York: University Press Syndicate Company, March 1992.

Barr, Stephen. "House Panel's Report Details Wasted Billions." *Washington Post*, January 25, 1993, p. A15.

Barringer, Felicity. "Rich-Poor Gulf Widens among Blacks." *New York Times*, September 25, 1992, p. A12.

Bayley, David H. *Forces of Order: Police Behavior in Japan and the United States*. Berkeley, CA: University of California Press, 1992.

Beck, Joan. "Learning a Lesson in Harsh Reality." *Chicago Tribune*, October 29, 1994, p. 17.

Belton, Sharon Sayles, and Norm Coleman. "Coming: An Urban Primary." *New York Times*, August 9, 1994, p. A23.

Berger, Joseph. "East Harlem Students Clutch a College Dream." *New York Times*, August 27, 1989, p. 1.

Berke, Richard L. "President's 'Victory Over Drugs' Is Decades Away, Officials Say." *New York Times*, September 24, 1989, p. 1.

_____. "Clinton Rebuffed on Plan to Reduce Election Spending." *New York Times*, February 4, 1993, p. A1.

Bernstein, Aaron. "Replenishing Our Human Capital." *Business Week/Reinventing America*, January 19, 1993, pp. 78–79.

_____, Richard Brandt, Barbara Carlson, and Karen Padley. "Teaching Business How to Train." *Business Week*, January 19, 1993, pp. 82–90.

Berrueta-Clement, J. R., L. J. Schweinhart, W. S. Barnett, A. S. Epstein, and D. P. Weikhard. *Changed Lives: The Effects of the Perry Preschool Program on Youths through Age 19*. Ypsilanti, MI: Highscope Press, 1984.

Birdsong, Bret C. *Federal Enterprise Zones: "A Poverty Program for the 1990s?"* Washington, DC: Urban Institute, October 1989.

Blanksteen, Charles L. "'Managed Competition' Is Not Healthy Answer." *New York Times*, December 10, 1992, p. A26.

Bolionis, Steve. "Rebuilding America: The Mind-Numbering Cost." *Business Week*, January 19, 1993, p. 196.
Borrus, Michael, "Investing on the Frontier." *American Prospect*, Fall 1992, p. 80.
Bourgois, Philip. "Just Another Night on Crack Street." *New York Times Magazine*. November 12, 1989, p. 53.
Brinkley, Allan. "Reagan's Revenge." *New York Times Magazine*, June 19, 1994, pp. 36–37.
Broad, William J. "Clinton to Promote High Technology, with Gore in Charge." *Science Times*, November 10, 1992, p. C1.
Broder, David S. "Fighting Drugs: Can Do. . . . " *Washington Post*, August 9, 1989, p. A23.
_____. "Clinton in Arkansas: A Closer Look." *International Herald Tribune*, July 6, 1992a, p. 4.
_____. "Congress Is Put on Probation." *Honolulu Advertiser*, November 25, 1992b, p. A3.
_____. "There's No Debate: These Efforts Made Voters Count in '92." *Milwaukee Sentinel*, December 29, 1992c, p. A10.
_____. "No Status Quo State Houses." *Washington Post*, February 7, 1993, p. C7.
_____. "Why We Lose with Term Limits." *Washington Post*, February 9, 1994a, p. A23.
_____. "To Save the Cities, Go Metro." *Washington Post*, July 10, 1994b, p. A27.
Brotman, Barbara. "Beethoven's 5th." *Chicago Tribune*, October 22, 1992. Section 5, p. l.
Califano, Joseph. "Break the Billion-Dollar Congress." *New York Times*, January 28, 1993, p. A21.
_____. "Wealthcare Reform." *Washington Post*, February 10, 1994, p. A27.
_____. "The Medicalization of Teen Pregnancy." *Washington Post*, February 8, 1995, p. A1.
Carnegie Corporation of New York. *A Matter of Time: Risk and Opportunity in the Nonschool Hours*. New York: Author, December 1992.
Carnegie Council on Adolescent Development. *Turning Points: Preparing American Youth for the Twenty-First Century*. New York: Carnegie Corporation of New York, June 1989.
Carnegie Foundation for the Advancement of Teaching. *An Imperiled Generation: Saving Urban Schools*. Princeton, NJ: Author, 1988.
Celis, William, III. "Governors Announce Plan to Help Preschool Children." *New York Times*, August 2, 1992, p. 22.
_____. "School Program for Poor Is Failing, a Panel Says." *New York Times*, December 11, 1992, p. 1.
Center on Budget and Policy Priorities. *Still Far from the Dream: Recent Developments in Black Income, Employment and Poverty*. Washington, DC: Author, 1988.
_____. *The Personal Responsibility Act: An Analysis*. Washington, DC: Author, 1994.
Centre for Legislative Exchange. *The Role of Legislators in Making Communities Safer from Crime*. Toronto: Author, 1990.
Chapman, Bruce. "National Service: It's Just Too Expensive." *Washington Post*, January 18, 1993, p. A29.
Children's Defense Fund. *The State of America's Children 1944*. Washington, DC: Author, 1944.
Chira, Susan. "The Nation: Housing and Fear Upend Integration." *New York Times*, February 14, 1993.
_____. "Study Confirms Worst Fears on U.S. Children." *New York Times*, April 12, 1994, p. A1.
Cities in Schools, Inc. *Research Brief: Description of Local CIS Evaluations*. Washington, DC: Author, 1989.
Clairborne, William. "Reclaiming the South Bronx, From the Grass Roots." *Washington Post*, November 8, 1992, p. A1.
_____. "'Citizens Jury' Demands Strong Action on Budget." *Washington Post*, January 21, 1993, p. A12.
Clines, Francis X. "Ex-inmates Urge Return to Areas of Crime to Help." *New York Times*, December 23, 1992, p. A1.
Clymer, Adam. "Clinton Tries to Learn from Carter and History." *New York Times*, December 6, 1992, p. E4.
_____. "War Foe to Oversee Military in House." *New York Times*, December 24, 1992, p. A12.
_____. "Savings at Pentagon May Finance Domestic Needs." *New York Times*, January 29, 1993, p. A13.
Cohen, Richard E. "Term Limits for the Hill's Baronies?" *National Journal*, December 7, 1991, p. 2979.
_____. "Congress's Poor Housekeeping on View." *National Journal*, March 14, 1992, p. 650.
Cohn, D'Vera, and Barbara Vobejda. "Few Blacks Reach Top in Private Sector, Census Finds." *Washington Post*, January 18, 1993, p. A1.
Committee for Economic Development. *Children in Need: Investment Strategies for the Educational Disadvantaged*. New York: Author, 1987.
"Funds Available for New Englanders to Replicate Three Model Projects." *A Common Ground*. (February 1991): 12.
Congressional Budget Office. *Reducing the Deficit: Spending and Revenue Options* (DOM-51). Washington, DC: Author, February 1992.
Connell, Christopher. "Bush Signs Bill for Urban Aid Summer Jobs." *Boston Globe*, June 23, 1992, p. 1.
Cunningham, William J. *Enterprise Zones*. Testimony before the Subcommittee on Select Revenue Measures, Committee on Ways and Means, U.S. House of Representatives, July 11, 1991.
Currie, Elliott. *Confronting Crime: An American Challenge*. New York: Pantheon Books, 1985.
_____. "The Re-Emergence of Methamphetamine." Testimony before the House Select Committee on Narcotics Abuse and Control, U.S. House of Representatives, October 24, 1989.

_____. *Reckoning: Drugs, the Cities, and the American Future.* New York: Hill and Wang, 1993.
Curtis, Lynn A., Ed. *American Violence and Public Policy: An Update of the National Commission on the Causes and Prevention of Violence.* New Haven, CT: Yale University Press, 1985.
_____. "Race and Violent Crime: Towards a New Policy." In *Violent Crime, Violent Criminals*, edited by Neil Alan Weiner and Marvin E. Wolfgang. Newbury Park, CA: Sage Publications, 1989a.
_____. *The National Drug Control Strategy and Inner City Policy.* Testimony before the House Select Committee on Narcotics Abuse and Control, U.S. House of Representatives. Washington, DC: Milton S. Eisenhower Foundation, November 15, 1989b.
_____. *Doing What Works.* Testimony before the Committee on Ways and Means, Subcommittee on Select Revenue Measures, U.S. House of Representatives. Washington, DC: Milton S. Eisenhower Foundation, July 11, 1991.
_____. *Lord, How Dare We Celebrate?* Testimony before the House Committee on Education and Labor, Subcommittee on Human Resources at the Reauthorization Hearings for the Office of Juvenile Justice and Delinquency Prevention, U.S. House of Representatives. Washington, DC: Milton S. Eisenhower Foundation, February 5, 1992.
_____. *Policy That Works Twenty-Five Years after the Kerner Commission.* Testimony before the Senate Committee on Banking, Housing and Urban Affairs. Washington, DC: Milton S. Eisenhower Foundation, April 28, 1993a.
_____. *Testimony before the House Committee on Government Operations on the Reauthorization of the Office of National Drug Control Policy.* House Government Operations Committee. Washington, DC: Milton S. Eisenhower Foundation, October 5, 1993b.
_____. "An Assessment of the Crime Bill." *National Neighborhood Coalition Newsletter*, June–July 1994, p. 1.
Cushman, John H. "Clinton Seeks Taxes on Hidden Profits." *New York Times*, October 24, 1992, p. A9.
_____. "Bankers Lining Up Lobbyists with Close Ties to Clinton." *New York Times*, January 10, 1993, p. 1.
Danziger, Sheldon, and Daniel Weinberg, eds. *Fighting Poverty.* Cambridge, MA: Harvard University Press, 1986.
Degler, Carol N. "In Search of the Un-hyphenated American." *Kettering Review*, Summer 1992, p. 39.
De Leon, George. "Therapeutic Community Treatment Research Facts: What We Know." *Therapeutic Community Association Newsletter*, Fall 1988.
_____. "Psychopathology and Substance Abuse: What Is Being Learned from Research in Therapeutic Communities." *Journal of Psychoactive Drugs* 2(April–June, 1989): 177.
_____, and Mitchell S. Rosenthal. "Treatment in Residential Therapeutic Communities." In *Treatment of Psychiatric Disorders*, Vol. 2., edited by T. B. Karasu. Washington, DC: American Psychiatric Press, 1989.
Denny, Jeffrey. "Democrats Play the Soft Money Game." *Common Cause Magazine*, Winter 1992a, p. 9.
_____. "Whatever Happened to Toby Moffett?" *Common Cause Magazine*, Winter 1992b, p. 12.
_____. "Who Needs Enemies?" *Common Cause Magazine*, Winter 1992c, p.30.
DeParle, Jason. "Richer Rich, Poorer Poor, and a Fatter Green Book," *New York Times*, May 26, 1991, p. E2
_____. "Talk of Cutting Welfare Rolls Sounds Good, but Progress Is Far from Sure." *New York Times*, October 17, 1992a, p. A9.
_____. "How to Lift the Poor. *New York Times*, November 10, 1992b, p. A20.
_____. "Trying to Make Teen-Agers Tomorrow's Skilled Workers." *New York Times*, November 26, 1992c, p. 1.
_____. "Whither on Welfare?" *New York Times*, February 3, 1993a, p. A16.
_____. "Census Reports Jump in Births Out of Wedlock." *New York Times*, July 14, 1993b, p. A1.
_____. "President to Campaign against Teenage Pregnancy." *New York Times*, June 10, 1994a, p. A12.
_____. "Study Finds That Education Does Not Ease Welfare Roles." *New York Times*, June 21, 1994b, p. A8.
_____. "Despising Welfare, Pitying Its Young." *New York Times*, December 18, 1994c, p. E5.
de Tocqueville, Alexis. *Democracy in America.* Translated by George Lawrence and edited by J. P. Mayer. New York: Doubleday, Anchor Books, 1969.
Devroy, Ann. "Clinton's Pledges on Campaign Finance Encounter Resistance among Democrats." *Washington Post*, February 4, 1993, p. A9.
Dewar, Helen. "In a System Divided, Partisan Politics Has Stranglehold on Progress." *Washington Post*, August 3, 1992, p. A1.
_____. "GOP Crime Strategy Fails." *Washington Post*, August 27, 1994, p. A1.
Dommel, Paul R., et al. *Decentralizing Community Development.* Washington, DC: U.S. Department of Housing and Urban Development, 1978.
Donahue, James P. "The Fat Cat Free-loaders." *Washington Post*, March 6, 1994, p. C1.
Donahue, John D. *The Privatization Decision: Public Ends, Private Means.* New York: Basic Books, 1989.
Dowd, Maureen. "Americans Like G.O.P. Agenda but Split on How to Reach Goals." *New York Times*, December 15, 1994, p. A1.
Dreier, Peter. "Redlining Cities: How Banks Color Community Development." *Challenge*, November–

December 1991, pp. 36–53.

———. *Putting Housing on the National Agenda*. Boston: World Trade Center, November 9, 1992.

———. "America's Urban Crisis." *North Carolina Law Review* 71, No., 5(1993): 327–341.

Drugs and Crime Data Center and Clearinghouse. *Fact Sheet: Drug Date Summary*. Washington, DC: Author, November 1992.

Dryfoos, Joy G. *Adolescents At Risk*. New York: Oxford University Press, 1990.

Duke, Lynne. "DC Youth Get Taste of Discipline." *Washington Post*, August 26, 1989, p. A1.

Dunham, Richard S. "From the Heartland a Cry of Disgust." *Business Week/Reinventing America*, January 13, 1992, p. 3.

Eck, John E., and William Spelman. *Problem Solving: Problem Oriented Policing in Newport News*. Washington, DC: U.S. Department of Justice, 1987.

Eckholm, Erik. "Teen-Age Gangs Are Inflicting Lethal Violence on Small Cities." *New York Times*, January 31, 1993, p. A1.

Economist: "Tax Gap," December 24, 1988, p. 83; "Not So EZ." January 28, 1989a, p. 23; "A Budget for Boring Brilliance." February 11, 1989b, p. 14; "Jack, the Swamp Fighter." September 30, 1989c, p. 21; "The Pentagon Goes on the Defensive." September 28, 1991, p. 25; "Life, Liberty and Try Pursuing a Bit of Tolerance Too." September 5, 1992, p. 22; "Getting His Way." November 7, 1992, p. 15; "Meanwhile, in South Central." November 14, 1992, p. 23; "The Future in Their Past: What America Can Learn from Martin Luther King and Malcolm X." November 21, 1992, p. 10; "The No-Hard-Choices Summit." December 19, 1992, p. 23; "New Congress, Old Habits." January 16, 1993, p. 32.

Edelman, Marian Wright. *Families in Peril: An Agenda for Social Change*. Cambridge, MA: Harvard University Press, 1987.

Egan, Timothy. "Violent Measures on Term Limits and Crime Draw Wide Support." *New York Times*, November 4, 1993, p. A24.

Eizenstat, Stuart E. "Aspirin in the Cabinet." *Japan Times*, November 15, 1992, p. 21.

Elliott, Michael. "The European Example." *Washington Post*, March 17, 1991, p. D2.

Fagan, Jeffrey. "Neighborhood Education, Mobilization, and Organization for Juvenile Crime Prevention." *Annals of the American and Political and Social Science* 494(November 1987): 54.

Falco, Mathea. *The Making of a Drug-Free America: Programs That Work*. New York: Random House/Times Books, 1993.

Family Service America. *A Commitment to Families: An Action Agenda for Supporting and Strengthening America's Families*, 1994–1995. Milwaukee: Family Service America.

Federal Bureau of Investigation. *Uniform Crime Reports*, 1992. Washington, DC: U.S. Government Printing Office.

Feldkamp, Robert H. "The War That Went Away." *Narcotics Demand Reduction Digest*, September 1992a, p. 1.

———. "Combatants in the Drug War Agree on the Need for More Treatment and Education." *Narcotics Demand Reduction Digest*, October 1992b, p. 1.

———. "Clinton Expected to Shift Federal Spending Priorities and Earmark More Dollars for Demand Reduction." *Narcotics Demand Reduction Digest*, November 1992c, p. 1.

———. "Clinton Must Make Major Decisions in Direction and Goals of Drug War." *Narcotics Demand Reduction Digest*, January 1993, p. 1.

Felner, Robert D., and Angela M. Adan. "The School Transitional Environment Project: An Ecological Intervention and Evaluation." In *14 Ounces of Prevention: A Casebook for Practitioners*, edited by Richard H. Price et al. Washington, DC: American Psychological Association, 1988.

Ferre, M. Isolina. "Prevention and Control of Violence through Community Revitalization, Individual Dignity, and Personal Self Confidence." *Annals of the American Academy of Political and Social Science*, 494 (November 1987): 27.

Fink, Arlene, Jacqueline Kosecoff, and Carol Roth. "An Evaluation of The Door: Summary." Santa Monica, CA: Fink and Kosecoff, Inc., 1983.

Fisher, Marc. "German Job Training: A Model for America?" *Washington Post*, October 18, 1992, p. A1.

Fiske, Edward B. "Paying Attention to the Schools Is a National Mission Now." *New York Times*, October 1, 1989, p. 22.

———. "Governor's Panel Will Seek Broader Preschool Program." *New York Times*, February 25, 1990, p. 22.

Ford Foundation. "The Common Good: Social Welfare and the American Future." *Ford Foundation News Letter* 20(August 6, 1989): 1.

———. "Fathers and Families: Forging Ties That Bind." *Ford Foundation Report*, Fall 1992, pp. 3–8.

Frankel, Glenn. "Foreign Officials, Press Criticize U.S. Over Rioting." *Washington Post*, May 2, 1992, p. A11.

Freedman, Marc. The Kindness of Strangers: Reflections on the Mentoring Movement. *Public/Private Ventures*, Fall 1991.

French–American Foundation. *French Approaches to the Urban Crisis*. New York and Paris 1992.

Friedman, Thomas L. "Clinton as U.S. Teacher: More Than a Talk Show." *New York Times*, December 15, 1992, p. A14.
_____. "'Clinton, Taking Over . . . Asks the Shareholders.'" *New York Times*, December 20, 1992, p. 1.
_____. "$15 Billion Jobs Effort Is Called Likely." *New York Times*, January 27, 1993a, p. A15.
_____. "Collider and Space Station Saved from Budget Ax." *New York Times*, February 6, 1993b, p. 8.
Furlong, Tom. "Enterprise Zone in L.A. Fraught with Problems." *Los Angeles Times*, May 19, 1992. p. D1.
Galster, George C. "Housing Discrimination and Urban Poverty of African-Americans." *Journal of Housing Research* 2, No. 2(1991): 196–211.
Garland, Susan B., and Christina Delvare. "A Way Out of the Morass." *Business Week/Reinventing America*, January 19, 1993, pp. 100–106.
Gelb, Leslie H. "Clinton's Security Trio." *New York Times*, December 20, 1992, p. E13.
Gifford, Bill. "Paradise Found." *Washington City Paper*, January 29, 1993, p. 20.
Gladwell, Malcolm. "Some Hear Black and White in Divergence of Spoken Word."*Washington Post*, April 29, 1991, p. A3.
Goldberg, Mark A., and Theodore R. Marmor. " . . . And What the Experts Expect." *Washington Post*, February 14, 1993, p. C3.
Gordon, Michael R. "Star Wars Fading as Major Elements of U.S. Strategy." *New York Times*, September 29, 1989a, p. A1.
_____. "The Military Mask of Peace in Our Times." *New York Times*, December 17, 1989b, p. B1.
Gottfredson, Michael, and Travis Hirschi. "Criminal Behavior: Why We're Losing the War on Crime." *Washington Post*, September 10, 1989, p. C3.
Greenfeld, Lawrence A. *Prisons and Prisoners in the United States* (NCJ-137002). Washington, DC: U.S. Department of Justice, Bureau of Justice Statistics, April 1992.
Greenhouse, Steven. "Lessons Across Six Decades As Clinton Tries to Make Jobs." *New York Times*, November 24, 1992, p. A1.
Greenstein, Robert, and Paul Leonard. "The Fiscal Year 1992 Bush Budget: Still Not Tackling the Nation's Problems." Washington, DC: Center on Budget and Policy Priorities, February 1992.
Greider, William. *Who Will Tell the People: The Betrayal of American Democracy*. New York: Simon and Schuster, 1992.
Gross, Jane. "A Remnant of the War on Poverty, the Job Corps Is a Quiet Success. *New York Times*, February 17, 1993.
Gueron, Judith M., and Edward Pauly. *From Welfare to Work*. New York: Russell Sage Foundation, 1991.
Gugliotta, Guy. "Saving HUD: One Department's Risky Strategy for Radical Change." *Washington Post*, February 6, 1995, p. A4.
Guskind, Robert. "Enterprise Zones: Do They Work?" *Journal of Housing*, January–February 1990, pp. 73–87.
_____. "The Economic Crisis of Urban American." *Business Week*, May 18, 1992, p. 45.
Haar, Charles M. *Between the Idea and the Reality: A Study on the Origin, Fate, and Legacy of the Model Cities Program*. Boston, MA: Little, Brown, and Co., 1975.
Hamburg, David A. "Fundamental Building Blocks of Early Life." *Annual Report of the Carnegie Corporation of New York*. New York: Carnegie Corporation, 1987.
Harrell, Adele V., and George E. Peterson, eds. *Drugs, Crime and Social Isolation: Barriers to Urban Opportunity*. Washington, DC: Urban Institute Press, 1992.
Harris, Fred R. *Plenary Presentation on the Kerner Riot Commission Twenty-Five Years Later*. Presentation at the Presidential Commission Anniversary Policy Forum Sponsored by the Eisenhower Foundation, Washington, DC: January 27, 1994.
_____, and Roger W. Wilkins, eds. *Quiet Riots: Race and Poverty in the United States*. New York: Pantheon Books, 1988.
Harris, Irving B. "What Can We Do to Prevent the Cycle of Poverty?" New Haven, CT: Child Study Center, Yale University, March 24, 1987.
_____. "Child Development and the Cycle of Poverty." New Haven, CT: Child Study Center, Yale University, October 25, 1990.
Harrison, Lawrence. "A Dream Not Really Deferred." *Washington Post*, January 17, 1993, p. C5.
Havel, Vaclav. "Politics and the World Itself." *Kettering Review*, Summer 1992, p. 8.
Hayes, John G. *The Impact of Citizen Involvement in Preventing Crime in Public Housing: A Report of the Department of Housing and Urban Development's Interagency Anticrime Demonstration Program*. Charlotte, SC: Housing Authority of the City of Charlotte, January 1982.
_____. *A Program Manual: The Resident Safety Department's Safe Neighborhood Awareness Program*. Charlotte, SC: Housing Authority of the City of Charlotte, May 1988.
Himmelstein, David, and Steffie Woolhandler. "'Managed Competition' Is Not Healthy Answer." *New York Times*, December 10, 1992, p. A26.

Hinds, Michael deCourcy. "Jobs Promised in '91 Bill Have Yet to Be Realized." *New York Times*, February 1, 1993, p. A12.
Hope, Tim, and Margaret Shaw, eds. *Communities and Crime Reduction*. London, England: Her Majesty's Stationery Office, 1988.
Hoffman, David, and David S. Broder. "Summit Sets Seven Main Goals for Education." *Washington Post*, September 1989, p. A3.
Hoffman, Saul D., and Laurence S. Seidman. *The Earned Income Tax Credit*. Kalamazoo, MI: W. E. Upjohn Institute for Employment Research, 1990.
Holmes, Steven A. "Birth Rate for Unwed Women Up Seventy Percent Since 1983: Study Says." *New York Times*, July 20, 1994, p. A1.
Horowitz, Michael. "States of Grace." *New York Times*, November 24, 1992, p. A17.
Howe, Irving. "Clinton, Seen from the Left." *New York Times*, January 20, 1993, p. A23.
Ifill, Gwen. "Kemp Announces Steps to End HUD Physical Abuses." *Washington Post*, October 4, 1989, p. A1.
_____. "Local Taxes Must Go Up, Many City Leaders Say." *Washington Post*, January 9, 1990, p. A5.
_____. "Also Set to Push a Revamping of Welfare." *New York Times*, February 3, 1993, p. C5.
_____. "Victory Over Crime, At Least Politically." *New York Times*, August 28, 1994, p. E1.
Isikoff, Michael. "Drug Survey Shows Rise in Use Among Students." *Washington Post*, October 1992.
_____. "Under Clinton, Drug Policy Office's Hot Streak Melts Down." *Washington Post*, February 10, 1993, p. A14.
Japan Times: "A New U.S. Emphasis on High-Tech." November 19, 1992, p. 20.
Jencks, Christopher. "Can We Put a Time Limit on Welfare?" *American Prospect*, Fall 1992.
Johnson, Dirk. "Voters Can't Find the Humor in Capital's Partisan Games." *New York Times*, August 27, 1994, p. A1.
Johnson, Haynes. *Divided We Fall: Gambling with History in the Nineties*. New York: W. W. Norton, 1994.
Jordan, Mary. "Ills of Big-City Schools Tied to Lower Spending." *Washington Post*, September 23, 1992, p. A3.
_____, and Ann Devroy. "Community Service Plan Scaled Back." *Washington Post*, February 4, 1993, p. A1.
Kaplan, Marshall, and James Franklin, eds. *The Future of U.S. Urban Policy*. Durham, NC: Duke University Press, 1990.
Karr, Albert R. "Job Corps, Long Considered a Success, Sparks Political Tug-of-War Over Costs." *Wall Street Journal*, June 1, 1992. p. A1.
Kaslow, Amy. "Corps for Troubled Youth Now Finds Itself in Trouble." *Christian Science Monitor*, February 2, 1995, p. 1.
Kauffman, L. A. "Democracy in a Postmodern World?" *Kettering Review*, Summer 1992, p. 25.
Kelly, Michael. "Clinton, After Raising Hopes, Tries to Lower Expectations." *New York Times*, November 9, 1992, p. A1.
Kennedy, Paul. *The Rise and Fall of the Great Powers*. New York: Random House, 1987.
Kennedy, Robert. *To Seek a Newer World*. New York: Pantheon Books, 1968.
Killborn, Peter T. "In Small Steps, Program Puts Homeless into Jobs." *New York Times*, January 28, 1990, p. A1.
Kingsley, Thomas G., and Margery Austin Turner, eds. *Housing Markers and Residential Mobility*, Washington, DC: Urban Institute Press, December 1992.
Kinsley, Michael. "Pony Excuses on the Deficit." *Washington Post*, January 14,1993, p. A29.
Kinzer, Stephen. "Germans' Apprentice System Is Seen as Key to Long Boom." *New York Times*, February 6, 1993, p. A1.
Klaidman, Daniel. "Is It Time to Take a Bite Out of McGruff?" *Illegal Times*, November 29, 1993, p. 1.
Kleiman, Mark, and David Cavenaugh. *A Cost-Benefit Analysis of Prison Cell Construction and Alternative Sanctions*. Report to the National Institute of Justice, BOTEC, Washington, DC, May 1990.
Kohn, Imre. *A Supplementary Analysis of Change at the Around the Corner to the World and Dorchester Youth Collaborative Programs*. Washington, DC: Milton S. Eisenhower Foundation, October 1989.
Kolata, Gina. "Despite Its Promise of Riches, the Crack Trade Seldom Pays," *New York Times*, November 26, 1989, p. A1.
Krauss, Clifford. "Newest Victim of Politics." *New York Times*, October 10, 1992, p. A1.
Kurtz, Howard. "Negative Ads Appear to Lose Potency." *Washington Post*, October 26, 1992, p. A1.
Kuttner, Robert. "Facing Up to Industrial Policy." *Industry*, April 19, 1992a, p. 22.
_____. "Cutting the Deficit Won't Cure the Economy." *Washington Post*, July 31, 1992b, p. A23.
_____. "The Welfare Perplex." *New York Times*, June 19, 1994, p. A21.
_____. "Instead, Close Loopholes." *New York Times*, February 8, 1995, p. A19.
Lacayo, Richard. "What Would It Take to Get America Off Drugs?" *Time*, November 9, 1992.
Lehman, Jane. "Think Tanks Pondering Housing Laws." *Washington Post*, July 22, 1989, p. F1.
_____. "Bill Clinton's Vision on Housing." *Washington Post*, November 7, 1992, p. E1.
Leonard, Paul, and Robert Greenstein. *Budget Assessment of Youth Investment and Community Reconstruction*. Washington, DC: Center on Budget and Policy Priorities, January 31, 1990.

Levitan, Sar A. *Programs in Aid of the Poor*. Baltimore, MD: Johns Hopkins University Press, 1990.
_____, and Frank Gallo. *Spending to Save: Expanding Employment Opportunities*. Washington, DC: Center for Social Policy Studies, 1992.
_____, Frank Gallo, and Isaac Shapiro. *Working but Poor*. Baltimore: Johns Hopkins University Press, 1993.
Lewis, Flora. "The Society Race." *New York Times*, August 6, 1989.
Lohr, Steve. "Lesson for a High-Tech President." *New York Times*, January 24, 1993, p. E3.
Los Angeles Times: "Unsure Prognosis for Term-Limitation Fever." November 9, 1992, p. A10.
Lurie, Theodora. *Fathers and Families: Forging Ties That Bind*, Vol. 23. New York: Ford Foundation Report, Fall 1992, p. 3.
Madrick, Jeff. "Why Knock Public Investment?" *New York Times*, January 19, 1993, p. A20.
Malcolm, Andrew M. "Crack, Bane of Inner City, Is Now Gripping Suburbs." *New York Times*, October 1, 1989, p. A1.
Mallar, Charles. *Evaluation of the Economic Impacts of the Job Corps Program: Third Follow-up Report*. Princeton, NJ: Mathematical Policy Research, 1982.
Manchester Guardian Weekly: "Time for a Serious Examination of Defense Spending." November 26, 1989, p. 1.
Mann, Paul. "U.S. Fraud Probe Rekindles Military Waste Controversy." *Aviation Weekly and Space Technology*, July 4, 1988a.
_____. "Voters Ready to Redefine National Security Threats." *Aviation Weekly and Space Technology*, October 31, 1988b.
Mann, Thomas E., and Norman J. Ornstein. *Renewing Congress: A First Report of the Renewing Congress Project*. Washington, DC: American Enterprise Institute and the Brookings Institution, 1992.
Marcus, Ruth. "President Pledges to Reform Welfare." *Washington Post*, February 3, 1993, p. A1.
Mariano, Ann. "Paradise at Parkside Reclaims Its Legacy." *Washington Post*, June 29, 1991, p. E1.
_____. "Report Calls HUD Cuts Crippling." *Washington Post*, December 19, 1992, p. E1.
Marquand, Robert. "GOP Puts Out Contract on Crime." *Christian Science Monitor*, February 3, 1995, p. 1.
Marshall, Will, and Martin Schram. *Mandate for Change*. New York: Progressive Policy Institute, Berkley Books, 1993.
Massing, Michael. "The Rehabbing of America." *New York Times Book Review*, January 24, 1993, p. 10.
Mathews, David. "Afterthoughts." *Kettering Review*, Summer 1992, p. 47.
Matthews, Jay. "Drop Out Prevention: Human Touch Helps." *Washington Post*, June 3, 1991, p. A1.
Mauer, Marc. *Young Black Men and the Criminal Justice System: A Growing National Problem*. Washington, DC: Sentencing Project, February, 1990.
_____. *Americans Behind Bars: One Year Later*. Washington, DC: Sentencing Project, February 1992.
McAllister, Bill. "Study: 1 in 4 Young Black Men Is in Jail or Court Supervised." *Washington Post*, February 27, 1990, p. A3.
McCombs, Phil. "A Delicate Operation." *Washington Post*, February 4, 1993, p. C1.
McFate, Katherine. *Poverty, Inequality and the Crisis of Social Policy*. Washington, DC: Joint Center for Political and Economic Studies, September 1991.
_____, with Cheryl Reed. *Black Crime, White Fear*. Washington, DC: Joint Center for Political and Economic Studies, 1992.
McNamara, Robert. "For the Record." *Washington Post*, November 25, 1992, p. A16.
Mecs, Helen, Director of Public Relations, The Argus Community. Memorandum to. *University of Denver Law Review*. New York, January 22, 1993.
Memmott, Mark. "Pros: Clinton Must Define Investment, Pork." *USA Today*, December 29, 1992, p. B1.
Milton S. Eisenhower Foundation. *Youth Investment and Community Reconstruction: Street Level Lessons on Crime and Drugs for the Nineties*. Washington, DC: Author, 1990.
_____. *Investing in Children and Youth, Reconstructing Our Cities*. A Report in Commemoration of the Twenty-Fifth Anniversary of the National Advisory Commission on Civil Disorders. Washington, DC: Author, 1993.
_____. *Community Policing and Youth Development*. Washington, DC: Author, 1995.
Milwaukee Journal. "You Can't Junk Welfare on the Cheek." May 8, 1994, p. J4.
Mollenkopf, John H. *The Contested City*. Princeton, NJ: Princeton University Press, 1983.
Morin, Richard. "Drug Abuse Leads Nation's Worries." *Washington Post*, August 23, 1989, p. A22.
Moyers, Bill. *The Public Mind. Consuming Images: Image and Reality in America* [Television] Public Broadcasting System, Washington, DC, November 9, 1989.
Moynihan, Daniel P. *Maximum Feasible Misunderstanding: Community Action and the War on Poverty*. New York: Free Press, 1969.
Mufson, Steven. "Clinton Confronts Dilemma Over Federal Budget Deficit." *Washington Post*, January 11, 1993a, p. A1.
_____. "Clinton Faces a Challenge in Business Tax Shortfalls." *Washington Post*, January 21, 1993b, p. A12.

———. "Goal to Cut Deficit Eluded Darman, Final Budget Shows." *Washington Post*, January 7, 1993c, p. D11.

———, and David S. Hilzenrath. "Clinton Backs Away from Tax Cut Vow," and "Clinton Advisers Back Sharp Cuts in Deficit." *Washington Post*, January 14, 1993, p. A8.

———, and Dana Priest. "Clinton Signals Intention to Confront the Federal Budget Deficit." *Washington Post*, December 19, 1992, p. A9.

Mulvey, Edward P. Michael A. Arthor, and N. Dickon Reppucci. *Draft Review of Programs for the Prevention and Treatment of Delinquency*. Washington, DC: Office of Technology Assessment, December 1989.

Nasar, Sylvia. "Tapping the Rich May Prove Tricky." *New York Times*, December 12, 1992, p. 39.

National Advisory Commission on Civil Disorders. *The Kerner Commission: Final Report*. Washington, DC: U.S. Government Printing Office, March 1, 1968.

National Commission on Children. *Final Report*. Washington, DC: Author, 1993.

National Commission on the Causes and Prevention of Violence. *The Eisenhower Violence Commission. To Establish Justice, to Insure Domestic Tranquility: Final Report*. Washington, DC: U.S. Government Printing Office, 1969.

National Housing Task Force. A *Decent Place to Live*. Washington, DC: National Housing Task Force, 1988.

National Institute of Justice. *Drug Use Forecasting: Drugs and Crime 1990 Annual Report*. Washington, DC: National Institute of Justice, 1991.

———. *Prevalence of Drug Use in the D.C. Metropolitan Area Household Population: 1990* (Technical Report No. 1). Washington, DC, National Institute on Drug Abuse, 1992.

National Institute on Drug Abuse. *Treatment Program Monograph Series. The Door: A Model Youth Center*. Washington, DC: Department of Health and Human Services, 1981.

National Journal: "Helping the Haves." April 14, 1990, p. 898; "Help for Aid May Have to Wait a Bit." April 25, 1992, p. 1001.

New York Times: "Philadelphia House of Umoja Praised for Role in Reducing Youth Violence." February 23, 1976, p. 21; "Rhode Island Offers Scholarship Plan for Poor." September 3, 1989, p. 25; "War: 1 Percent. Drugs: 54 Percent." September 28, 1989, p. A26; "For Poor Children: A Powerful Proposal." January 7, 1990, p. E24; "Almost Peace. One of Dividend?" February 4, 1990, p. E22; "Urban Schools Are Providing More Social Services." February 11, 1990, p. 47; "$150 Billion a Year: Where To Find It." March 8, 1990, p. A24; "$150 Billion a Year: How To Spend It." March 9, 1990, p. A34; "Private Cures for Public Ills." February 28, 1991, p. A24; "Pinch-Hitting for the Democrats: Invest in the Future? Yes, but How?" August 11, 1991, p. A16; "A Remnant of the War on Poverty, The Job Corps Is a Quiet Success." February 17, 1992, p. A1; "Report Says Poor Children Grew Poorer in 1980's." March 24, 1992, p. A22; "Define Needs, Not Glib Goals." April 12, 1992, p. E20; "Star Wars in the Twilight Zone." June 14, 1992, p. E18; "An Urban Aid Bill That Doesn't." October 26, 1992, p. A26; "National Security, Redefined." November 10, 1992, p. A22; "A Clinton Contradiction." November 22, 1992, p. E16; "A Foreign Notion for Washington: U.S. Needs Higher Taxes." November 29, 1992, p. E2; "Who Needs Four Air Forces?" November 30, 1992, p. A14; "The Clinton Anti-Gridlock Team." December 11, 1992, p. A38; "A Valuable Economics Seminar." December 16, 1992, p. A30; "No Delays for Public Trust." January 24, 1993, p. E16; "The Wine and Dine Congress." January 31, 1993, p. E16; "One Gun Per Month." February 4, 1993, p. A22; "Next: Campaign Finance Reform." February 8, 1993, A16; "Congress, Untie Yourself." February 10, 1993, p. A22; "Real Political Reform Can't Wait." February 21, 1993, p. 16; "Health Tinkering Is Not Reform." February 22, 1994, p. 813; "Poor Mother, Poor Child." June 17, 1994, p. A30; "Welfare as We've Known It." June 19, 1994, p. E4; "New Player in the Welfare Game." July 18, 1994, p. A14; "Orphanages Are No Solution." December 12, 1994, p. A18; "President Clinton's Welfare Waffle." January 9, 1995, p. A14; "Go After Corporate Welfare." January 17, 1995, p. A18.

Nisbet, Robert A. "The Contexts of Democracy." *Kettering Review*, Summer 1992, p. 15.

Nunn, Sam. *Nightline*, ABC News, January 4, 1990.

Offner, Paul. "Workfail." *New Republic*, December 28, 1992, p. 13.

Olson, Mancur. "The Interest-Free Solution." *Washington Post*, December 12, 1992, p. E1.

Oreskes, Michael, "The Civil Rights Act, 25 Years Later: A Law That Shapes a Re-Alignment." *New York Times*, July 2, 1989a, p. A16.

———. "What Poison Politics Has Done to America." *New York Times*, October 29, 1989b, p. E1.

———. "Grudging Public Thinks Tax Rise Now Must Come." *New York Times*, May 27, 1990, p. A1.

Overby, Peter. "Staking a Claim." *Common Cause Magazine*, Winter 1992, p. 8.

Passell, Peter. "What Counts Is Productivity and Productivity." *New York Times*, December 13, 1992, p. E1.

Pate, Anthony M., MaryAnn Wycoff, Wesley G. Skogan, and Lawrence W. Sherman. *Reducing Fear of Crime in Houston and in Newark: A Summary Report*. Washington, DC: Police Foundation, 1986.

Pear, Robert. "Clinton Offering Health Plan with Guarantee of Coverage and Curb on Private Spending."

New York Times, September 11, 1993a, p. A1.
_____. "Growing U.S. Debt Is Limiting Options Open For Clinton." *New York Times*, January 2, 1993b, p. C6.
_____. "Clinton Backs Off His Pledge to Cut the Deficit in Half." *New York Times*, January 7, 1993c, p. A1.
_____. "Budget Official Sees No Savings in Clinton's Health-Care Plans." *New York Times*, February 3, 1993d, p. A16.
_____. "Governors Deadlocked on Replacing Welfare." *New York Times*, January 31, 1995a, p. A14.
_____. "Governors Agree Children Must Be Protected No Matter What." *New York Times*, February 1, 1995b, p. A19.
Pearlstein, Steven. "'Investment Gap' Serves as a Rallying Cry." *Washington Post*, December 15, 1992. p. 14.
Peirce, Neal R., and Carol F. Steinbach. *Corrective Capitalism: The Rise of America's Community Development Corporations*. New York: Ford Foundation, July 1987.
Peters, Charles. "The Second Coming of Neo-Liberalism." *New York Times Magazine*, January 17, 1993, p. 30.
Petersilia, Joan, and Susan Turner. *Intensive Supervision for High-Risk Probationers: Findings from Three California Experiments*. Santa Monica, CA: Rand Corporation, 1990.
Peterson, George E., and Wayne P. Vroman, eds. *Urban Labor Markers and Job Opportunity*, Washington, DC: Urban Institute Press, 1992.
_____. *Big-City Politics, Governance and Fiscal Constraints*. Washington, DC: Urban Institute Press, 1993.
Peterson, Iver. "Older Cities Relying More on Suburbs' Taxes. " *New York Times*, February 12, 1993, p. A1.
Phillips, Kevin. *The Politics of Rich and Poor*. New York: Random House, 1990.
Pianin, Eric. "House Votes to Preserve Space Station Funding." *Washington Post*, July 30, 1992, p. A10.
_____. "President Vetos $27B Tax Bill." *Washington Post*, November 5, 1992, p. A3.
_____. "Clinton to Press Major Deficit Cut." *Washington Post*, January 12, 1993, p. A1.
Poliat, Denise F., Janet C. Quint, and James A. Riccio. *The Challenge of Serving Teenage Mothers: Lessons from Project Redirection*. New York: Manpower Demonstration Research Corporation, 1988.
Prestowicz, Clyde. "The New World Champion." *Far Eastern Economic Review*, January 1990, p. 18.
Priest, Dana. "How Hawaii Stands Above Health-Care Fray." *Washington Post*, October 18, 1992a, p. A4.
_____. "Foes of Health Care Change Are Warming to Clinton's Plans." *Washington Post*, December 5, 1992b, p. A1.
_____. "First Lady's First Task Breaks New Ground." *Washington Post*, January 27, 1993a, p. A6.
_____. "Managed Competition No Cure All: CBO Sees Little Change in Health Care Outlays Under Proposal." *Washington Post*, February 3, 1993b. p. A1.
_____. "Where Healthcare Reform Effort Failed." *Washington Post*, August 27, 1994, p. A1.
Price, Richard H., Emory L. Cowen, Raymond P. Lorion, and Julia Ramos-McKay, eds. *14 Ounces of Prevention: A Case Book for Practitioners*. Washington, DC: American Psychological Association, 1988.
Quint, Janet C., Judith S. Musick, with Joyce A. Aldner. *Lives of Promise, Lives of Pain: Young Mothers After New Chance*. Manpower Demonstration Research Corporation, January 1994.
Quint, Michael. "This Bank Can Turn a Profit and Follow a Social Agenda." *New York Times*, May 24, 1992, p. A1.
Rapoport, Robert N. *New Interventions for Children and Youth: Action Research Approaches*. Cambridge, England: Cambridge University Press, 1987.
Raspberry, William. "Head Start: A Program That Works." *Washington Post*, January 19, 1990, p. A21.
Rayburn, Paul. "EPA Report Calls Cigarette Smoke 'Substantial' Risk for Nonsmokers." *Washington Post*, January 8, 1993, p. A3.
Reich, Robert. "Secession of Successful." *New York Times Magazine*, January 20, 1991.
_____. "Accounting the Future." *American Prospect*, Fall 1992.
Reuter, P. H., J. G. Haaga, P. J. Murphy, and A. M. Prakac. *Drug Use and Drug Programs in the Washington Metropolitan Area*. Santa Monica, CA: Rand Corporation, July 1988.
Rich, Michael J. *National Goals and Local Choices: Distributing Federal Aid to the Poor*.Princeton, NJ: Princeton University Press, 1993.
Rich, Spencer. "Job-Training Program Is Paying Off—for Some." *Washington Post*, May 23, 1992, p. A11.
_____. "Runaway Training." *Washington Post*, February 7, 1993, p. C3.
_____. "Challenging a Theory on Welfare." *Washington Post*, August 12, 1993, p. A3.
Rose, Charlie. *Charlie Rose Show*. Public Broadcasting System, August 3, 1994.
Rosenbaum, David E. "Professor Moynihan Wakes the Class with Truth about Taxes." *New York Times*, January 21, 1990, p. E1.
_____. "Peace Dividend: A Dream for Every Dollar." *New York Times*, February 19, 1990, p. E1.
_____. "Clinton Weighing Freeze or New Tax on Social Security." *New York Times*, January 31, 1993, p. A1.
Rosenbaum, Dennis P. "Community Crime Prevention: A Review and Synthesis of the Literature." *Justice Quarterly* 5 (September 1988).
Rosenbaum, James E. "Black Pioneers—Do Their Moves to the Suburbs Increase Economic Opportuni-

ty for Mothers and Children?" *Housing Policy Debate* 2, No. 4 (1991).
Rother, Larry. "Homelessness Defies Every City's Remedy: Arrest-Free Zones in Miami, *New York Times*, November 22, 1992, p. E3.
Rotunda, Ronald D. "No Impediment to Term Limits." *Washington Post*, February 13, 1993, p. A31.
Rowen, Hobart. "No Peace Dividend?" *Washington Post*, January 25, 1990, p. A27.
Royko, Mike. "Crime Dog Puts Bite on Taxpayers." *Chicago Tribune*, January 7, 1993, p. 3.
Rua, Jim. *Treatment Works: The Tragic Cost of Undervaluing Treatment in the Drug War*. Washington, DC: National Association of State Alcohol and Drug Abuse Directors, March 1990.
Russell, Avery. "Making America Drug Free." *Carnegie Quarterly*, Summer 1992.
Schmidt, Susan. "RTC pays $35 an Hour for Photocopying Files." *Washington Post*, February 13, 1993, p. A1.
Schmidt, William E. "Study Links Male Unemployment and Single Mothers in Chicago." *New York Times*, January 15, 1989, p. 16.
_____. "Drug War Funds Arouse a Conflict." *New York Times*, November 12, 1989, p. 1.
Schmitt, Eric. "Clinton and Bush Agree on Trimming Armed Forces, but Their Paths Vary." *New York Times*, October 21, 1992, p. A20.
Schneider Keith. "Gore Making Administration More Environmentally Friendly." *New York Times*, December 15, 1992, p. A16.
Schinke, S., et al. *The Effects of Boys and Girls Clubs on Alcohol and Drug Use and Related Problems in Public Housing*. New York: Columbia University School of Social Work, 1991.
Schmidt, Susan. "RTC's Contracting Faults Led to Hugh Costs for Photocopying, Probe Finds." *Washington Post*, February 13, 1993, p. A1.
Schorr, Lisbeth B. *Within Our Reach: Breaking the Cycle of Disadvantage*. New York: Doubleday, 1988.
Schwartz, Tzivia. "Discrimination Built In." *New York Times*, November 8, 1993, p. A18.
Schweinhart, Lawrence J., and David P. Weikart. "The High-Scope Perry Pre-School Program." In *14 Ounces of Prevention: A Casebook for Practitioners*, edited by Richard A. Price, Emory L. Cowen, Raymond P. Lorion, and Julia Ramos-McKay. Washington, DC: American Psychological Association, 1988.
Sciolino, Elaine. "$30 Billion in Excess Equipment Stored by Military, Panel Asserts." *New York Times*, February 1990, p. A1.
Scruggs, Yvonne. *Then and Now, 1963–1993: Demographics and Data on Deficits*. Joint Center for Political and Economic Studies, August 1993a.
_____. "The Cities." In L.E. Heagerty, ed., *Eyes on the President* (pp. 106–125). Occidental, CA: Chronos, 1993b.
Seelye, Katharine Q. "Republicans Redesign Last Year's Crime Bill." *New York Times*, February 1, 1995, p. A18.
Segal, Troy, et al. "Look Who's Ahead of the Learning Curve." *Business Week*, January 19, 1993, pp. 92–98.
Sentencing Project. "Crime Rates and Incarceration: Are We Any Safer?" Washington, DC: Author, Spring 1992.
Shapiro, Isaac, and Robert Greenstein. "Making Work Pay: A New Agenda for Poverty Policies." Washington, DC: Center on Budget and Policy Priorities, March 21, 1989.
_____, and Robert Greenstein. "Selective Prosperity: Increasing Income Disparities Since 1977." Washington, DC: Center on Budget and Policy Priorities, 1991.
Shenk, David. "Putting Panels First." *Washington Post*, February 7, 1993, p. C1.
Shields, Mark. "Politicians and Plumbers." *Washington Post*, April 9, 1994, p. A21.
Silberman, Charles E. *Criminal Violence and Criminal Justice*. New York: Random House, 1978.
Silbert, Mimi. "Delancey Street Foundation: A Process of Mutual Restitution." In *Self-Help Revolution*, edited by Frank Riessman and Alan Gratner. New York: Human Sciences Press, 1984.
Sklar, Morton B. "Proposed JTPA Reforms Miss the Mark." *Youth Policy*, September–October 1989, p. 36.
Skolnick, Jerome H., and David H. Bayley. *The New Blue Line: Police Innovation in Six American Cities*. New York: Free Press, 1986.
Smith, R. Jeffery. "Two Missiles Unnecessary, Ex-Chiefs Say." *Washington Post*, February 3, 1990, p. A5.
Smolow, Jill. "Where Children Come First." *Time*, November 9, 1992, p. 58.
Southerland, Daniel. "Independent, Nonpartisan Panel Is Sought to Review Subsidy Programs." *Washington Post*, December 8, 1992, p. A17.
Spillett, R., et al. "Boys and Girls Clubs in Public Housing Projects." New York: Columbia University School of Social Work, 1991.
Stanfield, Rochelle. "The Forgotten Half." *National Journal*, May 2, 1992, pp. 1049–1052.
_____. "Battle Zones." *National Journal*, June 1992.
Stanley, Alessandra. "Words of Advice, Bittersweet." *New York Times*, January 14, 1993, p. C1.
Steinbach, Carol. "A Decent Place to Live Revisited: The State of Housing in America." *Enterprise Foundation*, October–November 1992, p. 23.
Struyk, Raymond Turner, Austin Margery, and Makiko Ueno. *Future U.S. Housing Policy: Meeting the Demographic Challenge*. Washington, DC: Urban Institute Press, 1989.

Sturz, Elizabeth Lyttleton. *Widening Circles*. New York: Harper and Row, 1983.
———. *Dealing with Disruptive Adolescents: Alternative Program in Congregate Care*. New York: Argus Community, 1992.
———, and Mary Taylor. "Inventing and Reinventing Argus: What Makes One Community Organization Work." *Annals of the American Academy of Political and Social Science* 959 (November 1987): 19.
Sugarman, Josh. *NRA Money-Firepower-Fear*. Bethesda, MD: National Press Books, 1992.
Sullivan, Liane. "Evaluation Report on the Phoenix House School-Based Drug Education and Prevention Project." Submitted to the U.S. Department of Education, December 30, 1988.
Sundquist, James L. *Constitutional Reform and Effective Government*. Washington, DC: Brookings Institution, 1992.
Sviridoff, Michele, and Jerome McElroy. *Employment and Crime: A Summary Report*. New York: Vera Institute of Justice, 1985.
Taggart, Robert. *A Fisherman's Guide: An Assessment of Training and Remediation Strategies*. Kalamazoo, MI: W. E. Upjohn Institute for Employment Research, October 1981.
Taylor, Paul. "Tax Policy as Political Battleground." *Washington Post*, February 18, 1990, p. A1.
Teitelbaum, Mel. "Invitation to Fraud." *New York Times*, November 8, 1993, p. A18.
Tidwell, Billy, J. *Playing to Win: A Marshall Plan for America*. Washington, DC: National Urban League, 1992.
Tolchin, Martin. "Mayors Press Clinton on Promise to Rebuild Nation." *New York Times*, January 25, 1993.
Toner, Robin. "Black Politicians Are Leaning Against Some Old Barriers." *New York Times*, November 5, 1989, p. E1.
———. "Los Angeles Riots Are a Warning, Americans Fear." *New York Times*, May 11, 1992, p. A1.
Treaster, Joseph B. "20 Years of War on Drugs, and No Victory Yet." *New York Times*, June 14, 1992a, p. E7.
———. "Some Think the 'War on Drugs' Is Being Waged on Wrong Front." *New York Times*, July 28, 1992b, p. A1.
———. "Experts Welcome Clinton's Move on Drug Policy Office." *New York Times*, February 10, 1993, p. A20.
———. "Drug Wars, Cont.: The Liberals Unlikely Ally." *New York Times*, February 5, 1995, p. E3.
Trento, Susan B. *The Power House*. New York: St. Martin's Press, 1992.
Turner, Margery Austin. "Discrimination in Urban Housing Markets: Lessons from Fair Housing Audits." *Housing Policy Debate* 3, No. 2 (1992).
———, Raymond Struyk, and John Yinger. *Housing Discrimination Study: Synthesis*. Washington, DC: U.S. Department of Housing and Urban Development, 1992.
Tyler, Patrick E. "Halving Defense Budget in Decade Suggested." *Washington Post*, November 21, 1989, p. A1.
Uchitelle, Louis. "Will All This Talk Lead to New Taxes?" *New York Times*, March 25, 1990, p. E1.
———. "The Real Challenge of the Deficit Is Deciding How to Live with It." *New York Times*, January 17, 1993, p. E3.
Urban Institute. *Confronting the Nation's Urban Crisis: From Watts (1965) to South Central Los Angeles (1992)*. Washington, DC: Author, September 1992.
U.S.A. Basics. *The Comprehensive Competencies Program: A High Tech/High Touch Approach to Basic Skills Master*. Alexandria, VA: U.S. Basic Skills Investment Corp. 1989.
U.S. Conference of Mayors. *Mayors Release New Lists of Transportation and Community Development Projects "Ready to Go" in Cities*. (news release). February 18, 1993.
USA Today: "Cut Federal Programs as Part of Deficit Fight." September 23, 1992a, p. 10A.
———. "Prevention Pays for Kids." December 18, 1992b, p. 10A.
U.S. Department of Health and Human Services. *National Household Survey on Drug Abuse: Main Findings 1990*. DHHS Publication No. (ADM) 91-1788. Washington, DC: National Institute on Drug Abuse, 1991.
U.S. Department of Justice. *Prisoners in 1988*. Washington, DC: Author, April 1989.
———. *Criminal Victimization 1988*. Washington, DC: Author, October 1989.
———. *Recidivism of Felons on Probation, 1986|N|89*. Bureau of Justice Statistics Special Report, NCJ-134177. Washington, DC: Author, February 1992.
U.S. General Accounting Office. *Foreign Economic Assistance Issues*. Washington, DC: Author, December 1992a.
———. *NASA Issues*. Washington, DC: Author, December 1992b.
———. *National Security Issues*. Washington, DC: Author, December 1992c.
U.S. House of Representatives. *Overview of Entitlement Programs: 1992 Green Book*. House Committee on Ways and Means, Washington, DC, May 1992.
Van Dijk, Jan, and M. Killias Mayhew. *Experiences of Crime Across the World: Key Findings of the 1989 International Crime Survey*. Boston: Kluewer, 1992.
Vobejda, Barbara. "Gains by Blacks Said to Stagnate in Last 20 Years." *Washington Post*, July 28, 1989, p. A1.
———. Children's Poverty Rose in '80s." *Washington Post*, August 12, 1992a, p. A3.
———. "Home Alone, Glued to the TV." *Washington Post*, December 10, 1992b, p. A3.
———. "Head Start Expansion Is Urged." *Washington Post*, January 13, 1994a, p. A4.
———. "Conservative Welfare Idea Criticized." *Washington Post*, June 24, 1994b, p. A18.
———. "Study Alters Image of Typical Family. *Washington Post*, August 30, 1994c, p. A3.

_____. "GOP Welfare Plan Would Shrink the System." *Washington Post*, December 7, 1994d, p. A22.
_____. "Republican Welfare Plan Is Termed 'Indefensible.'" *Washington Post*, January 11, 1995a, p. A4.
_____. "Child-Care Centers Get Low Ratings." *Washington Post*, February 6, 1995b, p. A1.
Walker, Gary. *Anatomy of a Demonstration*. Public/Private Ventures, 1992.
Waller, Irvin. *Current Trends in European Crime Prevention: Implications for Canada*. Ottawa, Canada: Department of Justice, 1989.
Wall Street Journal: "Clinton Faces Decision on Raising Gas Tax." December 28, 1992, p. A2.
Washington Post: "A Social Deficit Too." May 7, 1989, p. B6; "Life with Mikhail Gorbachev." May 14, 1989, p. C6; "More on Those Defense Cuts." December 19, 1989, p. A22; "Dropout Prevention: Human Touch Helps." June 3, 1991, p. 4; "A Senate Yes to the Brady Bill." July 1, 1991, A18; "Verbatim." May 18, 1992, p. A19; "Worst Bill of the Year." July 31, 1992, p. A22; "The President-Elect Should Listen to the Candidate." November 20, 1992, p. A4; "And a New Text at Education." January 4, 1993, p. A28; "Revitalizing Congress." January 6, 1993, p. A20; "Getting Welfare Right." January 7, 1993, p. A30; Cisneros Offers Urban, Ethnic Edge to National Role." January 12, 1993, p. A24; "A New Broom at HUD . . ." January 14, 1993, p. C4; "Short and Sweet." January 21, 1993, p. A22; "The Health Reform Issue . . ." January 27, 1993, p. A18; "Campaign Reform, Anyone?" February 7, 1993, p. C6; "Coloradan Pleads Guilty in HUD Scandal." February 10, 1993, p. A12; "The New Day Care Debate." April 8, 1994, p. A20; "Welfare Reform Meets the Deficit." May 2, 1994, p. A18; "A National Dialogue on Kids." July 31, 1994, p. C8; "Reforming Welfare, State by State." December 18, 1994, p. C6; "Welfare: A Case in Point." January 10, 1995, p. A16.
Weber, Bruce. *Kilos of Crack and $200 Sneakers: Young Dealers Confide in a Novelist*. September 6, 1992. p. E7.
Wertheimer, Fred. "From Campaign Pledges to Political Action." *Common Cause Magazine*, Winter 1992, p. 27.
Whittemore, Hank. "Hitting Bottom Can Be the Beginning." *Parade*, March 15, 1992, p. 4.
Wienk, Ronald. *Discrimination in Urban Credit Markets: What We Don't Know and Why We Don't Know It*. Paper presented at the Fannie Mae Annual Housing Conference, Washington, DC, 1992.
Wilkins, Roger. "Great Things That Gingrich Could Do." *Washington Post*, January 10, 1995, p. A17.
Will, George F. "Petrified Port." *Washington Post*, November 4, 1993, p. A21.
Williams, Terry. *The Cocaine Kids: The Inside Story of a Teenage Drug Ring*. Reading, MA: Addison-Wesley Publishing, 1989.
William T. Grant Foundation. "The Forgotten Half: Pathways to Success for America's Youth and Young Families." *Final Report on Youth and America's Future*. New York: Author, 1988.
Wilson, George C. "U.S. Begins Retooling the Military." *Washington Post*, November 26, 1989, p. A1.
Wynes, Michael. "Hi. Goodbye. This Takes 11 Weeks and $3.5 Million?" *New York Times*, November 22, 1992.
Young, Amy E. "Common Cause News." *Common Cause Magazine*, Winter 1992, p. 27.
"Young Unwed Fathers: They Are Not All Alike." Public/Private Ventures Newsletter, Summer 1994, p. 1.
Youth Indicators 1991. *Trends in the Well-Being of American Youth*. Washington, DC: U.S. Government Printing Office, 1991.
Youth Policy Institute. *Youth Policy*, Vol. 14, Nos. 7 and 8. Washington, DC: Author, December 1992.
_____. "JobStart: A Promising Program for School Dropouts." *Youth Record*, Vol. 1, No. 8. Washington, DC: Author, July 1989, p. 6.
_____. "The Progressive Housing Program." *Youth Record*, Vol. 1, No. 8. Washington, DC: Author, July 19, 1989, p. 6.
_____. "Defense Cuts in the 90s: Where Will the Money Go? Who Will Benefit?" *Youth Record*, Vol. 1, No. 18. Washington, DC: Author, December 19, 1989a, p. 1.
_____. "'The Congressional Black Caucus' 'Quality of Life' Budget." *Youth Record*, Vol. 1, No. 18. Washington, DC: Author, December 19, 1989b, p. 2.
_____. "Drug Dealers Provide Record 'Dividend' for New Federal Prisons." *Youth Record*, Vol. 1, No.18. Washington, DC: Author, December 19, 1989c, p. 12.
_____. "YouthBuild Program Prepares for Big Year in 1993." *Youth Record*, Vol. 4, No.22. Washington, DC: Author, November 29, 1992, p. 8.
_____. "Clinton Faces Many Options for School Reform, but Leans Toward Public School Choice." *Youth Record*, Vol. 4, No. 23. Washington, DC: Author, December 14, 1992, p. 23.
_____. "Chelsea Clinton's School Choice Rekindles Controversy." *Youth Record*, Vol. 5, No. 1. Washington, DC: Author, January 14, 1993, p. 4.
Zdenek, Robert O. "Community Development Corporations in the 1990s." *Future Choices: Toward a National Youth Policy* 1(Fall 1989): 66.
Zedleski, Edwin W. "When Have We Punished Enough?" *Public Administration Review*, November 1985: 216–229.
Zuckerman, Jill. "All about Enterprise Zones." *American Caucus*, August 31–September 13, 1992, pp. 16–35.